The Secret War for Texas

STUART REID

TEXAS A&M UNIVERSITY PRESS • *College Station*

The paper used in this book
meets the minimum requirements
of the American National Standard for Permanence
of Paper for Printed Library Materials, z39.48-1984.
Binding materials have been chosen for durability.

LIBRARY OF CONGRESS CATALOGING-IN-PUBLICATION DATa

Reid, Stuart, 1954–
    The secret war for Texas / Stuart Reid. — 1st ed.
        p. cm. — (Elma Dill Russell Spencer series in the West and
    Southwest ; no. 28)
    Includes bibliographical references and index.
    ISBN-13: 978-1-58544-565-3 (cloth : alk. paper)
    ISBN-10: 158544-565-7
    1. Texas—History—Revolution, 1835–1836. 2. Matamoros Expedition
(1835–1836) 3. Grant, James, 1793–1836. 4. Soldiers—Texas—Biography.
5. Scots—Texas—Biography. 6. Landowners—Texas—Biography.
7. Texas—History—Revolution, 1835–1836—Biography. 8. United
States—Foreign relations—1815-1861. 9. United States—Foreign
relations—Great Britain. 10. Great Britain—Foreign relations—United
States. I. Title. II. Series.
F390.R39   2007
976.4'03–dc22   2006014555

To the memory of

Dr. James Grant (1793–1836),

"a gentleman, scholar, patriot,

and gallant soldier"

Contents

Acknowledgments

THIS BOOK BEGAN WITH a not uncommon family mystery: the search for my three-times-great-grandfather, James Grant, a doctor from Scotland's Black Isle who once worked for the East India Company but then seemingly vanished from the records in the early 1820s. At first that search was no more than a casual distraction from more serious studies, but then quite by chance a tattered fragment of newspaper turned up with a curious story that he had been killed in Mexico. With that vital clue he was quickly identified as a major player in the Texas Revolution, yet one about whom surprisingly little was written or known.

As Sam Houston and others never tired of pointing out, Grant was not a Texan, and it soon became clear that his fate was bound up with the largely untold story of British efforts to keep Texas out of American hands. Earlier historians, such as J. L. Worley and Anton Adams, have long acknowledged England's interest in Texas at an early date. However, for both, that early date coincided with the establishment of Texas as a republic in 1836. Had they properly reflected that before this Texas was part of Mexico, and had they examined the voluminous Foreign Office files relating to that country, they would have found that Britain's interest was aroused from the very moment Stephen Austin brought his first colonists to the Brazos bottoms. And Britain's interest was anything but passive.

Foreign Office and Colonial Office files in London yielded a wealth of material. Beyond this, tracing James Grant's surprising role in the early history of Texas has of necessity been accomplished at some distance from the scene of the events. The task has been eased and rendered all the more agreeable by the advice, comments, and assistance freely given by a number of individuals and organizations, including but by no means confined to Stephen L. Hardin of Victoria College in Victoria, Texas;

Craig Roell of Georgia Southern University in Statesboro; the late Jack Jackson of Austin, Texas; Jim Boylston, Kevin Hendryx, Herb True, and David Webb of the Alamo Society; Thomas Ricks Lindley, often an adversary in debate but an indefatigable and generous researcher; reviewer Andrés Tijerina and an anynomous reviewer; and copyeditor Sally Antrobus. Thanks are also due to Warren Stricker of the Daughters of the Republic of Texas Library in San Antonio, who among other things provided one of the lighter moments with an electronic transmission of Reuben Brown's narrative of Grant's last fight, a story abruptly interrupted at the words: "We saw the enemy charging upon us from every direction. Wheeling around we . . ." It took another twenty-four hours before that particular cliff-hanger was resolved.

Closer to home, the staff of the National Archives at Kew, the Scottish Record Office in Edinburgh, the genealogy department of Inverness Public Library, and that wonderfully tranquil treasure house of curiosities, the library of the Literary and Philosophical Society of Newcastle upon Tyne, all provided their usual quietly efficient assistance.

Last and not least, I must also thank cousin Jennifer, whose newspaper clipping started me on the road to Mexico without either of us having the least idea of where it would eventually lead us.

The Secret War for Texas

Introduction

ON APRIL 2, 1836, Richard Pakenham, the British minister to Mexico, formally advised the foreign secretary, Lord Palmerston, of the latest news from Texas. As expected, San Antonio de Béxar and the Alamo had now fallen to General Santa Anna, and it was confidently anticipated that the rebellion would soon be at an end. To the British government this news was neither unexpected nor at all unwelcome, but Pakenham had more to tell. "Simultaneously with the taking of Bexar," he wrote, "a detached Party of Texans Commanded by a British Subject, of the name of Grant, who had become a Citizen of Mexico and distinguished himself in that part of the Country by a series of very disreputable transactions was cut off, and Doctor Grant and 42 of his Party killed in the encounter."[1] Pakenham clearly thought this news to be of equal importance to the fall of the Alamo, yet Grant was not the first or only British subject to have died in the troubles in Texas and northern Mexico. At least eight others had recently been executed at Tampico by the Mexican government, and of course more had just died at the Alamo itself, but they passed largely without comment.

What was so different about Dr. James Grant? What were those "very disreputable transactions," and above all why did Richard Pakenham know that the news of Grant's death would be of particular interest to Lord Palmerston?

Answering these questions requires a fresh look at the events that led up to that famous battle for the Alamo, because while its heroic defense against Santa Anna and his Mexican army is rightly described as the creation myth of Texas, the Texan Revolution was not quite the straightforward contest between embattled American farmers and their Mexican oppressors that has passed into popular legend. In a very real sense that Revolution began as an offshoot to a much wider Mexican civil war, and ultimately it was also part of the original "Great Game": a secret contest played out by London and Washington for more than fifty years to secure mastery of the North American continent and to determine whether the manifest destiny of the United States to stretch from sea to shining sea should be realized or frustrated.

That struggle began even before the last shots had been fired in the American Revolution, as both sides fought to establish the boundaries between British and United States territory in the "Old Northwest"; and indeed to settle the even more fundamental question of whether Canada should remain a British colony or be brought into the Union—by force if necessary. At first Britain and her native allies held the upper hand in the undeclared war against the nascent republic, but gradually a stalemate became established, and although the bickering along the border came to an end only as late as 1838 with the defeat of an American filibustering group called the Hunters, a new area of conflict had opened up in 1803. The vast but ill-defined Louisiana Purchase, closely followed by the subsequent American seizure of Florida, shifted attention to the Gulf of Mexico and to the Caribbean, brought war to New Orleans in 1815, and opened up the prospect that the manifest destiny of the United States to span the continent from sea to shining sea might soon be an attainable goal. Only two things stood in the way of American ambitions to reach the Pacific Ocean: the British claim to the Oregon country; and the vast but sparsely populated Mexican province of Texas.

The prospect of Texas being swallowed up by the United States and thereby upsetting the balance of power and trade in both North America and the Caribbean Basin was therefore viewed with almost as much concern in London as it was in Mexico City. Taking advantage of its emptiness, thousands of American settlers poured across the Sabine River into Texas between 1822 and 1835. Many, perhaps the majority, obtained legitimate land grants and for the most part dutifully became Mexican citizens, as was required of them. But they also determinedly retained their American identity, and when they eventually rose up in revolt in the 1830s it was only natural that they should look eastward to the Sabine and the Old Flag for assistance.

However, after their initial easy victories over the central government's forces in the autumn of 1835, and then the capture of old provincial capital of San Antonio de Béxar, the rebels found themselves at odds over what to do next. All, without exception, were in favor of

A planter or businessman, based on a sketch by the noted genre artist George Caleb Bingham, working in Missouri in the early 1840s. This provides a good illustration of the sort of clothing likely to have been worn by Grant and the other Texian leaders.

some kind of independence for Texas, but they were divided as to the form that independence should take and whether they should remain at least outwardly loyal to the Mexican federation and its suppressed liberal Constitution of 1824 or seek immediate annexation by the United States instead. At the turn of the year the most urgent question before the rebels was whether to stay put and consolidate their position or to march south to the Rio Grande:

"To descend upon the wealthy border city of Matamoros and capture and loot the place, seemed easy to accomplish and soon became the favorite theme, with many willing listeners and ready volunteers," recalled Captain Creed Taylor.[2]

But in the end, as the sequel shows, the attempt of this enterprise proved to be the mother of the greatest misfortunes that ever came upon the colonists of Texas. The wild idea first originated with

Dr. James Grant, erstwhile wealthy, but aggrieved ranchero of Parras, Mexico—posing as a Texas patriot—who, without the shadow of authority, marched away from Bexar with 200 volunteers, after having despoiled the handful of men left under Colonel Neill of ammunition, blankets, medical stores, and everything else worth taking, and proceeded to San Patricio, where he expected to be joined by Colonel Fannin, Frank Johnson, and others. This was early in January, 1836. Dr. Grant was a Scotchman who had lived several years in Mexico and owned large properties in the Mexican Republic. Just when and why he came to Texas and enlisted in the struggle for independence I am unable to say, but I was told that for the stand he took against Santa Anna in the Zacatecas affair, he was forced to fly for his life, and hence came to Texas and joined the colonial army. Grant was a shrewd schemer, and adept in the school of intrigue, and withal, a visionary. . . .

Then began a long series of misfortunes sufficient to cause every patriot to lose all hope for ultimate success. And these misfortunes—the breach between the council and the governor, the disasters at San Patricio, Refugio, Goliad, and San Antonio, may be traced and accredited directly to Dr. Grant and his wild scheme for the capture of Matamoros.

Despite his dramatic influence on events, and the enduring accusations that he fatally weakened the Alamo by stripping it of men, ammunition, and medical supplies, Grant remains an enigma; a shadowy and often sinister figure routinely condemned by historians and frequently dismissed out of hand merely as an unscrupulous land speculator. Yet a search for the real Dr. James Grant—Colonel Frank Johnson's "gentleman, scholar, patriot and gallant soldier"—soon reveals him as a surprisingly solid and altogether much more complex figure; and while it would be easy to assume that those "disreputable transactions" darkly alluded to by Pakenham related to the land speculation so rife at the time, the probability is that the diplomat was actually thinking of something else entirely, for Grant had been in Mexico a long time and was involved in some very surprising business indeed.

When he first arrived in the rebel camp outside Bexar in November 1835, his ostensible purpose was indeed to persuade the Texians to march on Matamoros and join with the Mexican Federalists, even if it meant engineering an all-out assault on the town first. By January 1 he had his army, but he had also precipitated that fatal "breach between the council and the governor"; between those rebels who would have settled for the recognition of Texas as an independent state within the Mexican federation and the newer, more militant arrivals clamoring for annexation by the United States. Hindsight aside, the unending flow of settlers across the Sabine River probably made it inevitable that if left to itself, Texas would one day become an American state rather than a Mexican one. Consequently Grant's determined efforts to ensure that Texas instead remained part of the Mexican federation, or even became part of a projected new republic of northern Mexico, made no sense to his opponents. His bitter enemy, the legendary Sam Houston (and through him Henderson Yoakum and generations of other historians), therefore charged that the expedition was only a scheme got up by Grant in order to recover his "princely" estates in neighboring Coahuila and to secure vast but corruptly obtained land grants in Texas itself.

Ultimately, although it is questionable whether he ever fully realized it, Sam Houston was right up to a point. It was only natural, of course, that Grant would want to regain his embargoed property in Coahuila, and it was certainly true that he was never a resident of Texas and was opposed to Texan independence. Far more important, however, he was not and never had been an American citizen either. Consequently it is one of the revolution's ironies that Grant would in the end be killed leading an army consisting predominantly of American filibusters, for he was actually a British agent, and indeed his cousin was the colonial secretary, Lord Glenelg. Moreover, when Grant and his men were ambushed and killed, they were not returning from a casual "mustanging" or horse-rustling foray but from a "secret expedition" to the Rio Grande and a failed rendezvous with the historical El Zorro. And the aim of that rendezvous was to trigger a much wider Mexican civil war that would lead to the creation of a new republic of northern Mexico and that would ultimately interpose an impenetrable barrier to American expansion along the Gulf of Mexico toward the Pacific Ocean.

This then is the forgotten story of Dr. James Grant and the twenty-year-long secret war for Texas; from his involvement in the "silly quixotic" Fredonian Rebellion to the bloody battles along the Atascosita Road, which effectively ended British hopes of stopping Manifest Destiny in its tracks.

1 • *Gone to Texas*

IN THE BEGINNING OF COURSE, Texas was Spanish territory, but in 1808 the French Emperor Napoleon invaded Spain, deposing and imprisoning its royal family and so beginning the terrible six-year-long Peninsular War. To the Spaniards it was their War of Independence, and that was exactly what it also became in their American colonies, for the various royal governors, effectively cut off from home, soon found themselves beset by liberal juntas keen to emulate their North American colleagues by proclaiming their own independence from the mother country. Mexico was no exception. On September 15, 1810, an obscure country priest named Miguel Hidalgo issued his famous *grito de Dolores* and then led a peasant army almost to the gates of Mexico City. Although often hard-pressed, the Royalists held their own, surviving more than ten years of liberal rebellions and American-led filibustering expeditions, until one day Spain suddenly lost control of Mexico in what can only be described as a fit of inattention.

In 1820 a mutiny at Cadiz among troops about to embark for the Americas rapidly became a revolution that brought a liberal government to power in Spain itself, forcing King Ferdinand to restore the voided liberal constitution of 1811 and to begin dismantling the enormous privileges enjoyed by the Catholic Church. In Mexico the Royalists, who had hitherto been winning, thus found themselves on the wrong side overnight, for ironically it appeared that the only way they could retain both their own power and that of the Catholic Church was by repudiating Spanish sovereignty! Thus the Royalist commander, General Augustín Iturbide, met with his rebel counterpart, Vincente Guerrero, and between them they issued El Plan de Iguala on February 27, 1821. Mexico was proclaimed to be an "independent, moderate constitutional monarchy," although only the first of these aspirations was ever to be fully realized. While there was some talk of justifying themselves by pledging allegiance to any convenient Bourbon princeling who might happen to be available, starting with King Ferdinand, it was General Iturbide who eventually announced himself to be the Emperor Augustín I of Mexico. Predictably, he did not last long, and late in 1822 one of his own generals, Antonio López de Santa Anna, helped proclaim a liberal republic. Although King Ferdinand was restored to the Spanish throne a year later, Mexico henceforth remained independent and in the following year adopted a liberal constitution that was closely and very consciously—but ultimately superficially—modeled on that of the United States.

This Constitution of 1824 was to be crucial to much of what followed. The small print is of little significance, since all sides would later interpret it, ignore it, or even discard it as they pleased. What was important was that it established Mexico as a federal republic, which like its northern neighbor was made up of a number of more or less sovereign states. Indeed Mexican politicians routinely referred to the two republics as the United States of the North and the United States of the South respectively. Unfortunately after fourteen years of revolution, counterrevolution, invasion, and civil war, the new republic was both economically and politically bankrupt, and the conflicts and contradictions inherent in that federal constitution erupted in Mexico a full generation before they tore North America apart.

In the meantime, the newly independent Mexico and indeed all of Spanish America was of considerable interest to the British government, and to the Board of Trade in particular, for the region offered attractive commercial opportunities. Between 1822 and 1824 Britain annually exported some £5,883,000 (about $30 million) worth of goods to the former Spanish colonies, and between 1825 and 1827 that average rose to about £6,605,000 a year, most of it going to Mexico.[1] British investment in the country and its silver mines was even more considerable and, despite the collapse of a short-lived boom in the late 1820s, would grow to something in excess of £70 million by 1836.[2] Yet that trade and investment was both informal and unprotected inasmuch as Britain had still to recognize Mexican independence. More important, no one in the British government was under any illusions as to the potential threat posed by the United States, which made no secret of its expansionist aspirations in the region or its desire to dominate or acquire the remains of the

Spanish empire. Florida had already been seized in a particularly blatant piece of filibustering, and covetous eyes were now being cast upon both Texas and the great island of Cuba, which was widely regarded as the key to the whole Caribbean Basin.

Clearly something would have to be done. Late in 1822 the then British foreign minister, George Canning, reluctantly determined to send a self-proclaimed confidential agent, Dr. Patrick Mackie, out to Mexico in order to open preliminary discussions with Iturbide on recognition. Canning was evidently dubious about Mackie, and with good reason, since the Glaswegian doctor's claim to be well acquainted with the emperor was almost certainly false, and there is some doubt as to whether he had even been to Mexico before. However, any unease was temporarily dispelled by the coincidental arrival in London of another Scots adventurer, Arthur Goodall Wavell, who turned out to be a quite genuine envoy from Iturbide himself.[3] Mackie was thereupon dispatched to Mexico in late November, but without being told anything of Wavell, who as it turned out was primarily concerned with securing a loan of $20 million for the Mexican government and also forwarding some private schemes of his own.

Inconveniently for all the parties concerned, Iturbide had in the meantime been toppled, and when Mackie exceeded his instructions by immediately entering into detailed negotiations with the new government, Canning seized the opportunity to repudiate him and to place the question of recognition on hold. The fact of the matter was that although anxious to reach an accommodation with Mexico, and so forestall American ambitions, the British government still considered that it had an obligation to offer continued support to its Spanish counterparts, who were now struggling against a renewed French invasion, this time in support of Ferdinand and the Royalists. Immediately recognizing the independence of Mexico and the other breakaway South American republics could have been a fatal blow to the Spanish liberals.

Then, on October 10, 1823, news reached London that Cadiz had fallen and the liberal junta with it. Those scruples became academic, and later that same day—without reference to the king and in defiance of France and the other European powers—Canning formally instructed an official commissioner, Lionel Hervey, to proceed to Mexico. Hervey's instructions had already been drawn up back in July, and while formal recognition of Mexico was still some time away (the treaty would not

Death of Mrs J. McIntosh,

Another of the oldest identities of this district passed away on Thursday morning. It will be remembered some five years ago Mrs Jamesina McIntosh met with a unfortunate accident, resulting in a fracture of the hip. It was thought that owing to her advanced age she would not survive many days as there was no hope of setting the broken limb. She surprised everyone by the patient manner in which she bore her painful injury, and during the five years, though bedridden, maintained a cheerful temperament, and was, up to a week ago, glad to converse with the many friends who called to see her. and on Thursday morning the end came very peacefully. Mrs McIntosh came to Clermont with her husband in 1864, the latter starting business a chemist, but died about six years r. The eldest son has also passed but Mrs McIntosh leaves six en and 10 grandchildren, who. ne exception. are all in Clar- present. Mrs McIntosh was ghter of Dr. James Grant, the head medical officer of a Hospital. He left that to go to Mexico at the xican war, a reward ereg by the Mexican e was arrested, and L. Edwards, was im- naged to escape, but murdered. Mrs er long residence respected. and her

This fragmentary obituary for James Grant's eldest daughter, which appeared in an unidentified Australian newspaper in March 1911, provides a vital clue linking Grant to Benjamin Edwards and the Fredonian Rebellion. Courtesy Jennifer Lentell.

be signed until December 26, 1826), the outcome of his negotiations was anticipated by the immediate accreditation of British consuls to the principal ports.[4] The reasons for the seeming haste, as Canning freely admitted in a December memorandum to the Cabinet, were his "apprehension of the ambition and ascendancy" of the United States and his belief that "we now have the opportunity (but it may not last long) of opposing a powerful barrier to the influence of the US by an amicable connection with Mexico, which from its position must be either subservient to or jealous of the US."[5]

And so it all began. That barrier took tangible form in Texas, which in Spanish days was a thinly settled province serving both as a buffer against the hostile Plains Indians and as a bridge between the Mexican interior and far-off Louisiana. A truly vast area then stretching from the Mississippi Valley to the Rocky Mountains and perhaps beyond, Louisiana was ceded to France by the Treaty of San Ildefonso in 1800, only to be almost immediately sold by Napoleon to the United States three years later. In itself this transaction was a worrying enough development for both Spain and anyone else with interests in the region, but it was immensely complicated by Napoleon's blatantly fraudulent inclusion of Texas in the deal. Not until the Adams-Onis Treaty of 1819 would the Americans formally accept that Texas formed no part of the Louisiana Purchase. Yet they were never truly reconciled to the fact and continued to harbor designs upon Texas that had ramifications far beyond the immediate seizure of Mexican territory and the removal of the barrier it presented to the westward expansion of the United States.

British concerns over those designs would be succinctly expressed by an anonymous pamphleteer, who pointed out in 1830 that "every thing lost to Mexico would be so much taken away from the only independent North American counterpoise to our great North American rival." He also went on to warn that the loss of this equilibrium would enable the United States to "overrule the policy and dictate, without fear of remonstrance, the tariffs of all America, and in the first place that of Mexico; and in what spirit those tariffs will be conceived, and with what strictness enforced, the present commercial code of Washington and the practice of New York may sufficiently teach us."[6] The Board of Trade could not have put it better.

The situation was further complicated by the fact that the decade of rebellion and civil war that preceded Mexican independence saw the

Hispanic population of Texas fall by more than half, largely thanks to Gutiérrez de Lara's invasion with an army of American mercenaries in August 1812, and General Arredondo's bloody counterattack in the following year. By 1819, in the wake of yet another American filibustering expedition led by a Dr. James Long, it was estimated that there were only some two thousand Tejanos left, and even they were under constant threat from the indigenous Comanche clans. Consequently, when the Federal Republic of Mexico was formally established in 1824, Texas was temporarily reconstituted as a mere department of a new combined state of Coahuila y Texas and was thereafter governed from Saltillo rather than from San Antonio de Béxar.

In a spectacularly successful attempt to arrest this disastrous demographic decline and so forestall the feared American expansion, first the Spanish and then the new Mexican government encouraged large-scale colonization of Texas through the medium of *empresario* grants, the first of which was awarded to a Missourian named Stephen Fuller Austin in 1822. The system was deceptively simple and better still, from the government's point of view, self-financing. Essentially, in return for a substantial grant of vacant public land, the empresario would bring in an agreed quota of settlers, each of whom, having promised to adopt the Catholic religion and to obey the laws of Mexico, would in turn be allocated a fixed share of the land. It may seem paradoxical that the Mexican government, concerned as it was about American ambitions and the increasing numbers of squatters already drifting over the Sabine, officially encouraged other Americans to settle in Texas. Nevertheless that, to some extent, was the point of the whole exercise. For by giving good legal title to those "respectable" colonists taking up Mexican citizenship, the Mexican government hoped to preempt the squatters and at the same time unequivocally demonstrate its own superior title to the province.

Moreover, Austin had in any case deliberately misled the Mexican government about the extent to which North Americans would settle his colony. His grant had originally been awarded to his father Moses, a sometime Spanish citizen when his home in Missouri was accounted part of Spanish Louisiana. However, the older Austin died before he could begin his settlement, and the transfer of the grant to his son was greatly assisted by none other than Arthur Wavell, who, having been kicked out of the Chilean army, had talked Iturbide into making him a general in the Mexican army. On July 4, 1822, Austin agreed to enter into a partnership with the general, who was to raise capital and recruit potential settlers in Europe, which was probably the real reason why Wavell then turned up so fortuitously in London.

Having spoken informally with Canning and secured the required Mexican loan from Berkeley, Hervey and Company within just two weeks of his arrival, Wavell at first encountered a lack of enthusiasm for the Texas business.[7] It was only one of many such schemes being promoted in the London money market at the time, and in February of 1823 he commented gloomily that his efforts were being particularly hampered by a scheme for a colony in the mythical Central American country of Poyais, dreamed up by an adventurer calling himself Sir Gregor MacGregor.[8] Nevertheless Wavell persevered and by May was able to report that "one of the largest and richest houses in this city" was prepared to advance "£20,000—say $100,000" for a half share in the colony.[9] To his dismay, Austin never responded. The truth was that the empresario was actually committed to finding all the colonists and capital he required in the United States.

On the other hand, having been alerted by Wavell to this substantial influx of American settlers to Texas, it was only natural that the British government should want to plant an agent in such a sensitive area. This was a frighteningly informal process at the time, for although there was a secret service fund or allocation, there was no proper government-run intelligence organization as such. Individual ministers appointed agents as and when required for a particular job and kept no official records, or at least none that have survived. Several British agents were apparently operating in Mexico at this period, but with one exception, identification of individuals is impossible since they were discreetly paid out of the "home" account rather than a separate Mexico account.[10] When pressed in Parliament in 1822 about this apparent lack of accountability, Canning's predecessor, Lord Castlereagh, declined to reveal any details of how the secret service money was spent and dryly commented that the question was "rather an Irish proposition, for it would then be secret service money no longer."[11]

In the circumstances it is hardly surprising that ministers preferred their agents to be gentlemen, who came personally recommended—which makes it all the more surprising that Patrick Mackie's rather dubious services were accepted in the first place. In finding an agent to go to

Texas, however, the recommendation must have come through the Board of Trade, which was the department most deeply interested in Mexican affairs. At the time the Board was presided over by the celebrated William Huskisson, another prominent critic of American designs on Texas—and Huskisson, as it happens, had some surprisingly weighty experience in this particular line of business. Although a lifelong liberal, he had begun his government career by running an extremely efficient spy network in Napoleon's Europe for nearly fourteen years between 1795 and 1808, and so he had a lively appreciation of the value of a good agent in the right place.[12] As for that Texas agent, who better for the job than "a shrewd schemer, and adept in the school of intrigue," with some knowledge of the cotton trade, a man who had a pressing desire to get out of the country and also just happened to be the footloose cousin of his fiercely abolitionist deputy, Charles Grant, the future Lord Glenelg.[13]

That cousin, Dr. James Grant, was yet another Scot, born in the tiny village of Milton of Redcastle in Ross-shire on July 28, 1793.[14] His grandfather, Alexander, was one of the warrior Grants of Shewglie in Glen Urquhart, a swashbuckling character who was among the first to join the Young Pretender, Charles Edward Stuart, and who fought at Culloden in 1746. Escaping afterward, he found rehabilitation in the service of the mighty East India Company, the first and arguably the greatest multinational corporation the world has ever known. It would also come to be run by a Scottish mafia, and Alexander Grant was one of those who set the takeover in motion. In India Captain Grant, as he swiftly became, narrowly avoided incarceration in the infamous Black Hole of Calcutta by literally being the last man onto the last boat to get away from the doomed fortress. He redeemed himself for abandonment of the doomed garrison by fighting at Plassey under Clive and so helped lay the foundations of the British Empire. Thus he came home with a respectable fortune and an illegitimate son William, who was promptly packed off to live with his Shewglie relatives in Glen Urquhart and then orphaned at the age of eleven when Alexander tried his luck in India a second time but instead found an early grave. Although all his father's money went to a wife acquired on the way back out to India, William's "acquirements" were said to be uncommon.[15] After marrying the illegitimate daughter of another relative, he moved to his cousin James's estate at Redcastle in 1791, where, like all the Shewglie Grants, he fathered a large brood during his "most exemplary and highly valued though humble life."[16]

Given the Shewglie family's strong connections with India, it was almost inevitable that in 1812 William's second son James, then a medical student, also entered the East India Company's service. Ordinarily the boy would have started his career as a surgeon's mate, but William's cousin Charles, who had gone out to India under Alexander's patronage, was by now not only a director of the company but one of the most influential chairmen in its long history as well as a liberal member of Parliament, evangelist, and abolitionist colleague of the famed William Wilberforce. Young James therefore went to sea not as a humble mate but as the surgeon of the *General Stuart.*

Between 1813 and 1819 James made three long voyages to India and China as a doctor on board the company's ships. In the course of those voyages, as was customary, he also did some trading on his own account in tea and cotton and perhaps a little opium on the side. In time he could have retired as a respectably prosperous man, but then in the early 1820s his life took an unexpected and completely different direction. While living in London in 1812 he hastily married Margaret Urquhart, the daughter of another East India Company official.[17] Although he subsequently fathered two children, Stewart Marjoribanks in 1817 and Jamesina five years later, the marriage was punctuated by long separations and was far from being a happy one. Urging his children to "study the character of any pretender well before they come under any engagement, and to attend to real instead of Showy or surreptitious merits," he later spoke in his will of "a long series of heart burnings in the marriage life which had an oppressive influence on me and my fortunes during the best period of my existence."[18] The result was that like a surprising number of others involved in the events ahead, he parted from his wife, entrusted both of the children to his own parents, and seemingly without explanation abandoned both medicine and the sea to turn up in New Orleans sometime in the late summer of 1823.[19]

Curiously, he neglected to resign from the service of the East India Company, which by this period was virtually an adjunct of the government. In the light of what followed this omission may be significant, for he must have sailed in about July at precisely the time when Lionel Hervey's instructions were being drafted by Canning.[20] At any rate from the Crescent City James quickly moved on into Texas and immediately proceeded to make the acquaintanceship of Stephen Austin himself. To all outward appearances he was examining the prospects for settling in the colony and for engaging in the growing or more likely the trading of cotton. By late March 1824, however, he was back in New Orleans, making encouraging noises about the quality of Texan cotton but complaining to Austin that "as my visit to your country has at this moment blighted my credit with my friends in this place; I hope you will be indulgent to me; and tho I do not come nor send out before the fall you will indulge me. . . . I shall either come myself or send my Brother [Hugh Grant] in the fall; Mr. Jones has my instructions to get a title for the Land." [21]

Although he was constantly declaring his determination "to be a Citizen of your country," there was always something to hinder him, and he did not stay in New Orleans. Instead he moved farther into northern Mexico. In January 1825, he was writing from Camargo, about one hundred miles up the Rio Grande, taking "the opportunity of Colnl. Milam, passing your way, to drop you a few lines respecting my interest in your Colony, I have been a great deal absent, but it has been completely out of my power to be there, my business in this part of the Country has been in such a situation that I have not been able to leave." He hoped to be with Austin in June, but July found him still on the Rio Grande at Reynosa, packing mule trains overland to the colonies, although this was a frustrating experience. On one particularly notable occasion he "went up the Country and bought Some Wool to bring on to the Settlement but by high waters and loosing Mules and Horses, it is only the other day I was able to get my Cargos and Mules Collected in Comargo." Even then, as he lamented to Austin, he was "again prevented by high waters all the Water Courses are up so that mules with Cargo cannot proceed and I am uncertain when I will be able to travel with my cargo there has been a great deal of Rain in this Country, the Rio Grande is very high and likewise the Nueces, and as I am unable to proceed, I have concluded to go down to Refugio and purchase a few goods, to see if I can make up my lost time." [22] If he hoped thereby to establish the practicality of a regular trade route between the colonies and the Mexican interior he was disappointed, but at least he was thoroughly familiarizing himself with Texas.

Once again he assured Austin in this letter that "I shall be with you as soon as is practicable; as I have since I first saw the Country been determined to become a Settler; and have refused some good offers to make money, in consequence of making all my arrangements to go and settle with you." Yet for all his professed determination those arrangements remained curiously intangible. His reluctance to commit himself is on the face of it all the more curious given the success of the colony, for by 1827 Austin would have fulfilled his contract by settling 297 families on his original grant. More empresarios followed in his wake, and by 1830 there would be an estimated sixteen thousand Americans in Texas and no end in sight to the influx.

However, while the empresario experiment was spectacularly successful in repopulating Texas, it was already backfiring disastrously in political terms. "By thus imprudently encouraging emigration upon too large a scale," wrote Hervey's successor, Henry Ward, "the Mexican Government has attained but little authority over the new settlers, established in masses in various parts of Texas, who being separated only by an imaginary boundary line from their countrymen upon the opposite bank of the Sabina, naturally look to them for support in their difficulties."[23] And so it proved. Far from serving as a barrier to Norte Americano expansion, the Texas colonies were encouraging it by attracting both settlers and squatters, and the traders and professional men—particularly the ubiquitous lawyers—needed to turn the new settlements into viable communities. Furthermore the majority of the legitimate colonists, although ostentatiously and in many cases genuinely professing their loyalty to the federal Constitution of 1824, had neither the opportunity nor the inclination to assimilate themselves into Mexican society and culture. They still thought of themselves as Americans.

This was justification enough for British concern and was recognized as such from the very outset. Hervey had barely arrived in Mexico before he began warning of the dire consequences, and Henry Ward, who came after him, fought a series of semiclandestine battles with Joel Poinsett, his American counterpart, while constantly badgering his own government for instructions on how to proceed with the Texas business. On September 6, 1825, Ward wrote, the treaty

> between the United States and this country, advances but slowly, though I am at a loss to understand, in what the cause of the delay consists. . . . While the Mexicans are . . . jealous in guarding against encroachments in the shape of a treaty, they are suffering, on the other hand, by an absurd mixture of negligence, & weakness, the

whole disputed territory, (between the Sabine and the Neches) and an immense tract of country beyond it, to be quietly taken possession of by the very men, whose claim to it, they are resisting here:—you will perceive Sir, by a reference to the Map, that the whole of the lands between the rivers Sabine and Brazos, have been granted away to American Settlers, and that the tide of emigration is settling very fast in the direction of the Rio Bravo. These grants have been made by the provincial Government of Texas, and retailed by the Original speculators to the hordes of their countrymen, which have already arrived there, at a moderate price of half a dollar an acre, by which however they have cleared 150 per cent profit. On the most moderate computation, six hundred North American families are already established in Texas; their numbers are increasing daily, and though they nominally recognize the authority of the Mexican Government, a very little time will enable them, to set at defiance any attempt to enforce it. . . . General Wavell has, I believe, a considerable share, but he is, I understand, almost the only Englishman, who has applied for land in Texas. The rest of the settlers are all American—Back-woodsmen, a bold and hardy race, but likely to prove bad subjects, and most inconvenient neighbors. In the event of a rupture between this country and the United States, their feelings and earlier connections will naturally lead them to side with the latter; and in time of peace their lawless habits, and dislike of all restraints, will, as naturally, induce them to take advantage of their position which is admirably adapted for a great smuggling trade, and to resist all attempts to repress it. In short, Mexico, though she may gain in point of numbers, will not, certainly, acquire any real strength, by such an addition to her population. . . . Not knowing in how far His Majesty's Government may conceive the possession of Texas by the Americans, to be likely to affect the interests of Great Britain, I have not thought it right to go beyond such general observations upon the subject, in my communications with this Government, as appeared to me calculated to make it perceive the danger, to which it is willfully exposing itself. Were but one hundredth part of the attention paid to practical encroachment, which will be bestowed upon anything like a verbal cession, Mexico would have little to fear.[24]

Then on March 18, 1826, he again announced: "With regard to Texas something must be done immediately, for so incomprehensible is the apathy of the Government that altho' it is in possession of facts which ought to determine it to adopt vigorous measures at once, unless a sort of factitious excitement be constantly kept up, it relapses into indifference, and pursues with the best intentions, the very course with Mr. Poinsett would trace out as most favourable to his plans."[25] As it happens Ward already had something in mind, and the very next day wrote another letter to Canning, outlining some direct action being taken to try to block the overland route between Texas and Louisiana:

> I was requested by General Wavell a few weeks ago to assist him in carrying through a project which he could not but regard as calculated to prove highly advantageous to this Country, provided the sanction, and co-operation of the Government were secured. He, General Wavell, had obtained from the Government of Texas a Grant of land, which it was his intention to colonise with Europeans, provided the President would add to it a valuable tract of Country situated in the vicinity of the Sabine, and Red River and which as comprised in the boundary line, the Supreme Government alone could dispose of. General Wavell stated that this Grant would effectually break the chain of communication which it was evidently the object of the Americans to establish, as it occupies a great part of the space which intervenes between the frontier of Louisiana and the lands already ceded to Messrs Edwards, Leftwich and Austin.[26]

The Mexican president, Guadalupe Victoria, was seemingly agreeable, on condition that Wavell "was not to admit upon it [the grant] a single North American Colonist." What was more, in a second letter of the same date Ward revealed that he had another ally, named John Dunn Hunter. A Cherokee by adoption, Hunter had been appointed as a commissioner to try to obtain a Mexican land grant for his people, who were moving westward to escape harassment by the "Backsettlers": "Hunter assured me," said Ward, "that they are . . . determined to resist all encroachments upon the part of the Americans, provided the Government will sanction and support them if necessary; I thought that a better opportunity could not easily be found of opposing a formidable obstacle to the designs of the United States upon Texas." Once again the president seemed "much pleased with the idea," but rather than "appear myself too much in the business," Ward introduced Hunter to Wavell. The two were natural allies, for the principal attraction of the scheme was that the establishment of the Cherokees would "complete this plan (Wavell's colony) by covering the whole line of the Red River, beyond the General's Grant."

It all looked very promising, and Ward could not resist closing by assuring Canning that "I have taken the greatest care not to commit myself in any way and that what I have written for Hunter was copied by himself in my sight, so that not only does his Petition appear in his own handwriting, but no proof exists of my having had anything to do with it."[27]

Plausible deniability was clearly nothing new, and at the same time Ward also helped engineer the appointment of General Mier y Teran to carry out what would be a far-reaching tour of inspection of the Texas colonies.[28] Teran was not to undertake his survey until 1828, but afterward, having seen the scale of the threat at first hand, he made a number of recommendations aimed at severely restricting American immigration and tightening Mexican control of Texas. In the meantime Ward himself had a book and a map printed at just this time, unambiguously titled *United States Designs on Texas*.[29] In gathering material for that book, and indeed in monitoring developments in Texas generally, Ward obviously depended heavily on the assistance of other less conspicuous agents, and the circumstances point to James Grant's involvement in the business. Grant was well acquainted both with Texas and with Benjamin Rush Milam, a Kentucky-born filibuster turned entrepreneur, who also happened to be Wavell's new partner. Since Milam frequently carried letters between Grant and Austin in the 1820s, he may also unwittingly (or not) have been the means by which Grant was able to pass information back to Ward, either directly or more likely through Wavell.[30]

Some of that information, moreover, could have been highly damaging. From Presidio del Rio Grande, Grant wrote to Stephen Austin on May 13, 1826, making his customary excuses for not visiting the colony "owing to my business," and disingenuously informing him that an American named George Nixon ("who is well known to you from the disturbance he tried to make when on the Rio Brazos"), having "taken particular pains to shew me all the documents, in order to draw me to his side," was trying "to represent your Conduct in a bad light" to the authorities.[31] He thus poisoned that particular well and encouraged Austin to "depend upon all my influence, and exertion, for the protection and welfare of the Colony."[32] It was probably Grant rather than Nixon who eventually used the papers to undermine the Americans in the end, for he boasted in the same letter that notwithstanding his bad Spanish, he was on intimate terms with an unnamed general and a priest "whose Uncle is one of the Secretaries of the department of Mexico."[33]

Hardly surprisingly, in October of that year Captain John Austin wrote from Saltillo to his namesake, complaining that "the English have left no method untryed but on the contrary have used every exertion to induce the Genl Govt to regard the Americans with jealousy and suspicion. They have used all their intrigue and influence to injure the Character of the Americans and many representations have been made in Mexico against Amer[ic]n Emigration." Nevertheless, he concluded that "the Govt. attributed it to Ambition and that natural antipathy the English possess towards us."[34] For his part, Ward gloomily admitted: "I have done everything in my power to frustrate them [the Americans] here, and shall still continue to do so. If I have not been successful, my failure must be ascribed not to any want of exertion on my part, but to the vanity and listlessness of those at the heart of affairs here."[35] Although he did not spell it out, his principal disappointment was the failure of the Mexican government to confirm the proposed land grant to the Cherokees, which he certainly suspected was due in part to Poinsett, "who is determined if possible to parry a blow the consequences of which might certainly prove highly injurious to his present schemes." What was more, the American government was insisting that Wavell's land grant was actually within United States territory.

Even as Captain Austin was warning that something was afoot, this obstruction now led Ward to involve himself directly in the scheme to try and impose a British-dominated buffer state between the Sabine and the colonies. There are only fleeting and tantalizing references to exactly what happened, but the outlines can be reconstructed clearly enough. The attempted coup was preceded by two wide-ranging tours of northern Mexico, ostensibly in order to carry out a detailed assessment of the various foreign-controlled mining operations there. These mines were legitimately one of the British government's principal concerns, and as far back as January 1824, Lionel Hervey had warned that unless American influence was checked, "the whole produce of the mines would in few years find its way through the Northern Provinces to New Orleans."[36] In themselves Ward's tours could therefore be plausibly presented as an important exercise to inform British economic strategy, but his superiors in London were unimpressed, and after the first one he was told in no uncertain terms that "although you were directed (in common with the other British Agents in the new States of America) to send to this Office information on the Subject of the Mines in Mexico, yet you were not authorized to take a journey and incur an expense on that Account."[37] Ward undoubtedly did collect a great deal of useful information on the mines, which he duly passed to London and later incorporated to some effect in his book, but the real purpose of his traveling north from Mexico City was something very different.

Back in April when the scheme to create the barrier colonies was being hatched, Ward had written a private letter to Charles Vaughan, the British minister at Washington, introducing Wavell, who "has been of great use to me here and can give you a very good idea of the state of affairs here at the present moment. His only fault is being almost too zealous upon the subject, & from this the only differences we have had have arisen."[38] The "subject" was of course Texas, and after briefing Vaughan on the settlement scheme, Wavell returned there by way of New Orleans, visiting Nacogdoches in the summer and then proceeding up the Red River. His timing was interesting, to say the least.

The Fredonian Rebellion is one of the more bizarre episodes in the early history of Texas, although in outline the facts seem straightforward enough. In April 1825, a Mississippian named Haden Edwards obtained an empresario grant to settle eight hundred families on lands around Nacogdoches in East Texas. As was customary he was required to respect any previous Spanish grants in the area, and inevitably the close proximity of the border meant a fair number of squatters. Therefore when he actually arrived there in September of that year with his first fifty families, Edwards peremptorily ordered that the existing settlers "immediately present themselves to me and show me their titles or documents, if any they possess, so that they can be received or rejected and if they do not do this, the said lands will be sold to the first person who occupies them." In the light of the quite breathtaking land frauds being almost openly practiced at that time by James Bowie in neighboring Louisiana, based on forged Spanish grants, this was a sensible precaution.[39]

Unfortunately his high-handed approach provoked trouble. Although relatively few claims were involved, an undignified row broke out between the old settlers and the new, which came to a head in December when Edwards successfully had his own son-in-law elected as *alcalde* of Nacogdoches. The old settlers then equally successfully challenged the result, and in March the election was reversed by the political chief in San Antonio, José Antonio Saucedo, and Samuel Norris was thus installed as alcalde in his place. Shortly after this Edwards returned to the United States, ostensibly in search of further financial backing, leaving the colony in the hands of his brother Benjamin, who proceeded to make matters far worse by falling out with the vice governor of Coahuila y Texas, Victor Blanco. The result was that in October Haden Edwards's grant was revoked by the government. Far from defusing the feud, this only brought matters to a head, and on November 22 some of Edwards's supporters, led by Martin Parmer, seized control of Nacogdoches, arrested Norris, and installed Joseph Durst as alcalde in his stead. As some 250 Mexican troops under Lieutenant Colonel Mateo Ahumada closed in, the rebels concluded an alliance with the neighboring Cherokee and proclaimed the independent Republic of Fredonia on December 21, 1826. It even had its own flag. The republic lasted just over a month before Ahumada reached the town on January 31, 1827, only to find that the rebels had fled across the Sabine to the safety of the United States.

"There never was a more silly, wild Quicksotic scheme than that of Nacogdoches," commented one observer. Seriocomic aspects notwithstanding, the historical significance of the Fredonian Rebellion appears to lie in its dramatic deepening of the growing distrust felt by the Mexican government toward its Texas colonists—despite the fact that Austin and his militia had joined with Ahumada to crush the revolt. It is also easy to see parallels with the earlier West Florida affair, where the proclamation of a rebel "republic" was the signal for American annexation. In reality it was the reason behind Ward's northern odysseys. Oblivious to the reprimand issued over his first trip, he abruptly embarked on another between November 31, 1826, and January 23, 1827, plausibly taking as his excuse the desirability of leaving Mexico City while elections were in progress. Rather less explicably he took his wife, an eighteen-month-old child, and a five-month-old baby, and all of the men in his party were heavily armed. What was more, although he properly relayed to his superiors a report of an attempted coup in the capital during his absence, he quite incredibly said absolutely nothing at all, either in his official dispatches or in his later book, about the crisis in Texas that erupted and then collapsed while he was in the north.[40]

The reason for this curious lacuna is not hard to discover. On January 24, 1827, just as the whole affair was about to fizzle out, a colonist named James Kerr, who had been sent to find out what was really going on, wrote to Austin reporting what he had just learned at first hand in Nacogdoches: "I bege leave to suggest that, there is a combination of men (some of whom call themselves Americans) but I believe them to be Englishmen principally—tho, some are perhapse French origin etc. . . . First I will identify one John D Hunter (commonly called Doctor Hunter), and one _____ Basset. These two men say they are Cherokees by adoption."[41] It was Hunter who concluded the extraordinary alliance between the "Fredonians" and the Cherokee, leading Austin to exclaim in horror: "Great God, can it be possible that Americans, high minded free born and honourable Americans will so far forget the country of their birth, so far forget themselves, as to league with barbarians and join a band of savages."[42] Austin's astonishment is understandable, but Hunter's involvement immediately raises the likelihood that it was he who initiated the alliance with the Edwards, rather than the other way around. And there was more. Kerr went on to warn:

> The Mexican nation granted a section of Hir territory to one Genl Waval to colonize, and I was informed by some of the out Laws while at Nachadoches that he Hunter had said, his great dependence, and hopes for assistance to revolutionize the department of Texas was on the British; that he expected in less than four months to be reinforced by 500 englishmen who would land at the mouth of the Brassos under the command of said Waval; that a Doctor *Somebody* who spoke French, English, and Spanish was then in the interior as a spy. That Hunter would act on the frontiers; stimulating to action our red Bretheren, while the British would land on the Coast and over power all opposition, and organise a Govt of their own formation and which as my informant said would be an effective one.

Not surprisingly, Kerr admitted that the scheme, and in particular the reported British involvement, sounded unlikely "when compaired with reason and common sence; yet," as he so rightly said, "we see some of its features demonstrated. . . . It is a well known fact that waval [*sic*] and Hunter were together in Mexico last winter and that Hunter said he was treated with more than ordinary politeness by said waval, and other Englishmen in Mexico." So he was, of course, and while there was no doubt some exaggeration in the claim of five hundred Englishmen about to land at the Brazos, all of what Kerr reported is entirely consistent with the plan outlined by Ward back in March to interpose a buffer zone along the frontier and with Wavell's appearance on the Red River earlier that summer. Moreover, while Kerr jumped to the conclusion that the "spy" was a Mexican Army doctor named José Luciano Oliver, it is plain from the context in which he appears that Kerr's informants were talking about a British agent, not a Mexican one. Instead, that "Doctor *Somebody*" must have been James Grant, who was indeed in the "interior" at the time, ostensibly to purchase half a league of land at Matagorda, for family sources firmly associate him in some kind of revolutionary activity with one or both of the Edwards brothers.[43]

Just how deeply Haden Edwards himself was involved in this scheme is open to debate. His initial troubles with the settlers at Nacogdoches were unquestionably of his own making and quite unconnected with Ward's clandestine maneuverings. On the other hand his later decision, or perhaps his brother Benjamin's decision, to initiate a rebellion certainly appears, on the strength of Kerr's report, to have been heavily influenced by promises of British support, which can only have come from Wavell and Grant. What authority the old soldier of fortune might have had to offer this support may be questionable, particularly in the light of Ward's warning that he was "almost too zealous." Ultimately, however, the diplomat must at least have been aware of what was going on, and so Grant's far from coincidental presence in Texas just at this moment indicates that once again, although close at hand, Ward was taking "the greatest care not to commit (himself) in any way." As he and Wavell were simply too prominent to appear in the business, it fell to Dr. *Somebody*—James Grant—to liaise with the rebels and perhaps offer those promises of British backing. At any rate when that support failed to materialize, the sudden collapse of the rebellion demonstrates the extent to which Edwards and his confederates may have been depending upon it. Had the proposed alliance with Wavell and Hunter actually come to fruition, the Republic of Texas (or Fredonia) might have been born ten years early as a British client state with an "effective" government hostile to any notion of American annexation.

Instead it all fell apart as those involved were scattered. The Edwardses and their American colleagues escaped across the border, but Hunter was repudiated and soon afterward killed by the Cherokees. Despite Kerr's denunciation, Wavell managed to avoid the subsequent fallout and persevered unsuccessfully with his land claims on the Red River. Ward, having so spectacularly overstepped the mark in interfering with Mexico's internal affairs, was recalled to London with a thunderous swiftness that might otherwise seem inexplicable.[44] All he could do was insist to the naval officer sent to fetch him home that he be carried by way of New York, "being exceedingly desirous to see his Majesty's Minister at Washington." In his subsequent book he would disingenuously describe the detour to New York as coming about purely by chance and so providing an entirely fortuitous opportunity to pay a pleasant social call on the minister, who happened to be his old friend, Charles Vaughan. In reality Captain Vernon was extremely reluctant to deviate so far from his intended course and did so only after Ward presented him with written orders stating that he regarded it "as in some measure essential to the good of the service that I should have this personal communication with Mr. Vaughan, as it is impossible for me to convey to him in writing all that I have to state."[45] Such an urgent conference can only have been to brief Vaughan on the Fredonia debacle, and when Vernon complained to his superiors on returning to England, they too were solemnly assured by the Foreign Office that the detour was indeed "necessary" and for the good of the service.

In fact the Fredonian business effectively marked the end of active British attempts to curb the Americans for the time being. Ward was replaced by Richard Pakenham, a cautious career diplomat who preferred to fret over such comfortably mundane matters as the unreliability of the postal system; Canning briefly became prime minister and then died in August; while both Charles Grant and his old boss, William Huskisson, left the government in the following year; none of their successors in office displayed much interest in the region. Lord Palmerston, who succeeded to the Foreign Office in 1830, was chiefly concerned with European and Near Eastern politics and singularly unconcerned over more distant trans-Atlantic matters.

There were still those both inside Parliament and out of it who would continue to warn against the dangers of American expansion, Henry Ward included. But to all outward appearances James Grant, for the moment at least, was cut adrift. He never returned to Scotland, and despite his having finally bought some land in Texas, there were no more letters to Stephen Austin offering excuses for his failure to visit the colony. Instead he remained in Coahuila, settling down at Parras with a Mexican woman, María Guadalupe Reyes, fathering a further seven children, and gaining a reputation as a "man of progress."[46]

2 • *Revolution*

SHEER HARD WORK was what earned James Grant his reputation as a man of progress. According to John Linn, Grant became the "resident agent of an English mining company," perhaps pointing to a connection with the iron ore mine at Encarnación, which Wavell and Milam leased to an English company at about this time. More likely, it refers to his becoming the general manager "of a number of extensive haciendas" forming the vast Aguayo estates in Coahuila and Zacatecas (map, next page). These were leased in September 1828, to a consortium of British companies headed by the famous banking house of Baring Brothers and by the Mexican-based Staples and Company.[1] Grant also purchased and developed his own Hacienda los Hornos—the Hacienda of the Furnaces, near Parras. An 1835 creditors' claim would mention wheat being grown there, and there were vineyards too, but it was primarily an industrial enterprise.[2] In addition to the *hornos* or furnaces that gave the hacienda its name, Grant obtained a ten-year concession to manufacture cotton and wool in the three departments of Saltillo, Parras, and Monclova and would be in the process of setting up a cotton mill there in partnership with a Daniel Toler when the final crisis broke.[3] The whole enterprise was reputedly valued at $105,000 in 1838.[4] As if all that were not enough, in 1833 Grant entered into partnership with an Englishman named Dr. John Charles Beales to settle eight hundred European families on that part of Coahuila lying between the Rio Grande and Nueces rivers and so create the settlement of Dolores, near Presidio del Rio Grande. It was little wonder therefore that he should adopt the Spanish style of Don Diego Grant or that Linn should remark that "at his home in Coahuila he lived like a lord and entertained like a prince."[5]

Grant also formally became a citizen of the state on September 21, 1830.[6] Just two years later he was elected to the state legislature of

MEXICO
1835

Mexico in 1835.

Coahuila y Texas, as one of the three deputies for the department of
Parras. Notwithstanding the accord patched up at Iguala nearly ten
years before, Mexico at this time was still bitterly and to a large extent
unavoidably divided on ideological lines into two mutually antagonistic
factions, distinguished as the Federalistas and Centralistas. The former
were regarded as liberals, were largely anticlerical, and were conspicuously keen to take a progressive approach to trade and industry. The
Centralistas, on the other hand, not only stood in opposition to these
tenets but were sometimes accused of being the "Spanish" party and in
favor of a return to rule from Madrid. Fundamentally though, the two
parties were probably not very far apart on most issues, save for the all-
important one of the states' rights enshrined in the Constitution of 1824.
Mexico was a huge country of many contrasts, comparatively thinly populated, and uncertainly held together by an extremely ramshackle infra-
structure. Unsurprisingly, federalist sentiment was strongest far away
from Mexico City in the outlying states, which through circumstances
as much as politics became accustomed to a considerable degree of
autonomy. The ultraconservative Centralistas, in contrast, believed with

some reason that only a strong central government, underpinned by an equally powerful Catholic Church, could hold the republic together by preventing those states from breaking away.

In January 1833, Major General Antonio López de Santa Anna became president of the republic on a federalist ticket, but he promptly and prudently retired to his hacienda, leaving his deputy, Valentín Gómez Farias, in charge of the government. Farias equally promptly but far less prudently embarked on a wide-ranging program of liberal reform, which, as so often happens, succeeded in alienating both the Church and the landed gentry or *hacendados,* while failing to deliver any tangible benefits to the poor. Both his credibility and his popularity plummeted, and in April 1834, Santa Anna walked back into office, sacked Farias, and soon afterward invoked the emergency powers in the constitution to rule by decree. Some time later he justified his actions by declaring that Mexico was not yet ready for democracy: "A hundred years to come," he remarked to his Texian captors after the Battle of San Jacinto, "my people will not be fit for liberty. A despotism is the proper government for them."[7] On various pretexts he also began progressively dissolving the state legislatures and so, quite effortlessly, not only switched sides but assumed leadership of the Centralistas.

Naturally enough, opposition to this unexpected coup came principally from the federalists of the northern states, including Coahuila y Texas. Complicating matters enormously were the growing number of increasingly restless American settlers in Texas. Despite the ban on immigration from the United States that followed Mier y Teran's inspection, squatters had continued to flood across the Sabine, and Mexican attempts to retain some control over the situation led to violent clashes at Anahuac and Nacogdoches in 1832. As pressure grew for a formal measure of autonomy, a constitutional convention sent Stephen Austin to Mexico City in November 1833, with a mandate to seek resolution of a number of long-standing grievances and to urge the case for restoring statehood to Texas. On most of the issues he found the government to be surprisingly receptive, but when rebuffed on the all-important matter of statehood he was indiscreet enough to write home recommending that Texas should set up a state government anyway. Unfortunately the authorities at Bexar were rather more alarmed than excited by this proposition and denounced him instead. Consequently he was arrested at Monterrey and sent straight back to Mexico City.

James Grant immediately responded by lending him two hundred dollars and was then instrumental in the spring of 1834 in passing a number of laws in the Coahuila legislature that were intended to dampen the underlying demands for secession.[8] Texas was reorganized into three departments (Bexar, Brazos, and Nacogdoches) rather than one, thus increasing Texian representation in the legislature; English was declared an official language; and provision made for trial by jury. For the colonists this new policy of accommodation was a considerable and welcome advance, and Grant soon developed a reputation as a friend to the Texas colonies and a firm advocate of their interests. On April 15, 1835, Green De Witt wrote to his Gonzales colonists, assuring them that he had been endeavoring to secure legal rights for their lands, "which I have every reason to think will now be accomplished by the assistance of Dr James Grant the Deputy of the Department of Parras and other members of Congress. . . . Dr Grant will in all likelihood visit our Colony in the fall of the year and will be able to give you satisfactory information on all points in which you and myself are equally interested."[9] Indeed many of the other Texian settlers' leaders, such as John Linn, John M. Durst, and of course Stephen Austin himself, regarded Grant with considerable respect at this time, which is at odds with the unsavory reputation later accorded him by Sam Houston.

Unfortunately, Grant's efforts did little to ease the situation, and his promised visit to Texas in the fall would be unavoidably delayed by events. Ultimately the colonists still wanted to form an autonomous English-speaking state, and in theory the 1824 constitution could have accommodated this. The union of Coahuila and Texas was acknowledged from the start to be a temporary one, and when Austin broached the subject, Santa Anna himself appeared not entirely unsympathetic; but it was the one thing the central government was not prepared to concede. The official reason was that Texas still lacked anything approaching the eighty thousand inhabitants clearly required under the terms of the constitution to qualify for statehood. In reality, of course, the refusal sprang from a well-founded fear that federal autonomy would only be the inevitable prelude to secession—and ultimately to annexation by the United States.

In the meantime matters were further inflamed when the near bankrupt Coahuila legislature hit upon the happy notion of selling off some of the vast swathes of as yet unclaimed public land in Texas. This began with an act of March 26, 1834, to sell land at auction in lots of one *labor* (177 acres) with a reserve price of ten dollars per labor, which was subsequently amended on April 23 to allow the land to be sold at the reserve by private treaty in the event of no bidders coming forward. Although the provisions drew little notice at the time, the sales would afterward be denounced in Texas as corrupt, and there is no doubting the role of a relatively small group of speculators in using private treaties with the state governor to buy up the lots offered. Nevertheless both these and the later land sales need to be seen in their proper context. The simple fact was that the legislature genuinely required a great deal of ready cash in order to defend itself against growing centralist pressure, which was why, on June 26, the executive was authorized to levy and organize a civic militia "for the defense of the federal institutions."

Back in March 1833, the federalist legislature had succeeded in transferring the state capital from Centralista-dominated Saltillo to the far more congenial surroundings of Monclova; James Bowie and other land speculators reputedly had a hand in this move.[10] Now, encouraged by Santa Anna's assumption of power, the Saltillo Centralistas retaliated by forming their own rival legislature in July 1834. Almost as a matter of form they also proclaimed the acts of the Monclova legislature annulled. In response the Federalistas began arming, and James Grant was designated *jefe* or chief of the civic militia of Parras.[11] Before any fighting took place both factions submitted the matter to Santa Anna for arbitration. He, pragmatically, confirmed that Monclova should now be recognized as the state capital but ruled that fresh elections should take place. Following those elections, which only confirmed the federalist ascendancy, the legislature reconvened on March 1, 1835, and this time Grant was installed as one of the secretaries on the executive council, where he played a prominent role in the events that followed.[12]

Finding that "there was not even a dollar in the coffers of the state to meet the principal and most indispensable expenses, owing to the large disbursements the past administration had to make on account of the turbulent revolt produced by one town of the state against its supreme authorities, and legislative and executive acts during the preceding two years term," another act was passed on March 14, 1835, authorizing the immediate sale of a further four hundred leagues of vacant land, this time "for attending to the present public exigencies of the state."[13] In view of the increasing urgency of the situation—no one in Coahuila was

A teamster dressed in jeanscloth working clothes—easily identifiable by the creased appearance. Many of the Texian soldiers, especially those coming from the United States, were dressed in this fashion. Based on a George Caleb Bingham sketch.

under any illusions that a fight could be avoided—the legislature was once again authorized to dispense with the restrictions imposed on the previous act of March 26, 1834. The land would simply be sold at the asking price, not by auction, and there was no limit on how much a single individual could buy.

The whole business was denounced as corrupt not only by the Centralistas but this time by the Texians as well, although the historian Eugene C. Barker has argued convincingly that the whole business was inflated out of all proportion. He points out that contrary to some contemporary claims, the crisis in Texas was not engineered by Grant or any of the other speculators to further their own aims. Indeed he questions whether the transactions really amounted to speculation at all and suggests that they may have constituted an attempted revival of the empresario system by other means.

Notwithstanding all the heat and passion aroused in Texas, the real reason for the opposition was that the lands were required not for the benefit of individual immigrants but to secure substantial loans from New Orleans bankers. In other words, the Texians also intended that the land should be used "for attending to the present public exigencies of the state"—but the state they had in mind was an independent Texas![14]

Establishing the extent of Grant's involvement in the land business is not easy. Even at the time of his death, his brother's agent, James Ogilvie, found it difficult to get straight answers from Grant's surviving associates. The most prominent of the speculators was John T. Mason, the sometime agent for the New York–based Galveston Bay and Texas Land Company, who had purchased the first of no fewer than four hundred leagues in June 1834, and then sold fifty of them to Grant.[15] Closely associated with Mason was the celebrated James Bowie, whom Grant probably first met in Saltillo in 1830, since Bowie obtained his letters of citizenship there on September 30, just a week after Grant did so. At the time Bowie may well have persuaded Grant to buy shares in his projected Coahuila Manufacturing Company, and when they were both in Monclova in December, 1834, Bowie is reputed to have borrowed considerable sums of money from Grant in return for the promise of one hundred leagues of Texas land.[16] This particular scheme was "never perfected," but on April 16, 1835, in the dying days of the Monclova legislature, Grant put Hacienda los Hornos up as security for the purchase of three hundred leagues. One third of them were reserved for him, and another hundred leagues went to John M. Durst, the Nacogdoches deputy in the legislature.[17] The remainder were passed to another noted speculator, Samuel M. Williams, who was apparently to retain half and sell the rest for Grant.[18]

In the meantime the Centralistas, understandably angered at these proceedings, again withdrew from the legislature in protest and attempted to establish a rival administration at Saltillo. This time they were supported by regular troops commanded by Brigadier General Martín Perfecto de Cos, and on April 7, Grant and the rest of the executives, hearing that Cos was on the march, formally authorized the legitimate governor, Augustín Viesca, to call out the civic militia. A few days later Grant and the militia confronted the regulars outside Monclova. James Bowie was there too and reportedly "did every thing in his power to bring on a battle."[19] But Cos, who found himself badly outnumbered and may have been under orders not to fight, backed off. Subsequently he even assured the legislature that he would "support the existing order of things in every respect" and would "lend his aid in person and influence to secure and continue the peace and security of the State."[20]

No one was under any illusion that the crisis was over, for April 7 had also brought an appeal from the neighboring state of Zacatecas. At the end of March Santa Anna's government placed a ceiling on the size of the civic or state militias, limiting them to a maximum of one recruit for every five hundred citizens. Predictably this aroused considerable opposition, and Zacatecas took the lead in authorizing its governor, Gonzáles Cosco, to "use all of the State Militia to repel any aggression." Equally predictably, having stirred up the conflict he wanted, Santa Anna began preparing a military expedition to bring the dissidents to heel. At first Coahuila's response to these moves was relatively muted and merely took the form of "expositions" or protests to Mexico City, denying that the militias were a threat to political stability. Otherwise it might have seemed as if business as usual prevailed.[21] But there were considerable undercurrents, and on April 27 the Saltillo Centralistas were formally denounced. The following day another decree called for a forced loan of twenty thousand dollars from the state's "capitalists."[22]

Against this increasingly tense background, Grant's "joint speculation of considerable magnitude" with Williams and the others looks very like insurance against the Monclova legislature's increasingly probable demise. On May 2 he collected the land certificates, and then he simply disappears from the records for two weeks. There may be a perfectly straightforward explanation, perhaps reflecting a routine rotation of cosignatories to decrees; but as Creed Taylor remembered, it was widely believed at the time that Grant took a stand against Santa Anna in the "Zacatecas affair."[23] This is plausible enough, for it would be only sensible for Viesca to send an envoy or two to liaise with Zacatecas as the crisis approached. In light of his prominent role in what followed, Grant, who already had his own contacts in Zacatecas from his days with the Aguayo estates, is by far the most likely choice for that envoy.

The war began in earnest on April 18, when Santa Anna marched north from Mexico City with some four thousand regulars. By May 9 he was approaching the village of Guadalupe, four miles to the south of the state capital. The Zacatecan commander, Don Francisco García, had a similar number of militia, well equipped from the revenues of the state's silver mines, and on May 10 he drew up his men on a thousand-yard-wide front on the east side of Guadalupe, with his left flank covered by the mountains and his right by a ravine. When Santa Anna came up he announced to García that he intended to quarter his army in Zacatecas that night and that the Federalistas therefore had eight hours to disband and surrender their weapons. García naturally refused and declared that he was standing by the Constitution of 1824, but Santa Anna delayed fighting. Instead he thoroughly reconnoitered the Zacatecan position before attacking early the next morning under cover of a drizzling rain. While a cavalry demonstration pinned down García's right flank, Santa Anna crushed the left flank with his infantry and artillery. It was all over within a couple of hours; estimates of the Federalista dead and wounded ranged as high as 1,200, while Santa Anna claimed 2,723 prisoners and turned his men loose on Zacatecas for two days of unrestrained murder, rape, and pillage.

Grant, if indeed he was present, managed to make his escape, but in an ugly foretaste of what was to come, Santa Anna ordered the summary execution of any Norte Americanos found among the prisoners. Intriguingly enough, included among them was a British subject named Magrath, whose demise aroused more than ordinary indignation at the Foreign Office. Although Richard Pakenham failed to elicit any satisfaction from the Mexican authorities in the end, the keenness with which this case was pursued—in marked contrast to the relative indifference the Foreign Office later displayed toward the Tampico prisoners— suggests that, like Grant, Magrath was one of their own.[24]

Santa Anna returned in triumph to Mexico City, leaving General Cos to deal with Monclova—properly this time. On May 20, with the Centralistas again closing in, the state legislature resolved to adjourn and the next day formally authorized the executive to establish itself "at any other place in the state than the capital," which everyone understood to mean San Antonio de Béxar. Unfortunately Viesca then dithered, delaying his departure from Monclova until May 25. When he did eventually go, it was in a coach accompanied by the state archives and an escort of 150 militia, who were probably Grant's men. He got only as far as the Hacienda de Hermanas, where they all met Mason and Bowie coming from Matamoros with forty thousand dollars in coin to pay for their earlier land grants.[25] There Viesca learned that Cos had forbidden him to cross into Texas, and for some reason they initially accepted this order quietly and returned to Monclova, where Grant prudently obtained a receipt for his thirty thousand dollars from the state secretary, José María Irala, on May 30.[26] Then the governor changed his mind yet again—or more likely had it changed for him. Leaving behind the archives and the militia but accompanied by Grant and a number of Texians, he secretly set off for a second time, only for the whole lot to be intercepted and arrested by General Cos at Gigedo on June 5.

As he and his men triumphantly marched into Monclova the general announced and justified himself in a proclamation charging "two or three designing and naturally turbulent foreigners, somewhat crafty in their machinations," with bringing about the crisis. It has been suggested that he may well have had Mason, Williams, and Bowie in mind.[27] But while that particular trio certainly made up the most prominent of the land speculators, they were not regarded as much of a political threat. Instead, Mexican sources firmly point to Dr. James Grant, his old friend Ben Milam, and perhaps Dr. John Cameron as the men actually fingered by Cos. Whether or not the Mexican government was aware that Grant was a British agent, he was certainly a "jefe de las armas" and a noted liberal, reputed to have fought against Santa Anna in Zacatecas.[28] Not only was he a prominent member of Viesca's council, but at the time of his arrest he was being described as "deputy president of the legislature," which confirms the impression that he, rather than the ineffectual Viesca, was the prime mover in the recent events.[29] Some months later *El Mosquito Mexicano* would even refer to the Scotsman in rather sinister fashion as "the never-well-thought-of Don Diego Grant."[30] As for the others, Ben Milam was a notorious filibuster and known associate of Grant, with an even longer history of troublemaking stretching all the way back to Long's ill-fated invasion in 1819, while Cameron too was a "foreigner" who had been living in Mexico and Texas since 1827 and was currently a secretary in the executive department of the Coahuila legislature. That alone may have been sufficient to damn him in Cos's eyes.

At any rate all three were held along with Viesca in nearby Monterrey, where Grant was soon in deeper trouble. Having paid more than thirty thousand dollars to the state treasury for the land certificates, or at least having persuaded Irala to sign a receipt for that sum, he redeemed Hacienda los Hornos and then, in a vain attempt to safeguard it, promptly signed the property over to María Guadalupe Reyes.[31] Unfortunately, as soon as Cos arrested him, all of his properties "lacking a head" were seized and "placed under the assistance of the Collector of Revenue" at Parras—or, as Grant himself rather more bluntly put it, "embargoed by my enemies." This was the signal for his creditors to begin gathering, and despite his attorney's protests that there were both sufficient credits and stock in hand to meet the debts, a receiver was appointed on September 17. To cap it all, Guadalupe gave birth to daughter shortly afterward, a daughter whom Grant was almost certainly destined never to see.[32]

James Bowie and most of the other American speculators were carried off in the opposite direction, down to the port of Matamoros near the mouth of the Rio Grande. This might have been with a view to their eventual deportation, for they were lightly guarded there, and within a day or two all of them got clean away, perhaps with the help of some of Mason's forty thousand dollars. If Cos or one of his officers was persuaded to turn a blind eye to their escape, it soon proved to be a costly mistake, for most of them fled straight to Texas, where an all-out revolt was on the point of breaking out.

Threatened for some time, the revolt finally began rather uncertainly on the evening of June 30, with a comically inept amphibious attack on the Mexican customs post at Anahuac in Galveston Bay, led by none other than William Barret Travis, the future defender of the Alamo. The post's commander, Captain Antonio Tenorio, managed to surrender to the Texians before anyone actually got hurt, and rather to the chagrin of the principals, the local colonists were more embarrassed than excited by the affair. If anything they tended to side with Tenorio, who briefly found himself the hero of the hour.[33] A similar lack of revolutionary fervor was demonstrated two weeks later, on July 13, when about one hundred men assembled in the public square at Nacogdoches in eastern Texas, elected the recently escaped James Bowie to be their colonel, and seized a quantity of arms from a government warehouse.[34] Just as at Anahuac, however, the rebellion initially received only muted support from those who were not directly involved. Moreover, once the arms were seized, the rebels seemed to be left at something of a loose end; Bowie eventually took himself off to Louisiana to attend to some pressing personal business.[35]

Quite coincidentally however, that same day Stephen Austin was released from prison in Mexico City, where after eighteen months in jail he was freed by one of those random amnesties that balanced the outward severity of the Mexican justice system. Returning home by way of New Orleans, he landed at Velasco on September 2, 1835. Embittered by his long imprisonment and thoroughly convinced that negotiation was no longer an option in the present circumstances, he reversed his previous conciliatory policy and issued a call to arms. "War is our only recourse," he announced. "War in full!"[36]

It was not long in coming. In mid-September, General Cos had landed with a number of small cavalry units at Copano and then moved inland to establish his headquarters at Bexar. Waiting for him there was the local commander, Colonel Domingo Urgatechea, with one under-strength regular infantry battalion and a few more cavalry, to give him a combined total of some two hundred infantry, four hundred cavalry, and a few gunners.[37] At the outset the Texians professed themselves unimpressed with the quality of these troops. They commented adversely on the preponderance of officers and the way in which the ranks were filled out with conscripts and worse. They were also downright unsettled by the fact that the Morelos Battalion even had a fair number of Negroes serving in its ranks, including one who held the rank of first sergeant. It was probably all the more galling therefore that most of those men would soon prove to be well-trained and doughty fighters.

Initially Cos's real problem was not the quality of his soldiers but the significant differences in the fighting methods practiced by his own men and the insurgent forces. Most of his regular infantry were armed with British-made .75 caliber India Pattern muskets. These were good sturdy weapons, noted by Henry Ward to be "in very good order" when they were purchased from his government in 1826.[38] Since the British Army considered these muskets to have a useful working life of about twelve years, those carried by Cos's infantry, and by Santa Anna's men who came after them, should still have been in good and serviceable condition. Stories of worn-out and damaged weapons, more dangerous to those who carried them than to the enemy, really originated during the Mexican War of ten years later. The problem in 1835, as the Texians noted, was that Mexican gunpowder was mixed with too much charcoal and was therefore far inferior to the Du Pont rifle powder they themselves favored. More pertinent, although the smooth-bored India Pattern was a formidable man-stopper, its optimum tactical range was something under fifty yards, and its admitted effectiveness on Napoleonic battlefields depended on the opposition standing their ground to engage in a close-range firefight in which the sheer weight of fire counted for far more than careful aiming. The Texians rarely cooperated. The majority of those who fought in the early battles were untrained militia armed with small caliber "country rifles." Although organized in companies they did not form up shoulder to shoulder as the Mexicans did, or even adopt any recognizable military formation at all, but instead fought pretty much "on their own hook," usually from behind cover; and as far as possible they kept their distance so that neither muskets nor bayonets could be used against them effectively. Only Cos's cavalry had the mobility needed to engage the Texians in the open, but their short-barreled *escopetas* and British-made Paget carbines were hopelessly outclassed by American rifles.

A few of those cavalrymen were involved in the first real clash, which finally occurred at Gonzales on October 2 in a rather petty fight over a worn-out little cannon. The settlers were ordered to be disarmed; so it had to be handed over. They refused and instead invited Lieutenant Francisco Castañeda, the Mexican officer sent to fetch it, to join them and declare for the federalists. He in turn politely declined, and when the shooting ended two of his men were dead and the Texians still had their cannon. Now it was time for them to march on Bexar.

The following day, October 3, 1835, the Supreme Government in Mexico City proclaimed the Constitution of 1824 void, but despite the crushing of Zacatecas and the arrest of the Coahuila federalists, resistance to Santa Anna was by no means confined to Texas. Plans were already well under way for a series of insurrections all across northern Mexico and for the widening of the Texian uprising into a full-scale civil war. From their prison in Monterrey, both Grant and Viesca were heavily involved in this planning through the medium of a Dr. Canilo Gutiérrez, although responsibility for actually initiating the revolt would lie with a group of exiles based in New Orleans. These included such luminaries as General José Antonio Mexía, Colonel Jorge Fisher, and even the former vice president, Valentín Gómez Farias. They in turn were closely involved with the erstwhile "speculating faction," including Mason and Williams, and—more important—with William Christy and Adolphus Sterne, two of the foremost supporters of the Texian colonists and themselves founders of the committee known as the "Friends of Texas."

Unsurprisingly both Mexía and Fisher spoke out at the famous meeting in Banks' Arcade on the evening of October 13, 1835, that resulted in the immediate enlistment of the first two companies of American volunteers to go to Texas, companies later famous as the legendary New Orleans Greys. The "first object of the attention of the Committee," wrote Fisher in the course of a long and rambling letter to Stephen Austin, "is the immediate dispatch of the Texas volunteers to Nacogdoches & Brasoria, and the southern expedition will be the secondary object, altho' myself and Mexía, and even Gomez Farias are anxious to see Matamoros taken by the expedition, and to cut off Cós from his resources by land and sea."[39] Once Tampico and Matamoros were in federalist hands, he went on, "our intention is that Gomez Farias should be called by the Texians, as the legitimate and constitutional Vice-President, of the Mexican Federation, and invested with Supreme executive power of the nation, forming his ministry and organizing his Government in Texas."

In view of the way things were going it was rather optimistic to expect such an invitation by the Texians, and in fact the "Friends" would effectively betray their Mexican colleagues in the coming months, but this assumption was fundamental for the federalists' plans, for Fisher also revealed that there were few troops in Monterrey, "where Col. Dn. Valente Gomez, (a liberal) is the Commandante, and Tente. Col. Agustin Mora de Basadre, formerly Secretary and aid to Genl. Mexía, is Mayor de la Plaza, which by a masterly management with Genl. Cos, previous to his departure from Matamoros we have achieved, with an avowed intention that he (Basadre) should protect the escape of Governor Viesca and Doctr. Grant, for Texas, and proceed with them thereto."

As it happened, Philip Dimitt, the recently installed Texian commander at Goliad, had already written to Stephen Austin, proposing just such an expedition: first to capture the fort at Lipantitlán, near San Patricio, and then perhaps to move on Matamoros, which would have "the most important consequences to the present and future repose of Texas."[40] Consequently when Mexía wrote to "the Gentlemen Directors of public affairs in Texas" announcing his intention of sailing for Tampico, Austin immediately applauded the move, declaring on November 5 that "nothing will aid Texas as much as an expedition to Matamoros under General Mexía—it is all important. I recommend that every possible effort be made to fit out such an expedition if it has not already been done, as I hope it has been."[41] He was so enthusiastic that he repeated himself even more forcefully two days later; "I know of no movement," he said, "that would serve Texas so efficiently as an expedition against Matemoras or Tampico by Gen. Mexía."[42]

In the meantime, the escape of Grant and Viesca was preceded by that of Ben Milam, who got away sometime in early October. According to the traditional story Milam was placed in the charge of an old friend, presumably Colonel Basadre. "This officer gave him the freedom of the city and furnished him with a horse. The water for washing purposes was about a mile from the prison, so Milam asked and secured permission from this old friend to take his clothes to the stream for laundering. All evidence is pretty conclusive that the Mexican officer knew what Milam intended doing, and it is probable that he was even furnished with food for the trip. Anyway, when he escaped, no attempt was made to capture him."[43] Traveling by night, Milam fortuitously joined the Texian revolutionaries as they were about to attack Goliad on October 9, and just as they intended, Basadre was able to use Milam's escape as an excuse for ordering Grant and Viesca placed under a stricter guard and sending them off to Vera Cruz a few weeks later. Supposedly they were to be imprisoned there in the grim island fortress of San Juan de Ulloa, but instead the transfer provided all three with their own opportunity to escape, and they took it. "Governor Viesca was an affable gentleman, a thorough scholar, an eloquent writer, and a sagacious statesman," wrote John Linn.[44] But he was also weak to the point of timidity, and hopelessly indecisive. Grant on the other hand was by all accounts shrewd and forceful, while the commander of their twenty-man cavalry escort, Colonel José María Gonzáles, was himself a committed federalist. He too must also have been involved in the plot from the start, for at La Rinconada the colonel and his soldiers changed sides, released their prisoners, and ran for Texas.

General Mexía for his part sailed from New Orleans on November 6, aboard the unheroically named *Mary Jane*. He had a crew of fifty, three cannon, and 150 men under Colonel Martín Peraza, "armed and equipped, for land service, and all in good spirits." Like the New Orleans Greys, they had been recruited in the Crescent City from "all nations," and at least some of them were under the naïve impression that they too were bound for Texas.[45] Not until they were out at sea, declared a Londoner named James Cramp, were they introduced to the general and informed of their true destination.[46] They were organized into at least three companies: the "Grenadiers" were commanded by a Kentucky-born mercenary named John M. Allen, while the "Sharpshooters" elected George Dedrick as their captain, and a third company, largely formed of Creoles, was commanded by a Captain Lambert or by Octave Blache, a son of the New Orleans city treasurer.[47] Cramp also mentions that he and his comrades were issued with what were probably Mexican uniforms, for the survivors were afterward referred to as the "Tampico Blues." This was done in order to ensure that they appeared as federalists rather than filibusters. With good reason Mexía regarded this point as being important, and before he sailed he hoped "to pick up some more Mexican sailors, and some deserters of Col. Piedras Batallon formerly at Nacogdoches, and mix them with the crew and soldiers we are going to get for the expedition, in order to give some colour of nationality, and not to appear entirely a foreign invasion."[48]

After touching in briefly at Belize the filibusters arrived off the mouth of the Pánuco River on November 14, only to go aground while trying to pass over the bar under cover of darkness. No lives were lost, but both the "crazy old schooner" and an accompanying steamboat were totally wrecked. Fortunately, instead of rounding them up, the garrison of the nearby fort, commanded by Captain Luis Guerra, promptly declared for the Constitution of 1824 and joined the rather bedraggled filibusters. Much of the following day was then spent in salvaging stores from the wrecks while Colonel Peraza went off to try to make contact with the local Federalistas and his old Pueblo Viejo Batallon.

Unfortunately it soon transpired that the revolt timed to coincide with Mexía's arrival had begun prematurely and had been suppressed within hours, so by late afternoon the general impatiently decided that his men's arms were sufficiently dried out and marched on Tampico itself. There James Crawford, the British consul, reported "the most active exertions were in progress to resist the expected attack, as well as guard against the treachery of the *Pueblo Viejo* Corps."[49] In fact Mexía later claimed it was Crawford who warned of the filibusters' approach, and when the attack went in at about half past one the following morning, it quickly stalled and degenerated into a confused firefight. Mexía admitted afterward that he had only had eight dry rounds per man and this little supply was soon exhausted. By half past three it was all over. A brief cessation of the firing gave Mexía some hopes of victory and he "believed himself to be master of the Place; but as the firing very soon after again became brisk, that was not the case." Seemingly just four of the garrison were killed, including the artillery commander, Colonel Murguia, while as Crawford observed, "two or three" of Mexía's men were left dead on the streets when daylight "discovered to the garrison that the invaders had retired." Even the withdrawal turned into a debacle, for "being all ignorant of the roads many lost themselves and were taken by the Rancheros and Cantoneros, and others were barbarously murdered, whilst all the prisoners were brutally used, cut and beaten."[50]

A curious stalemate then ensued. Mexía had failed to carry the town in the first gallant rush and so dug in at the fort to wait and see if the local Federalistas would rally to him after all. The garrison, too weak to attack him by themselves, sat in the town and waited for reinforcements of their own. In the end, by a process that remains tantalizingly unclear, Mexía chartered another American schooner, the *Halcyon*, which carried off most of his surviving filibusters and Guerra's company as well on November 26. Behind him, however, he left thirty-one of his men in Centralista hands, of whom three succumbed to their wounds before the others, including James Cramp, were taken out and shot on December 14.[51]

Rather more fortunately, by November 8 James Grant and his party had safely reached San Patricio on the then border between Tamaulipas and Texas along the Nueces River. There Viesca borrowed some money for the subsistence of Gonzáles and his troopers.[52] Adding a little company of Texians recruited by Ira Westover to their band, they moved on to the newly established rebel post at Goliad. But almost as soon as they arrived there on November 11, 1835, they clashed with Philip Dimitt.

At first things seemed promising enough, for Dimitt provided horses so that Robert Morris and his New Orleans Greys might escort them into town. However, although Viesca's release had been one of the original demands made by the insurgents at Anahuac back in June, the Texians had by now elected Henry Smith to be their own provisional governor of their self-proclaimed federal state. Consequently, despite his initial courtesy, Dimitt, who even at his best was a rather difficult and contentious character, flatly refused to recognize Viesca's authority.

This immediately led to an acrimonious falling out between Grant and Dimitt, which would have serious repercussions later on, and to a flurry of correspondence between the seat of the provisional government at San Felipe and Stephen Austin's headquarters outside San Antonio de Béxar. At Austin's request Grant also wrote an optimistic summary of what he understood or at least claimed to be the situation in the interior. "Zacatecas is oppressed," he acknowledged, "but ready to take advantage of the first opportunity to revenge her wrongs. Durango is also ready, as soon as she can hope for assistance. Tamaulipas and Nuevo Leon rise the moment an attack is made on Matamoras; and San Luis Potosi will instantly follow." He also described illusory uprisings in the south, where a general named Alvarez was said to have taken Acapulco, while "Guzman and Montenegro have an army of 2100 liberals, in the state of Guadalaxara, and must, by this time, have driven the central troops and centralists out of that territory." Having set the scene, he then went on to argue:

> The central government is sadly distressed for funds to carry on their despotic dispositions; and if one or two of their ports are taken, they will have to yield without striking a blow. Their army is scattered, and cannot be united with safety. A number of liberal and able officers are devoted to the cause of liberty; and when the principles on which the freemen of Texas have taken up arms, are known, i.e., the defence of the Constitution of 1824, the whole republic will rise at once, and the final destruction of Santa Anna, centralism and the Spanish party, may be considered as the immediate result.[53]

In short, if the Texians marched south to carry the war into the interior, victory was assured.

A Missouri raftsman dressed in jeanscloth pants and a shirt but no coat. Again, his appearance is typical of those serving in the Texian forces. Based on a George Caleb Bingham sketch.

In marked contrast, however, the next day Dimitt also wrote to Austin, flatly contradicting Grant's cheery predictions. "In a former communication," he grumbled "I hinted at the policy of a dash to Matamoros, hoping from what I had then heard, that the movement would be approved and sustained by a majority of the people in that section of the country. But now I hear it would not be."[54] Two or three days later Viesca in turn responded by declaring his intention of resolving the impasse by appealing directly to the Texian General Council, and in preparation for this meeting Grant managed to get himself elected as one of the Goliad delegates to the council.[55] How he achieved this in the face of Dimitt's hostility is one of the minor mysteries of the affair, but he may well have had a solid block of support in Westover's men, and others could have voted for him precisely because he was at odds with the abrasive Dimitt. To judge from later events, Morris may also have been an early convert to his cause. However, once elected, Grant immediately changed his mind. Since the crisis had first broken out in Coahuila and Zacatecas he had relished his newfound role as a man of action, and no doubt recognizing that his voice would carry little weight amid the wordy clamor at San Felipe, he resolved instead to ride north and join Stephen Austin and the rebel "Army of the People" then sitting outside Bexar.

In the wake of the Gonzales affair that army had come together on Cibolo Creek, where the embattled farmers elected Stephen Austin to be their commander. He was unquestionably the natural choice to unite them, but he was also sick and exhausted. Nor did he have any real military experience, at least not in commanding large bodies of men who (to anticipate a later commentator on those who fought in the American Civil War) would obey a reasonable order but only because it was reasonable—not because it was an order. On top of that he had to deal with the political maneuverings of Sam Houston.

Born in Virginia in 1793, Houston had been taken to Tennessee when he was fourteen and later served for a time in the U.S. Army under Andrew Jackson. Afterward he turned to the law and soon gravitated to politics; he was elected to Congress in 1823 and became governor of Tennessee in 1827. All was going well, but two years later it suddenly turned sour when his marriage broke up after just four months, triggering a latent but crippling instability. Throwing over the governorship and with it his political career, he went west to Arkansas. In his youth he had spent a number of years with the Cherokee, and he now sought an alcoholic refuge among them. It was three years before he returned. Then, reinventing himself as a diplomat of sorts, he went to Texas late in 1832, seemingly at the behest of his old mentor, Andrew Jackson. His youthful affinity with Native Americans had by now developed into something of an obsession, and officially his mission for Jackson was to carry out some fairly nebulous negotiations with the far-off Comanche. However, having gone through the motions of talking to them he settled in Nacogdoches, practiced law, and became a prominent advocate of exchanging Mexican for U.S. sovereignty. As such he was elected as a delegate to the constitutional conventions that prepared the ground for Texas' secession, and unsurprisingly, he too journeyed to the rendezvous on the Cibolo.

There, to everyone's surprise, he proceeded to use "every art to discourage the army; he even attempted to scare the soldiers to their homes by insinuating that the northern Indians in Texas were about to commence hostilities."[56] More to the point perhaps, he claimed that the army lacked both the men and the artillery to take on Cos at Béxar and argued that they should instead all fall back behind the Colorado River and wait until the spring. This was a theme to which he would return time and again over the coming months, and it was widely assumed he did so in the expectation that once the army settled behind the Colorado he would be able to gain control of it himself. While this was very likely true up to a point, it is equally probable that his real object in advocating the "temporary" abandonment of western Texas was to bring about a physical separation of the American colonies in the Brazos and the Redlands from the predominantly Hispanic department of Béxar. Throughout the Texas Revolution and long afterward, Houston was consistently to display an almost paranoid unwillingness to have any kind of involvement in Mexican affairs, and he may have reasoned that annexation by the United States would be much easier to bring about if it involved only the American colonies.

Be that as it may, Houston's appeal to the army on October 25 was stoutly rebutted by several officers and decisively rejected by the volunteers, but he returned undaunted to the convention at San Felipe and there persuaded the provisional governor, Henry Smith, to appoint him as major general and commander-in-chief of the Texian army on November 12. Frustratingly for the newly minted general, his authority was limited to a proposed regular army that did not yet exist and was not acknowledged by the volunteers sitting outside Bexar. Nevertheless it did give him the opportunity to poach officers such as James W. Fannin, William B. Travis, and his old friend Bowie and to renew his campaign to pull the army back behind the Colorado.

All this meant that when Grant arrived in the Cibolo camp on the evening of November 17, 1835, he immediately became embroiled in more trouble. Discipline was virtually nonexistent, desertion was so endemic as to be almost unremarkable, and worst of all, Austin turned out to be living on borrowed time. When the convention at San Felipe adjourned on November 14 in favor of a provisional government consisting of Governor Smith and a General Council, Houston's position was greatly strengthened. Partly at his urging, one of the new government's first acts was to appoint Austin as one of the commissioners to be sent east to seek aid from the United States. This was a shrewd move, for Austin was in many ways an ideal ambassador and under other circumstances might have embraced the opportunity wholeheartedly. Nevertheless, although he was advised of his selection on the afternoon of November 18—in a dispatch carried by James Bowie—Austin at first concealed the news from the army; ill as he was, he feared that the army would probably disintegrate without him. Instead, hoping that some real action would pull the volunteers together, he began planning for a full-scale assault on the town four days later, early on the morning of November 22.

3 · *Bexar*

AMONG ALL THE OTHER PREPARATIONS recorded in Austin's order book for November 21 is a short note directing that "the battery ordered to be erected within 300 yds of the walls of the fortifications [the Alamo] will be commenced this night, under the command of Capt. Cheshire assisted by Dr. James Grant as engineer." This is Grant's first known appearance as a soldier of Texas; beyond the ad hoc appointment, he had as yet no official standing in the army.[1] Nevertheless he was evidently playing a much more active part in the proceedings than this casual reference suggests, for another staff officer named Colonel William T. Austin (unrelated to Stephen Austin) recalled that "Dr. James Grant, who was a very skilful man and scientific engineer, had lately joined our army, and rendered very important service in devising the plan of attack, etc."[2]

Unfortunately, shortly before that attack was due to begin in the early hours of November 22, one of the officers in charge, Lieutenant Colonel Philip Sublett, reported that his men were refusing to move, and on further investigation other units evidenced a similar reluctance. According to Colonel Austin, "this wonderful and sudden change had been produced in the minds of the men secretly by some designing persons from motives of ambition and jealousy, which at the moment could not be precisely understood." Some historians have all too readily placed the finger of suspicion on Grant, but William Austin himself was in no doubt at all that the real villain of the piece was actually Wharton, the army's sometime judge advocate. "At this time," he explained bitterly; "General Sam Houston and William H. Wharton were intimate friends, and there can be no doubt that a perfect understanding prevailed between these two men to prevent, if possible, the objects of General Austin being accomplished, so that the laurels might be reserved for General Houston, who was electioneering at San Felipe for an appointment to the command of the Texas army."[3]

Despite his earlier rejection as regimental commander at the beginning of the month, this was also reckoned by some to be one of the reasons why James Bowie, another Houston supporter, had carried the letter informing Austin he was to be sent to the United States. Certainly a dispatch rider named George Patrick, who was one of Bowie's companions on that occasion, reckoned "he wanted to be in the Camps, yea and present when Genl Austin resigned command of the army." However, continued Patrick, "unfortunately for his prospects; he had access to strong drink from the city of San Antonio the night of our arrival. On the morning of the electing . . . Col. B. was drunk which secured the election of Genl. Burleson which doubtless was all for the best."[4] As Stephen Austin had long ago discovered to his despair, the Texian volunteers were far too fond of corn liquor, and indeed any other liquor on which they could lay their hands; perhaps for that very reason, they preferred their leaders to be sober and consistently voted accordingly. Consequently it was a respected Indian fighter named Ed Burleson who succeeded Austin as commander, although Bowie was consoled with a temporary staff appointment as adjutant general.

Notwithstanding his own equivocal role in the November 22 fiasco, Burleson was not one of Houston's men, and both his photograph and his reputation mark him as a stubborn and determined individual. But he too faced daunting odds in holding an increasingly demoralized army together, and soon there were more immediate worries. A couple of weeks before, Colonel Urgatechea had slipped out of Bexar to gather reinforcements, and Texian scouting parties had been looking out for his return ever since. Suddenly on the morning of November 26 one of those scouts, "Deaf" Smith, came galloping into the camp to report the approach of a substantial pack train escorted by as many as five hundred soldiers. Jumping to the understandable conclusion that this was the expected reinforcement, Burleson immediately sent out forty cavalry under Colonel Bowie to try and stop them as far away from the town as possible, while Captain William Jack followed with about one hundred infantry drawn from a variety of companies.

No eyewitness account records what part James Grant was to play in the fight, and he is not mentioned in Burleson's official report. Nevertheless it is inconceivable that "our brave Scot," as a New Orleans Grey named Herman Ehrenberg called him, should have attained the degree of influence he afterwards enjoyed had he remained behind in the camp. He could have ridden out with his old friend James Bowie, but that particular relationship must already have been turning sour. On the other hand, ever since they had served as an escort on Viesca's arrival at Goliad, Grant had been closely associated with Robert Morris's company of the New Orleans Greys, and judging by what followed, it is probable that he fought with them on this occasion.

Bowie went into action first. His so-called cavalrymen were really mounted infantry armed with a mixture of rifles and shotguns, and after the first ineffectual exchange of fire they dismounted and took cover in some dried-up streambeds. The Mexicans did likewise, then both sides sat tight and waited for reinforcements. Unfortunately, as Thomas J. Rusk reported, "Some cavalry had been seen a moment before Bowie's engagement commenced and something was said about taking a favorable position to fight them," but it was all very vague. Meanwhile Cos too had sent out some infantry of his own to rescue the cavalry, who were not Urgatechea's men at all but merely a grass or foraging party belonging to the garrison—and numbering something less than one hundred at that. Then, when Captain Jack and his infantry, double-quicking forward to the sound of the guns, got within about half a mile of the fight, the firing ceased.

This caused an unexpected problem, for aside from the watercourses the terrain was relatively flat and featureless except for clumps and groves of mesquite and other shrubs. Both parties had completely disappeared from view. Consequently, complained Rusk, "We were not apprized of the position Bowie occupied and marched in between the grass party and the reinforcement, who were apprized of our situation and we not of theirs. They waited very quietly until we passed a little eminence that was between us and them and then gave us a general fire which threw our Men into confusion."[5]

The Mexicans were in a good position behind some mesquite bushes, but after that initial moment of confusion in which some called out to retreat and others threw themselves flat on the ground, the Texians rallied, charged the Mexicans, and dispersed them. "Our forces were by this time scattered over about one hundred acres of ground," reported Rusk, "and in small parties, every man fighting pretty much on his own hook. We, however kept advancing upon the enemy and they falling back." That is, until the Texians were charged by some mounted Mexican cavalry and then attacked by a detachment of the Morelos Battalion: "These men advanced with great coolness and bravery under a destructive fire from our men, preserving all the time strict order and exhibiting no confusion. They got up in about twenty yards of our position; all our guns and pistols had been fired off and we had no time to reload and must have tried the butts of our guns against their bayonets but for the fact that some of our men who were fighting in a different place hearing the steady fire . . . at that point attempted to come to them and in coming across the field ran nearly upon the enemy's cannon."

The Mexican regulars thereupon fell back to protect their guns, and subsequently withdrew in good order into the town. The Texians made no attempt to pursue them but instead eagerly ran about capturing the abandoned pack mules. A rumor had got up that the mules were loaded with silver to pay Cos's men, but to their intense disappointment the Texians found only fodder. Thus, declared Creed Taylor, "this ludicrous affair was then dubbed and is since known in our history as the Grass Fight."

Four Texians were wounded in the fight and a fifth ran away, but by their estimation as many as sixty Mexicans were killed. Cos admitted to losing just three men, and while the Texians crowed that they had "flogged them like Hell," it was not much of a victory when all was said and done. Cos had sallied out of the town, rescued his foraging party, and then retired in his own sweet time. All that the Texians had to show for their efforts was the grass, and laugh as they might, this only added to the already widespread malaise. "Bread stuff, Coffee & Sugar some salt and Winter-Clothing," were all in short supply, desertions multiplied, and even at headquarters talk began to turn to retiring into winter quarters.

The militia simply wanted to go home, but the men belonging to the three American volunteer companies serving with the Texians saw matters differently. As Herman Ehrenberg complained, "dissatisfaction and restlessness prevailed in our ranks; furthermore, our inactive life wearied us, and the uncertainty into which we were thrown by the aimlessness of our chiefs depressed and irritated us." Grant, on the other hand, was anything but uncertain or aimless. From the beginning he had had a clear objective in mind and had made no secret of it. Now the volunteers began to consider following him south to Matamoros and the "interior."

On November 29 the highest-ranking of the volunteer officers, Grant's friend Robert C. Morris, wrote to Houston, declining a transfer to the regular army. At the same time he stoutly affirmed that his men, who "without exaggeration form the best disciplind corps now in Texas," were ready to march into the interior and "to them I promised to be the one of those who lead them on the road to Matamoros & who declare in the most positive manner that should this not be undertaken they will return home direct from hence."[6] Despite their close association, Morris's declaration was not a threat to abandon the siege prematurely in order to follow Grant. Paradoxically, although regarding the regular service as a "perfect Bugbear," Morris and the other American volunteers acknowledged Houston as the Texan army's commander in chief. "There was no-one," he continued, "more ardently wished you as a leader in the Camp." Rather he was serving notice that the volunteers had come to Texas to fight. None of *them* were going to spend the winter sitting idly in some God-forsaken camp on the Guadalupe or even the Colorado. Burleson, faced with the imminent prospect of the army falling apart, decided to attack Bexar in the early hours of December 4.

Once again the operation quickly dissolved into a fiasco. Shortly before the assault was due to begin, Robert Morris, who was now major of a provisional battalion comprising the volunteer companies, reported that one of his sentries had seen a man go from the camp into the Alamo. No one else had seen him, however, and notwithstanding his martial pretensions, Morris was something of an alarmist. It was even unkindly suggested by one of his own men that the shadowy figure was only a stray cow. Nevertheless, his insistence that the attack had been compromised was enough. Like Austin before him, Burleson was informed that his officers had no confidence in the success of the operation. This time there could be no mistaking what that meant. The siege would have to be abandoned. At daylight he called a general meeting of the troops and told them that there was no alternative but to break camp and retire to Gonzales. That much is certain, but perhaps precisely because it was such a dramatic turning point in Texan history, there is at first sight little apparent agreement on exactly what happened next.

So far as most of the remaining Texian militia were concerned, the long siege was now over, and with few obvious regrets they struck their tents, loaded their baggage, and started heading out down the Gonzales road. The American volunteers, on the other hand, were angry and bewildered by the sudden collapse of the whole operation. Herman Ehrenberg wrote that with discontent growing; "Colonel Grant, formerly an officer in the Scottish Highlanders and afterwards a citizen of Mexico, induced Burleson to call a general assembly of the whole army." Ehrenberg's narrative, written long afterward, is often distorted for dramatic effect, and it is uncertain whether he was describing the initial meeting that morning when Burleson announced that the army was to withdraw or the later decisive one. "Loud cries of disappointment broke out among the men," he continued, "and Grant himself, our brave Scot, shared our bitter disappointment." Since General Mexía and the survivors of his ill-fated expedition had only just reached the Brazos the day before, Grant, like everyone else at Bexar, was as yet ignorant of their failure to take Tampico. From his viewpoint; if the army did withdraw now, the opportunity to cooperate with the Federalistas down in the interior might be irretrievably lost, and with it the war. While no other narrative suggests that he was directly responsible for calling the assembly that followed the announcement, Ehrenberg's testimony shows that Grant was at the very least engaged in stirring up the volunteers' anger and dismay and encouraging them to take some kind of positive action.

The first claim to have initiated that action was afterward made by Captain William G. Cooke, who had succeeded Morris as commander of the 2nd Company of the New Orleans Greys. By his own account the camp was dissolving into anarchy when "I returned to my company and addressed them in a few words to ascertain whether they would follow me into town even if we were not sustained by the balance of the troops. With a unanimous shout they answered in the affirmative. We were immediately joined by the other volunteers from the United States, commanded by Capt. Breeze and Peacock, and I then marched them up and down the lines calling on volunteers to unite with us. We succeeded in raising about 300. I then marched them to Head quarters and halted them, and proposed the name of Benjamin R. Milam as the leader in the attack. He was elected unanimously."[7]

Unlike Ehrenberg, Cooke made no mention of Grant's intervention, no doubt because by the time he made his own appeal the Scotsman had moved on to find the other key player in the drama; Ben Milam. The most detailed account of what happened next comes from the new adjutant general, Frank Johnson, who claims, incidentally, to have been the lone voice dissenting from the decision to withdraw. Curiously enough

Johnson is also alone in explicitly denying that there was any disturbance in the camp. "About the middle of the afternoon," he wrote, "when most of the baggage wagons were loaded, and everything in readiness for the march on the next day, a Lieutenant of the Mexican army, a deserter, entered our camp, and was taken to General Burleson's quarters. He reported the defenses of the town weak, and that the place could be taken easily. After hearing his report, Colonel Johnson suggested to Colonel Milam to call for volunteers, that 'now is the time.' Most of the army had gathered at the headquarters of General Burleson. Milam called in a clear, loud voice, 'Who will go with Old Ben Milam into San Antonio?'"[8]

It was a famous moment indeed, and but for the later defense of the Alamo it might have become the defining act of the Texan Revolution. But the two versions of the story appear quite different until Grant's part in the proceedings is factored in. In the first place Milam's own dramatic appearance at headquarters at that moment, supposedly on returning from a scout, may not have been quite as fortuitous as the way it is usually represented, and nor was his call to arms as spontaneous as legend portrays it. Not only did William Austin recall that Burleson actually gave Milam and Johnson permission to go out and ask for volunteers, but in April of 1839 James Ogilvie had a long discussion with John Durst, the Nacogdoches deputy who had known Grant in Coahuila. In a contemporaneous note of their conversation, Ogilvie wrote that Durst spoke of Grant "with the utmost feeling of kindness & praise—says that *Milam was entirely directed by the Doctor who proposed calling for volunteers to attack Bexar through Milam—Dr Grant was the chief promoter of all great works.*"[9] If true—and given Grant's long association with Milam there is no reason to doubt it—this means that the old filibuster, "directed by the Doctor" rather than by Johnson, strode out to issue his famous rallying cry just as Cooke and the volunteers, urged on by their same "beloved Scot," came marching up in search of a leader.

About three hundred men responded in one way or another to the call, but only 210 were actually to take part in the assault. That night, recorded a Virginian named "Mag" Striff, one of the New Orleans Greys, they elected their "head officers for two divisions."[10] One was commanded by Ben Milam and Robert Morris and the other by Frank Johnson and James Grant—which is eloquent enough confirmation of the important part he had just played in engineering the attack. However, this election may only have been a matter of agreeing which officer was to go with which division, for Grant was already a colonel. Just when and how this elevation came about is unclear, but the General Council afterward noted that it was Ed Burleson who appointed "Dr. Grant, his aid-de camp, who was thereby entitled to rank as Colonel."[11] While they claimed this appointment was made subsequent to Burleson's own formal appointment by Governor Smith on December 9, it must actually date from the reshuffle following Bowie's departure from the army just a day or two after the Grass Fight in November, which would explain Grant's presence at Burleson's headquarters when the decision to attack was made.

According to Frank Johnson's subsequent official report:

The volunteers for storming the city of Bexar, possessed by the troops of General Cos, entered the suburbs in two divisions, under the command of Colonel Ben R Milam. The first division under his immediate command, aided by Major R. C. Morris, and the second under my command, aided by Colonels Grant and Austin, and Adjutant Brister. The first division, consisting of the companies of Captains York, Patton, Lewellyn, Crane, English, and Landrum, with two pieces and fifteen artillerymen, commanded by Lieutenant-Colonel Franks, took possession of the house of Don Antonio de La Garza. The second division, composed of the companies of Captains Cooke, Swisher, Edwards, Alley, Duncan, Peacock, Breeze and Plácido Benevides, took possession of the house of Verramendi."[12]

Before recounting how they got there, it may be helpful to consider the layout of Bexar as seen through the eyes of one of its attackers, the ubiquitous William T. Austin:

The town of San Antonio at that time was laid off in a square, with a row of rock buildings around it, some twenty feet high; the streets, passing through these buildings from different directions, were all closed by barricading as high as the tops of the houses, with wide and deep ditches immediately outside the barricading; port-holes were made in these barricades and cannon planted there for the purpose of raking the streets in the event of an assault. The tops of the houses were flat, with rock breastworks around the edges of the roofs, intended to be occupied by their infantry. They had cannon mounted on pivots at the church and upon other commanding house-tops. The country immediately about the town is an open prairie. The Alamo was a fort situated on the opposite bank of the river, and was occupied by the enemy's cavalry. At this fort they had upwards of thirty pieces of cannon, mounted upon the walls behind facades, many of which were pivot guns and commanded the whole surrounding country.[13]

The main Mexican position thus described by Austin consisted of two immediately adjacent squares, the Plaza de Armas, more commonly referred to as the Military Plaza, and the Plaza de las Yslas or main square, lying on either side of the church of San Fernando. Solidly fortified or at least well barricaded as it was, the position had certain weaknesses. First, Cos's "citadel," the Alamo, was at some distance from the town and separated from the main fortified area by the San Antonio River, the only link between the two positions being a single long and easily blocked street (map, next page). Second, the fortified houses ringing the twin plazas were themselves surrounded a sprawl of slums. While this outer area was patrolled and covered by a number of outposts, there were simply not enough men available to hold it properly, since Cos apparently had his headquarters in the eastern section called La Villita, and most of the cavalry were either there or at the Alamo. Colonel Nicolás Condelle therefore had little more than two hundred men of his Morelos Battalion and perhaps as many more hastily recruited local militia with which to hold both the plazas and the approaches to them.[14] The seeming disparity in numbers between attackers and defenders was thus more apparent than real.

The plan itself seems simple enough, and given the way in which Ben Milam was "entirely directed by the Doctor," it may well have been the same one that Grant originally devised for Stephen Austin's abortive attack two weeks earlier. Those men not volunteering to join the two attacking divisions were formed into a third or reserve division under Colonel Burleson's command, and while some of them mounted a diversionary attack on the Alamo, the two assault divisions were to enter the town from the north under cover of darkness, moving along parallel streets with the object of pushing as far as possible into the town without being detected. Rather than attacking the more heavily fortified

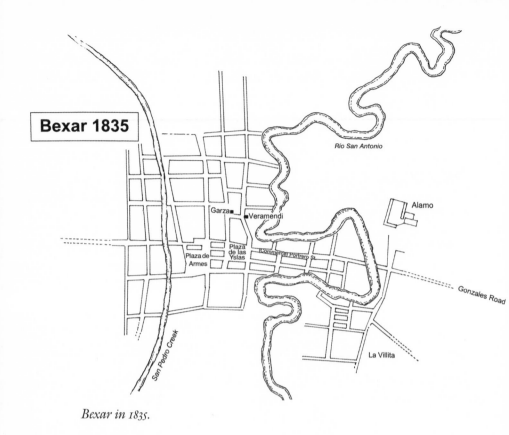

Bexar in 1835.

Military Plaza, the direction of Ben Milam's advance was aimed at the more makeshift fortifications of the Plaza de las Yslas. At the same time it appears that Johnson and Grant may have been attempting to effect a lodgment on Portrero Street (later Commerce Street) just at the east end of the plaza. Running in a straight line from east to west through a narrow peninsula formed by a loop in the San Antonio River, this road was the only link between the fortified plazas and the Alamo. If the Texians did succeed in reaching and blocking this road, the two positions would effectively be cut off from each other.

That night the weather turned bad as one of those Texas storms known as a blue norther swept over the camp, dampening the enthusiasm of many of the volunteers. At 2:00 A.M. those who stuck it out were roused and formed up in two columns in the cornfields north of the town. There they waited, shivering, for the reserve to get into position in front of the Alamo, before dropping their coats and blankets and moving forward.

Ehrenberg recalled:

> Our silent and fireless wait lasted an hour. At three o'clock we hur-
> ried noiselessly through the cornfield on our way to the city. There
> were many Mexican sentries scattered around the Alamo, not very
> far from us, but evidently they suspected nothing and thought they
> had faithfully discharged their duties if they shouted at intervals,
> "Centinela alerta." Their monotonous cries and the howling of the
> storm were the only sounds around us as we ran briskly across the
> field. The exercise warmed us and made us less sensitive to the cut-
> ting edge of the north wind. The feverish excitement into which
> the thought of the coming attack had thrown us also kept us from
> paying much attention to the unpleasantness of the chilly weather. A
> little after our start from the camp, the password for the day, "Bexar"
> went down our column, each man whispering it to the other. When
> we were near the middle of the cornfield we heard a deafening
> noise—not the sharp hiss of the storm, but a loud, booming crash.
> This explosion did not take us unaware, for we had expected it. It
> merely told us that the other contingent was doing its share of the
> work and bombarding the Alamo.[15]

That first cannon shot was fired at about 5:00 A.M., by James C. Neill,
probably from the battery originally constructed by Grant and Cheshire
in preparation for the abortive attack on November 22.

"The hollow roar of our cannon was followed by the brisk rattling
of drums and the shrill blasts of bugles," continued the young German. "Summons, cries, the sudden trampling of feet, the metallic click
of weapons mingled in the distance with the noisy blare of the alarm
and the heavy rumblings of the artillery. Our friends had done the trick.
Their cannonading had put the Mexicans on the alert, and many of them
would probably rush to the defense of the fortress. The success of this
first part of our scheme encouraged us, for we thought that in the midst
of the din and confusion we should have a better chance of slipping into
the city unnoticed."

Suitably distracted by the diversion, Cos did indeed send up rockets
to summon assistance from Condelle's garrison in the town. However
far from rushing to his defense, the garrison very properly sat tight.
Worse still, as Johnson and Grant's division crossed a brush fence at the

edge of the cornfield they were spotted by two Mexican sentries, who raised the alarm.[16] Consequently, Johnson reported, the "division was exposed for a short time to a very heavy fire of grape and musketry from the whole of the enemy's line of fortifications, until the guns of the first division opened their fire, when the enemy's attention was directed to both divisions. At seven o'clock, a heavy cannonading from the town was seconded by a well directed fire from the Alamo, which for a time prevented the possibility of covering our lines, or effecting a safe communication between the two divisions."[17]

Guided by the Mexican defector, Lieutenant Jesús Cuéllar, Johnson and Grant tried to advance up Soledad Street, but the fire was so heavy that they were soon obliged to leave the street and seek cover in adjacent houses. Johnson's report states that they took over James Bowie's old home, the Veramendi House, and this is confirmed by "Mag" Striff of the New Orleans Greys, but Ehrenberg rather casually describes their first refuge as an "old guard house," which suggests that the Veramendi House was the stone building stormed that evening by Peacock's and Breece's men. This would also explain why two rolls recording the names of those taking part in the battle noted, curiously enough, that while "those persons who volunteered and formed the first Division in the attack on San Antonio de Béxar . . . entered the House of La Garza on the morning of the 5th of December 1835 . . . those persons who Volunteered and formed the Second Division in the Attack on San Antonio Béxar . . . entered the house of Berramander on the night of the 5th of Dec 1835."[18] Whatever the actual timing, at least Johnson and Grant's men were doggedly heading in the right direction. In contrast, Milam's division, also coming under artillery fire while advancing up Acequia Street, hastily turned aside to occupy the de la Garza house, as the roll records. In so doing they must have become disoriented, for to reach it they had to turn east and so ran into Johnson and Grant's division, with the inevitable result that the two divisions ended up shooting at each other for a time.

The mistake was soon realized, but the problem now was the classic one confronted by all troops fighting in built-up areas. It was simply too dangerous to move about in the open streets. Milam's division had brought two cannon, but one, a twelve-pounder, was disabled right at the outset. The other, commanded by a German named William Langenheim, did get in a few useful shots, but he and his gunners were also soon forced to take shelter in the adjoining buildings. As for the vaunted Texian riflemen, they too were frustrated by the fortresslike design of the houses and by the confined spaces, which hindered them from getting a clear shot at the Mexican defenders without venturing right out into the bullet-swept yards and roadways.

At first the obvious answer seemed to be to get themselves up on the flat roofs of the houses. Unfortunately, in a complete reversal of the usual situation, the low parapets that surrounded the house tops offered the Texians no protection from Mexican sharpshooters stationed up in the church with excellent British-made Baker rifles. Of the ten men from Johnson's division who initially scrambled onto the roofs, five, including "Deaf" Smith, were wounded at once, encouraging everyone else to scramble back inside. Another of the casualties may have been James Grant, since he was also recorded by Johnson as having being "severely wounded" at some time during the first day.[19] However, the only other surviving reference to Grant's deeds that day relates to an incident that apparently took place rather later on.

"Mag" Striff afterward recalled that "the morning we entered Bowies house, we were destitute of supplies, and could not obtain them without exposing ourselves—a Mexican woman discovered our Situation, and offered her services to get us a Bucket of Water, She got the water and on her return to the house which we occupied, was shot through the arm by the Mexicans, and did not reach our Station; We did not get water until night." Ehrenberg recorded the same incident but added the useful detail that "Colonel Grant as well as the volunteers would not at first hear of her doing such a thing, for we feared that the Mexicans would show her no more mercy than they had shown the rest of us." This would indicate that Grant was still exercising command at that time and was not wounded until later, either by a random shot or perhaps even during the storming of the Veramendi House that evening. Whatever the circumstances, the fact remained that unlike his critics—Sam Houston included—Grant fought and bled in the battle, and that would count for a lot in the weeks that followed.

Two days later it was old Ben Milam's turn. He was shot dead by a Mexican rifleman while he stood in the garden of the Veramendi House. This left Johnson and Morris in overall command of the troops in the town; and although steady progress continued to be made in clearing Mexicans out of the other houses, it was still a painfully slow business.

The only way they could move forward was in short rushes from one house to the next, and more often than not by burrowing through the walls rather than risking exposure outside. What was more, since the fighting was concentrated on the north side of the town, Colonel Urgatechea was able to evade the Texian covering parties and get in on the south side with the long-awaited reinforcements on December 8. He brought more than six hundred men in total, which in other circumstances might have been sufficient to break the virtual stalemate and clear the Texians out of the town; but more than two thirds of them were raw conscripts. Some were even reported to have been marched there in chains and were variously described as prisoners from Zacatecas or even ordinary convicts. In any event, they proved worse than useless.

That night Captain William Cooke captured what was called the Priest's House and at last gained a lodgment on the main plaza. A hasty counterattack collapsed in confusion without getting anywhere, and Cos, who had come down to see for himself, ordered the town evacuated. To his credit he at first intended to continue the fight up at the Alamo, but instead his army dramatically fell apart. Quite coincidentally Colonel José María Gonzáles, the federalist officer who had helped Grant and Viesca escape from Monterrey, had just arrived outside Bexar and immediately made contact with the garrison, appealing to them to change sides. In response, a sizable number of Cos's cavalry, including at least two and perhaps even three complete *presidial* companies led by their officers, suddenly defected to the Texians—or rather to the Federalistas! Unable to rely on those who remained, Cos realized that he would not be able to extricate his remaining infantry from the town and ordered Colonel Sánchez Navarro to "go and save those brave men. I authorize you to approach the enemy and obtain the best terms possible." Colonel Condelle angrily protested to him that "el Batallon Morelos has never surrendered."[20] But there was no real alternative, and at about 7:00 A.M. on the morning of December 9, 1835, the white flag was raised. Bexar had finally fallen.

The happy news of General Cos's surrender reached San Felipe and the General Council on December 15, triggering a comedy of errors that would eventually have tragic and disastrous consequences. In the full flush of enthusiasm over the victory, Governor Smith immediately "appoints and commissions, without the advice or consent of the Council, Edward Burleson, Commander-in-Chief of the volunteer army at

Bexar."[21] Ed Burleson, however, was no longer there. No sooner had he seen General Cos off the premises, as it were, than he turned over command of the army to Frank Johnson on December 15 and headed for home. Oblivious to this, on the same day Smith equally unilaterally ordered Sam Houston, as commander in chief, to take formal charge of the projected expedition to Matamoros. Despite the failure of Mexía's expedition, Jorge Fisher was still assuring the General Council "that in February next there is a general plan of revolutionising all over Mexico," and that the capture of Matamoros would be sufficient to trigger it.[22]

Even Philip Dimitt had recovered his enthusiasm for the project. Rather than sit at Goliad waiting for the Mexicans to turn up, he argued on December 2, the Texians should immediately cross the Rio Grande, where they could "hurl the thunder back in the very atmosphere of the enemy, drag him, and with him the war out of Texas. The liberals of all classes would immediately join us, the neutrals would gather confidence, both in themselves and us, and the parasites of centralism, in that section, would be eventually panic-struck and paralyzed." Rather more prosaically, he added that the substantial customs revenues from the port would also come in very handy.[23] Stephen Austin concurred somewhat more quietly: "The best interests of Texas, I think require that the war should be kept out of this country and beyond the Rio Grande." No one was going to disagree with that; and he went on to recommend that "head quarters should be fixed at Goliad, and that a federal auxiliary army should be collected there, and offered to the federal party [in Mexico] should it be needed by them."[24]

Now it was Sam Houston's turn to get involved. He obviously knew that Smith had ordered Burleson to take charge of the volunteers at Bexar, and may even have drafted the orders himself, for on December 15 he wrote to a member of the council that he intended to locate a "field officer in command of San Antonio de Bexar with a sufficient number of troops for the defense of the station."[25] He had also, some time previously, sent James Bowie to Goliad in order to inspect the defenses and investigate various complaints being made about Dimitt's high-handed behavior. While not holding a regular commission, or indeed holding any real commission at all, Colonel Bowie was a trusted subordinate. It therefore made sense to delegate to him the job of organizing the Federal Volunteer Army—pending Houston's own arrival on the scene. Bowie's instructions were to assemble as many volunteers as necessary at

Goliad, then march on Matamoros and, having captured the city, hold it until further orders. Alternatively, should this not be possible Bowie was at least to push as far as he prudently could toward the Rio Grande and establish himself at Copano, north of Corpus Christi Bay, and there harass any Mexican troop movements on the nearby Atascosita Road.[26] Unfortunately, by the time these orders arrived at Goliad, Bowie, like Burleson, had gone back to San Felipe, and it took a long time for them to catch up with him.

For the moment neither of these missed appointments made much real difference, for at Bexar an army was already taking shape in any case. In January Colonel James Neill was to complain from Bexar to the governor and council: "You have doubtless heard from various Sources of the arbitrary rule of the Aide de Camp of Genl. E. Burliston, F. W. Johnson, and James Grant. The Town was Surrendered on the 9th Decr and So long as they remained in command there was not a move made by them to restore or organise harmony or to re-establish the civil functions of Govt."[27] In the circumstances this was hardly surprising, for neither Grant nor Johnson intended to stay there any longer than absolutely necessary. On December 17, just two days after Burleson's departure and only a week after the surrender, Grant's condition was downgraded to "slightly wounded" by the chief surgeon, Dr. Amos Pollard, and the same day Johnson wrote to the governor and council, requesting proper commissions for the officers of the "Federal Volunteer Army of Texas." He enumerated four companies of infantry and two of artillery.[28] But like all the other correspondence flying about at that stage, the list was out of date almost as soon as Johnson sent it off, for more volunteers were arriving from the United States all the time—and Grant found them a receptive audience.

In glowing terms he related to the boys the possibilities of the contemplated expedition. Matamoros was an opulent city. It was the port of entry for a vast territory embracing a quarter part of Old Mexico and all of New Mexico. Merchants and mine owners from Santa Fe, Taos, El Paso del Norte, Monclova, Monterrey and Chihuahua thronged this great maritime mart, while Spanish hidalgos and Mexican dons reveled in oriental splendor. Matamoros was but a few hundred miles from Bexar. The country was level; grass, game and wild cattle and horses abounded, and the march to the

Rio Grande would not be difficult, but rather a journey of pleasure. With a force of five hundred men—two hundred from Bexar joined with three hundred Texans whom he expected to meet him on the Nueces—he could defy any force the Mexican government might be able to throw behind the walls of the coveted city. He dwelt upon the present condition of the troops; their inactivity; their want of supplies; the glowing prospect for pay, and the utter inability of the provisional government to render their condition any better. The taking of Matamoros would remedy all these evils. Its wealth and treasures awaited their coming and would more than compensate for all the toil, time and expense of the present and past campaign. . . . These glowing representations had the desired effect. The minds of these young men from the "states" became inflamed with a desire for conquest, military glory, and loot. They were penniless, clad in rags, and had about exhausted the resources of the scant population of Bexar. It was a long stretch from San Antonio back to the "states" and no particular blame can be attached to the course they took.[29]

Thus by Christmas Eve of 1835, Colonel Johnson was able to write to the Military Committee: "I will make immediate arrangements for the expedition against Matamoros as we are fortunate enough to receive your recommendations to take such a step. It will, however, be necessary to await the arrival of reinforcements on the road to enable me to leave a sufficient garrison at this important point [Bexar]. The difficulty which presents itself does not consist in a lack of volunteers, but on the contrary, persuading a sufficient number of garrison duty to remain behind—All, all wish to achieve new victories and to raise the glory of the army of Texas as well as to assist the friends of liberty in the interior in throwing off the yoke of tyranny."[30] The next day he also wrote to advise the council:

The Expedition which you propose against Matamoros can be undertaken speedily with every rational prospect of success and every man in this garrison would willingly volunteer to proceed to the interior, but as the position which we occupy [Bexar] is all important to maintain, it will be desirable to await the arrival of considerable reinforcements now on the road to have a sufficient number for other purposes and in the meantime every necessary preparation of suitable artillery, arms and stores be made, all the animals required to convey the same procured. An expedition of this nature you point out has occupied our attention for some time and a small division of observation leaves this place today for the Nueces to occupy the attention of the enemy at Rio Grande and Laredo, to open and keep up communication with the liberals of the frontier—and above all to procure positive information of the forces at each point, their condition and every other particular that can serve to guide us in our future operations.[31]

The "division of observation" consisted of Colonel Gonzáles and his men, including the recent defectors, together with a Tejano spy company recruited by Don Plácido Benavides, who were sent off with orders "to scour the country between San Antonio and the Rio Grande."[32] Unfortunately, no sooner had they set out than it all turned nasty. Three days earlier Sam Houston had written directly to James Neill, ordering him to take command "of the Post of Bexar and make such disposition of the troops there as you may deem proper for the security & protection of the place."[33] About five days separated San Felipe from Bexar, so Neill's orders cannot have reached there before December 26, or perhaps even a day or so later, but when they did arrive, they sparked an immediate confrontation that rapidly grew into a crisis.

When he wrote those orders, Houston must have known that Johnson had perforce succeeded Burleson in command of the troops at Bexar and that they were even then being readied to march on Matamoros, yet he made no acknowledgment of this. It is perfectly understandable, of course, that he should want to appoint one of his own regular officers to command the post after the volunteers had gone, and there is no doubt that Neill was the right choice for that particular job. At the same time, in his own letters of December 24 and 25, Johnson readily acknowledged the necessity of maintaining a permanent garrison in Bexar. Indeed his December 17 request for proper commissions for the officers had been accompanied by a formidable shopping list of defense stores as well as an order for 100 artillery uniforms comprising blue jackets, vests and pants, 150 gray suits for infantry, and 50 green suits for riflemen.[34] He was even prepared, as he made perfectly clear, to delay his march until an adequate garrison for Bexar could first be organized. Regardless, Houston gave no clear directions as to how the forces assembling at Bexar might be apportioned between those required to form the garrison and those, if any, who could be released to march on Matamoros. His orders simply stated that Neill was to take command "of the troops there." Conflict was therefore inevitable, for in effect Neill, on the authority of Houston and ultimately Governor Smith, was ordered to use the volunteers as a garrison, while Johnson and Grant, on the authority of the General Council and its Military Committee, were ordered to march those very same volunteers to Goliad and thence to Matamoros—under Houston's command!

It is little wonder then that however well-intentioned, Neill's appointment and instructions plunged the volunteers into a destructive conflict that would eventually engulf both governor and council and would lead to a series of near fatal military disasters. Since neither Neill nor Johnson would acknowledge the authority of the other, their soldiers were inevitably forced to take sides. Neill must at some point have proposed calling for a general vote, for in a private addendum to a letter of January 14 he complained to Houston that "we will learn what Sneaking and Gamboling has been done, to operate against you by J[ohnson] & G[rant]. You will hear all about the Houston flag, and the Houston House in Bexar, for fear you would be elected Commander of the Volunteer Army. They never would let it come near an Election, but Shuffled it off, and threw the army into Confusion Several times, and the responsibility on the heads of the Several Captains."[35]

The worsening atmosphere notwithstanding, Grant was determined to march, and on December 29 wrote his will "on the Eve of marching on an expedition." Johnson decided at the very last moment to go to San Felipe himself, in an attempt to clarify exactly what the position was and to obtain explicit sanction to march the volunteers to Goliad despite Houston's apparent counterorders. Accordingly he left the next morning, and the whole mess promptly exploded behind him. No sooner had Johnson ridden out of sight than Neill announced that he was formally assuming command of the garrison. He made it abundantly clear that so far as he was concerned it comprised all of the troops then assembled at Bexar. As William Cooke recalled, any reluctance Grant might have had to put matters to a vote now vanished in the face of this crisis. "In the latter part of December 1835," Cooke wrote, "Col. F. Johnston left for the Seat of Govt. (then at San Felipe,) and Col. Grant was left in command—On about the 30th of Decr. he proposed to the troops to march to the Rio Grande, and unite with the Federalists who were then forming an army to operate against the Centralists, and form a new Confederacy of the Northern Mexican States & Texas—To this the larger portion of the troops consented—they were all volunteers, from the U.S."[36]

All in all six of the volunteer companies now elected to follow Grant, leaving Neill with just his own gunners, commanded by Almeron Dickinson, along with Captain Robert White's Bexar Guards; a small rump of Peacock's United States Invincibles, now led by his old lieutenant, John Chenoweth; and perhaps less than half of the New Orleans Greys, led by William Blazeby. The next day Blazeby and his supporters hurriedly met to recognize Neill as their "commander-in-chief," and in three successive resolutions declared that they considered it "highly essential that the existing army remain in Bejar"; that they should continue to have the privilege "of electing our own company officers"; and that "we consider the above highly essential for the unity and interest of the existing volunteer army in Bejar."[37]

Grant's response to this countermeeting was brutally eloquent. Ignoring the furious denunciations of Neill's faction, he ruthlessly stripped the Alamo of more than two thirds of its garrison; marching from Bexar on the first day of January 1836, at the head of more than two hundred men, all the horses and supplies he could lay hands on, and at least one wagon "pressed" from a man named John Gilbert "for hauling baggage, arms and ammunition for the said volunteers in their expedition against Matamoras, as authorised and contemplated by the General Council."[38]

4 • *Contending Chieftains*

TEXAN HISTORIANS have not been kind either to James Grant or to the expedition that he now led, and most have taken their cue from Sam Houston, who some time later charged in a vitriolic letter to Henry Smith: "Is he not a Scotchman who has resided in Mexico for the last ten years? Does he not own large possessions in the interior? . . . Is he not deeply interested in the hundred league claims of land which hang like a murky cloud over the people of Texas?"[1] Up to a point all of this was perfectly true. Although he was the possessor of half a league of land on the Colorado near Matagorda, Grant did indeed live south of the border rather than in Texas, and he also had a financial as well as a political stake in the restoration of a federalist government in Monclova. Frank Johnson was quick to respond—that Grant "was one, of many others, who bought land of the state of Coahuila and Texas, is a matter of fact and has not, so far as we know, ever been denied by him or others."[2] But the charge that land speculation was a significant factor in driving the expedition forward was nevertheless both plausible and damaging.

At the outset of the revolt, back in October, Houston had successfully urged both the closure of the land offices throughout Texas and a suspension of all the land grants made by the Coahuila y Texas legislature since 1833. Ostensibly this was done to protect the interests of the existing settlers, legitimate or otherwise, and of those joining them from the United States, but it also served notice that the authority of the Coahuila legislature was no longer recognized in Texas. Conversely, many of those now promoting cooperation with the Mexican liberals—and to some degree underwriting the revolution—including Mason, Williams, McKinney, and of course James Grant, were equally anxious to validate those land grants by restoring the federalist government in Monclova. Nor can there be any doubt that Grant wanted to recover his other "large possessions" in Mexico and to be reunited with Guadalupe Reyes and his children. However, to charge that his self interest was the real or sole motivation for the Matamoros expedition overlooks the true complexity of his motives and ignores the wider political context in which the expedition had first been conceived and planned by the Mexican liberals and only later taken up by all parties in the Texian ranks.

What was more, long before Houston or anyone else denounced Grant as an unscrupulous speculator, the Texians had already become split between those professing continued loyalty to the Mexican federation and those advocating complete independence. As is so often the case, if personal antipathy were set aside, in the end the differences between the two viewpoints came down to degrees of emphasis rather than to diametrically opposed principles. There is no doubt at all that the Texians were united or at least agreed in taking up arms to effect the separation of Texas from Coahuila, but where and how far they were to go from that point was another matter entirely. As early as October 5, 1835, Stephen Austin wrote that "I hope to see Texas forever free from Mexican domination of any kind—It is yet too soon to say this publically—but that is the point we shall aim at—and it is the one I am aiming at."[3] Nevertheless, at the turn of the year Texas was still acknowledged by the rebels to be part of Mexico, and the provisional government still publicly adhered to the principles of the Constitution of 1824 and its supposed guarantees of autonomy to the individual states of the Mexican federation.

The importance of holding to this seemingly cautious policy, in public at least, was twofold. In the first place, by demonstrating in their *grito* or "declaration of causes" on November 7, 1835, that they were behaving strictly within the terms of Mexico's existing constitution, the Texians invested their actions with a clearly recognizable legitimacy. In marked contrast, their more precarious legal status after the Declaration of Independence on March 2, 1836, would lead the British foreign secretary, Lord Palmerston, first to remark rather haughtily that "we must see whether the Band of outlaws who occupy Texas will be able to constitute themselves into such a community as it would be decent for us to make a Treaty with" and then to underline the point by concluding: "At all events it would not do for us to make a Treaty with a self-denominated State, till events had proved such a state could permanently maintain its independence."[4]

Second, as long as the Texians continued to cleave to the Constitution of 1824, they could also look for the support of their fellow liberals in the interior. Indeed the second section of their declaration of causes expressly pledged their own support to any other Mexican state that rose in revolt against the Centralistas, and Stephen Austin endorsed the Matamoros expedition by advising that the Texians' "federal auxiliary army" should be "offered to the federal party should it be needed." By thus making common cause with the Mexican liberals under the constitutionalist banner, they could deflect the inevitable charges that the revolt was being stirred up by land speculators, or was even the beginning of the long-feared American seizure of Texas; and should those liberals follow the Texians' example by rising up themselves, the fighting might, as Austin hoped, remain safely south of the Rio Grande and might ultimately lead to the total defeat of the Centralistas. Back in November James Grant had of course been at some pains to assure Austin of the prospects for just such a wider civil war, and how far he was now prepared to go to maintain the policy of active engagement with the liberals is a moot point.

At San Felipe both governor and council seemingly regarded the capture of Matamoros as the limit of their ambitions, but some of the Mexican liberals had a far bigger scheme in view. Since Mexico had broken away from Spain as an unstable aggregate of former colonial possessions, there was no reason why it should remain an indissoluble whole. Far better, they argued, that it should be broken up into more manageable units. In his letter of October 20, briefing Stephen Austin on the Federalistas' plans, Jorge Fisher asserted that "Tamaulipas, with the [Lt. g]overnor Dn. Vital Fernandez is decidedly in favor not only of the Federation, as a measure to act in concert with Tejas, Coahuila, Neuva Leon &c but even, for an intire separation of the northern Confederated States from Mexico, viz. from Rio Panico [i.e., Tampico], drawing a line to San Blas on the Pacific Ocean. This is a grand project which has the warmest wishes and best desires of all the proprietors of Matamoros and Tampico, and of the whole estados internos de Oriente and Occidente, Chihuahua y Neuvo Mexico."[5] Grant, as we have seen, was among those involved in devising this "grand project" and, according to a number of witnesses, was still actively promoting it among the footloose volunteers at Bexar in mid-December. Once Matamoros was in their hands, he is said to have claimed, "their ranks would soon be swelled by thousands of patriotic Mexicans who would hail the Americans as deliverers from the tyranny of Santa Anna, and it would only be a question of time when Tamaulipas, Nuevo Leon, Chihuahua, Coahuila, and New Mexico, would unite with Texas and form a new republic with Matamoros as its seat of government."

By turning the original concept around to suggest that the other northern Mexican states would join with a victorious Texas, rather than that the Texians should join the proposed confederation, Grant was in effect promoting a republic of Greater Texas, covering the whole of what would eventually become the southwestern United States as well as northern Mexico. It was a bold, even an exciting idea, not least because by whatever name it might be known, that proposed new republic happened to encompass most of Mexico's silver mining districts where he had been so active before the war. Yet as far as an increasingly assertive Texas was concerned, becoming involved in a civil war deep in the interior of Mexico made little sense. Sam Houston saw this all too clearly when he sagely wrote of the proposal: "It is the project of some interested in land matters, very largely, for Texas to unite with some three or four of the Eastern States of Mexico, and form a Republic—This I regard as worse, than our present, or even our former situation. Their wars would be our wars, and their revolutions: While our Revenues, our lands, and our lives would be expended to maintain their cause, and we could expect nothing in return; but prejudice, and if we relied upon them disappointment. Let Texas now Declare her independence, and it will cost her less blood, and treasure to maintain it; than it would cost her to maintain her integral interest in such a confederacy."[6]

Houston was also opposed to the project because although he was working for a complete and irrevocable separation of Texas from the rest of the Mexican federation, independence was not to be an end in itself. It was merely the first step toward annexation by the United States. Thus on March 7, only five days after the declaration of independence, he would write to James Collinsworth, then chairman of the government's Military Committee, asking: "What say you of a resolution, that Texas is part of Louisiana, and the U. States by treaty of 1803?"[7] Opinion is still divided as to whether Houston came to Texas in the first place with the sole object of securing it for the Union; this far from subtle hint and his behavior throughout the revolt certainly suggest that he did. Ordered by Austin at the outset to muster a militia company at Nacogdoches, he instead issued an appeal for volunteers from the United States, and without the slightest shadow of authority promised generous land grants to those who responded.

He was not alone, of course, in calling for assistance from beyond the Sabine, but next to Austin he was certainly the best known of the Texian leaders, and hundreds responded to the call. "Armed bands have been permitted to proceed from different parts of the United States openly and avowedly, to join in the contest, without the least degree of molestation;" thundered the noted American abolitionist Benjamin Lundy, "and even when complaints have been officially made by accredited Mexican agents, nothing has been done to arrest them except the formal transmission of orders to the District Attorneys, to which they paid not the slightest attention."[8] The Neutrality Act of April 24, 1800, did in fact provide for the imposition of fines of up to a thousand dollars and imprisonment for up to three years for those American citizens who enlisted under a foreign power—and three times as much for actually mounting or outfitting a military expedition. But there was also a convenient loophole in the act whereby individual offenders could be prosecuted only after the event, once they had provided the supplies or recruited and dispatched the soldiers. Accordingly, those doing the outfitting of the volunteers and the supplying of the rebels "in country" were always scrupulously careful to advertise for emigrants, not for soldiers. Nor were most of the supplies and equipment they forwarded unambiguously warlike in character. Flour and corn might both be vital to sustain the rebels, but the most zealous customs official would be hard-pressed to classify these as contraband. The shoes and clothing shipped to Texas, besides being individually purchased by many of the volunteers, such as the New Orleans Greys, Mobile Greys, and Alabama Greys, was simply ordinary workwear of brogans and grey fustian jackets and pants, rather than anything recognizable to early nineteenth-century eyes as proper military uniforms.[9] Even Du Pont's famous rifle powder was a legitimate requirement for frontier communities. Some unmistakably military material, such as the occasional cannon, was undoubtedly carried illicitly if not entirely clandestinely to Texas, but otherwise the cynical might well argue that the neutrality laws acted only to punish those who failed.[10]

Consequently those "armed bands" came over the border openly and even downright aggressively, cheerfully proclaiming themselves as

Peacock's (later Chenoweth's)[11] United States Invincibles, and as Law-rence's United States Independent Cavalry Company, or simply naming themselves after a score of states, cities, and counties in the Mississippi Valley. What was more, in blatant defiance of the Neutrality Act, all too many of the filibusters, far from being restrained or hindered by the U.S. government, were being equipped not with "country rifles" but with proper military weapons supplied from state arsenals. Captain Jack Shackleford's Alabama Red Rovers, for example, paid the state authori-ties six hundred dollars for fifty muskets and sets of accoutrements, while the Huntsville Volunteers managed to borrow another "fifty first rate U.S. muskets" from the same source—and they were not the only ones.

Little wonder then that the tumultuous arrival of these men, all but openly flying the Stars and Stripes, appeared to observers on both sides of the Atlantic to be clear evidence of an American plot to seize Texas. To those who knew the history of the past twenty years, events were follow-ing a worryingly familiar pattern. Texas was not the first piece of Spanish territory to be swallowed up in this way. Taking advantage of Spain's being overrun by French armies, a gang of American filibusters led by Reuben Kemper and his two brothers had organized a rebellion among the handful of settlers in West Florida in 1810 and had proclaimed an independent republic, complete with its own flag. More armed volun-teers promptly came flooding over the border to the aid of the rebels, and when the beleaguered Spaniards appealed to the United States gov-ernment to halt or restrain them, Washington responded by dispatch-ing U.S. regulars, not to arrest the adventurers but to "protect" them against the indigenous Seminoles! Those same Seminoles then provided a convenient pretext for Andrew Jackson to lead a series of military expe-ditions deep into Florida proper, with a pointed disregard for such nice-ties as observing international borders. Spain was only bowing to the inevitable when it formally ceded the whole area to the United States in the Adams-Onis Treaty of 1819. Notwithstanding the supposed final settlement of the boundaries between Spanish and American territory in that treaty, some ambiguities remained, and all too many Washington politicians were making no secret of their designs on both Texas and Cuba.

Understandably therefore, the influx of armed volunteers aroused strong suspicions that something similar to the Florida business was in the process of being attempted again, particularly when a Louisiana newspaper brazenly asserted that General Houston had gone to the Texas country specifically for the purpose of "revolutionizing" it, and went on to predict: "We may expect, shortly, to hear of his raising his flag." Even more explicitly, a Charleston paper opined: "It is not improbable that he [President Jackson] is now examining the propriety and practicability of a retrocession of the vast territory of Texas, an enterprise loudly demanded by the welfare of the west, and which could not fail to exercise an important and favorable influence upon the future destinies of the south thereby increasing the votes of the slaveholding states in the United States senate."[12] And thereby too, a new and altogether uglier factor was introduced into the equation, for although slavery was officially forbidden in Mexico, the prohibition was all but ignored in Texas—and Texian slave owners were now some of the most prominent advocates of revolution. One radical London paper observed after the event:

> Texas has long been the Naboth's vineyard of Brother Jonathan. For twenty years or more an anxiety has been manifested to push back the boundary of the United States territory, of which the Sabine river is the agreed line, so as to include the rich alluvial lands of the Delta of the Colorado, at the head of the Gulf of Mexico. There are stronger passions at work, however, than the mere lust of territory, deeper interests are at stake. Texas belongs to a republic which has abolished slavery; the object of the Americans is to convert it into a slave-holding state; not only to make it the field of slave cultivation, and a market for the Maryland slave trade, but, by annexing it to the Federal Union, to strengthen in Congress the preponderating influence of the southern slave-holding states. This atrocious project is the real origin and cause of the pretended contest for Texian independence—a war, on the part of the United States, of unprovoked aggression for the vilest of all purposes."[13]

Although there is no direct evidence that he personally linked the issue of slavery with frustrating American expansion beyond the Sabine, this was a sentiment with which James Grant would no doubt have agreed, had he lived to read it, for he was raised as an abolitionist in an influential political circle that included the patron saint of the antislavery movement, William Wilberforce himself.

A great many prominent people in London were passionately opposed to the prospect of an American annexation of Texas. Although out of government, William Huskisson had remained an important and vocal critic of both slavery and American designs on Texas right up until his unfortunate demise under the wheels of a railway locomotive in 1830. His speeches on the subject were still widely quoted, especially by Benjamin Hoy, the member of Parliament who finally forced a debate on the subject in August 1836. Hoy in turn was firmly supported by Dr. Stephen Lushington, another abolitionist of the old Wilberforce circle, as well as by our friend Henry Ward, himself now very much back in the game as a radical MP. Unfortunately all of them spoke as individuals, for in the decade since George Canning had first spoken of his "apprehension of the ambition and ascendancy" of the United States and of the need to oppose a powerful barrier to its westward expansion, the policy of the British government had dramatically changed. Lofty disdain for the Texian rebels notwithstanding, the foreign secretary, Lord Palmerston, was not only chiefly preoccupied with European and Near Eastern matters but was personally sympathetic toward the Americans—and consequently disinclined to get involved in the approaching crisis. The *Times* reported how in his last speech, Huskisson had ringingly declared:

> The possession of the Floridas by the United States, has long since given rational cause of uneasiness to England, from regard to the safety of our West India Islands; and we agree with Mr. Huskisson, that when the government of Washington intimated its repugnance to seeing Cuba transferred from the feeble Ferdinand to the vigorous grasp of George IV, the United States should have been informed that if Cuba were to continue permanently Spanish, so Texas, and in general the whole shore along the Gulf, should ensure to the Mexican republic. . . . With Spain we have a defensive alliance, ready made and consolidated by the most obvious interest, to prevent Cuba from falling a prey to the systematic aggrandizement of the United States. With Mexico, we are equally identified in resistance to the attempts of the same States upon Texas.[14]

Palmerston, by contrast, now blithely expressed confidence in the ability of the Mexican government to deal with the rebellion by itself. He contended, no doubt rightly, that in any case by that stage the whole matter would be settled before any meaningful intervention could take place. "To us perhaps it does not signify what becomes of Texas," he remarked privately, "though in a Political view it would be better that Texas should not be incorporated within the Union; commercially it would make little difference."[15]

What was more, in the debate of August 5, 1836, Palmerston would make the astonishing claim that "no correspondence had been laid before the House with regard to the progress or diminution of the slave trade, supposed to exist in Texas. . . . The fact was so; and the explanation he had to offer was, that his Majesty's Government had no agent in the province of Texas, and they had only lately received information from the British Minister at Mexico bearing on the illicit trade in slaves supposed to exist in Texas."[16] This was of course humbug, barely justified by the unofficial status of Grant, who was in any case dead by then, and it was certainly not a stance shared by a number of his parliamentary colleagues. Grant's cousin Charles, recently ennobled as Lord Glenelg, was now back in government as secretary of state for the Colonial Department and as such very concerned indeed about an upsurge in Caribbean slave trafficking, which was largely being fuelled by the ease with which slaves could be clandestinely run into the United States through Texas.

Slavery was not the only matter of concern in London. Not only was Cuba still suspected to be at risk, but at one point Benjamin Hoy also invoked the new and interesting specter of an American takeover of Texas and the other Mexican states north of the Rio Grande bringing the United States within six weeks' sail of China. One of the more intriguing aspects of British interest in the Texas Revolution was the close connection of so many of those involved with the East India Company. Among them were Lushington and Hoy. James Grant had also served the company and perhaps still did so even while in Mexico, while his cousin, Glenelg, spent four years as president of the East India Company Board of Control before moving to the Colonial Office and had secured the renewal of the company's charter in 1833. The price of that renewal was the loss of the company's trading monopoly in the China Seas, which was good news for the independent shipping interests—and for the Americans. Until that point American interlopers into the enormously valuable China trade had always been regarded as a nuisance, but no more than that. In the 1820s just one "China ship" had cleared

Acapulco or San Blas each year, and the sheer distance involved limited the number of those sailing from the U.S. eastern seaboard. But the opening up of the China trade coupled with the as yet theoretical prospect of an American presence on the California coast was infinitely more worrying to those with East India Company interests than Palmerston's offhand comment would indicate.

In short, all the concerns about American territorial and economic expansion articulated over the previous ten years and more by Canning, Huskisson, Henry Ward, and their colleagues and followers were rapidly coming to be vindicated, just at the very time when the foreign secretary was affecting a determined indifference to the issue. As a close friend of Palmerston's, and with a direct political and personal interest in the matter, Glenelg should have been able to exert some influence upon him. Unfortunately contemporaries were united in criticizing Glenelg's weakness, dilatoriness, obstinate irresolution, and sheer incompetence.[17] Protocol certainly forbade any public disagreement with another member of the government, and if Glenelg did make private representations, they were rebuffed. Grant therefore was very much on his own. How much contact he actually had with Britain at this point is unknown, but he must have been aware of developments within the East India Company and of the growing concern both inside and outside Parliament over the prospect of the Americans establishing themselves not just in Texas but in California as well.

Whether Grant could still be said to be operating with his government's official or even tacit sanction in now renewing his efforts to frustrate American expansion into Mexican territory is an interesting question, although the Foreign Office was certainly aware of his projected republic of northern Mexico.[18] The absence of a professionally run British intelligence service meant that throughout the first half of the nineteenth century and beyond, a surprising number of confidential agents sent to various parts of the globe by one administration would inconveniently remain there to embarrass the next. One of the most notable was another Highland Scot named David Urquhart, who came from the same part of the country as Grant and may even have been distantly related. Urquhart spent upward of a decade and a half on the fringes of the Turkish empire before Lord Palmerston finally tried to disown him, only to be forced to admit during a parliamentary debate in 1838 that the Scottish agent had good and sufficient grounds for believing "he was acting in accordance with the secret wishes of the Government"—and at this moment Grant was in an exactly similar position.[19]

It was clear enough that the long threatened crisis was now at hand and that he had to act decisively, without waiting for instructions that might never come. And so, as he rode south from Bexar in January of 1836, James can have needed little encouragement, tacit or otherwise, to believe that like Palmerston's principal *bête noire*, David Urquhart, he was indeed "acting in accordance with the secret wishes of the Government."

His Texian colleague Frank Johnson had no such comfort, for arriving in San Felipe on January 3, 1836, he walked straight into a political row that was about to tear the provisional government apart. In mid-November the Consultation, having set matters on what it considered a proper footing, had resolved to adjourn until March 1, leaving a small caretaker administration to conduct affairs in the meantime. That provisional government consisted of a governor, Henry Smith, and an Advisory Council presided over by the lieutenant governor, James Robinson. Unfortunately, perhaps because the arrangement was so temporary, their respective positions were never properly defined, and from the outset Smith and the council seemed intent on going their own ways. Smith, perhaps with some slight justification, took the view that he was invested with full plenary powers and was therefore entitled to exercise them unhindered by the council, whom he regarded merely as "devisors of ways and means." Conversely Robinson and his colleagues considered themselves to be the real government and deplored Smith's frequent acting "without the advice and consent of the Council." One result had of course been the conflicting orders given by the two parties to the troops at Bexar. Now Grant and Johnson were about to make things infinitely worse. Although he had written to the governor and council jointly in mid-December, it was now to the council alone that Johnson reported at San Felipe, requesting their formal authorization to proceed to Matamoros.[20]

Johnson's personal motives at this point are at best uncertain, and his own memoirs are astonishingly uninformative on the subject. He angrily insisted that James Grant was "a gentleman, scholar, patriot, and gallant soldier" and that "no man entered the service of Texas more heartily, zealously, or for purer motives than did Doctor Grant."[21] He also wrote to the council of his hopes of placing "Texas in a situation to dictate to the neighboring states." This clearly suggests that when he went to San Felipe, he had been won over by Grant's beguiling vision of those states attaching themselves to a Greater Texas. However, his assertion to the council that "we can calculate with certainty on our [Mexican] liberals" still sits uneasily with the fact that as recently as November 6, he had headed a petition demanding the exclusion of Mexicans from the camp outside Bexar. Consequently, his present eagerness to march south may also have been connected—as Sam Houston charged—with his involvement in the Coahuila land business, for Grant referred in his will to "a speculation set on foot between myself, Cameron and F. W. Johnson." Moreover, although Houston once more had a hand in them, there were persistent rumors both then and later that the principal object of the expedition was "plunder." On balance, therefore, while Grant had good political as well as personal and financial reasons for his actions, there remains a strong impression (reinforced by his wavering) that Johnson's advocacy of the Matamoros expedition lacked genuine conviction, and that personal ambition was the principal motivating factor in guiding his approach to the council.

As it happens James Bowie had already briefed the Advisory Council on the broad outlines of Houston's plan just a week earlier on December 28, and he had consequently been authorized to raise "an auxiliary volunteer corps" for the purpose. Now, Wyatt Hanks and the Military Committee, having interviewed Johnson, swiftly reported to the rest of the council on the evening of January 3 that "it is an expedition of the utmost importance at this time. It will give employment to the volunteers, until a regular army, sufficient for the protection of our country, can be raised and organized." They also recommended that Johnson should be given command "of all the troops that he can raise for that purpose" and went on to warn: "Delay at this time on our part would be dangerous. For if the volunteers on their march for Matamoros were defeated, the consequence resulting from it might prove fatal to Texas. But every one must foresee the benefit that would result from occupying and keeping possession, of that important and commercial depot. It would not only deprive our enemies of the immense revenue at that place, but aid us greatly in supporting our army. It would also carry the war into the enemies country; and with the vessels that will be floating upon the Gulf of Mexico in the service of Texas in one month, will give us the entire command of the Gulf, from Matamoras to New Orleans."[22]

So far so good, and as will become apparent, the authorization to raise troops was not necessarily the same thing as being placed in charge of the expedition. But at this point Johnson started to realize that the council might not actually have the power to do so in any case. Johnson's original list of officers proposed to be commissioned in his Federal Volunteer Army had been received by Henry Smith on December 23 and properly forwarded straight to Sam Houston, who was after all the commander in chief. This was just two days after Houston had himself ordered Neill to take command at Bexar on December 21, and perhaps for this very reason, he did nothing about it. Now Johnson tried again and was particularly keen to obtain proper commissions both for James Grant, who had been left in charge of the troops, and for his own adjutant, Nathaniel Brister. The council, however—by now only too aware of the problems caused by the earlier conflicting orders and appointments—turned cautious, particularly when on the morning of January 6, James Bowie suddenly "exhibited to the Council, orders from the Commander in Chief of the Army, to proceed against Matamoras."[23]

Despite Bowie's earlier briefing, the fact that he actually held written orders from Houston seemingly came as a complete surprise to the members of the council, who scrambled to obtain a transcript before he left that evening for Goliad. His decision to reveal those orders now must have been prompted by the arrival of Stephen S. Blount the previous day. On January 1, as Grant led the Federal Volunteer Army south out of Bexar, Colonel Neill had sent Lieutenant Blount racing eastward to find Sam Houston. The letter he carried, if it was the only one, was astonishingly brief and innocuous, outwardly no more than an introduction and a recommendation for promotion, but a postscript added by Green B. Jameson, the Alamo engineer, told Houston: "You are particularly refered to Lieut. Blount for information as regards the Conduct of Johnson & Grant at this Garrison of late and any statement on that subject may be relied on."[24] Presumably, with no time to write a more detailed report, the real message was a verbal one, alerting the commander in chief that Grant had gone, taking the better part of the army with him. Blount probably reached San Felipe sometime late on January 5, only to find that Houston was at Washington-on-the-Brazos. Nevertheless Governor Smith, galvanized into action by the letter, told Bowie to return to Goliad at once and sent a fresh rider straight on to

Washington with a similar message to Houston. The next day, while Bowie was packing his bags and astonishing the council, Smith wrote to Major William Ward, the commander of a small battalion of Georgia volunteers lying at Velasco, to tell him:

Every one that wishes to supercede the commander-in-chief, or not recognise him his proper place, distrust him! I have anticipated them and ordered the commander-in-chief forthwith to proceed to the frontier, take charge of the army, establish his headquarters at the most eligible point, and to immediately concentrate his troops, at the different points, so as to be in readiness for active operations, at the earliest possible date. A descent will be made on Matamoros, as soon as it can possibly be fitted out. . . . Some men of whom I have cautioned you [presumably Grant and Johnson] are making bold moves to become commander-in-chief of expeditions. I will rob them of the army and they will be flat.[25]

For once recognizing the urgency of the situation, Houston immediately got on the road to Goliad. In the circumstances—with the governor's furious denunciations ringing round San Felipe; with Bowie displaying unambiguous orders from the commander in chief to take charge of the expedition; with that same commander in chief declining to ratify his list of commissions; and with his own motives uncertain—it is hardly surprising that Johnson should have ended the day by "declining any participation in the contemplated expedition to Matamoras."[26]

Had that been the end of Johnson's involvement, events might yet have taken a different course, but now the council turned instead to Colonel James W. Fannin. A prominent colonist and sometime West Point cadet from Georgia, Fannin had commanded a company called the Brazos Guards in the fight at Concepción, before Houston lured him away with a colonel's commission in the regular army. Currently he was its ranking officer next to Houston, and had the army actually existed, Fannin would have been second in command. However he was also ambitious, and on January 7 seemingly had little hesitation in accepting an appointment "as an agent for and on behalf of the Provisional Government of Texas, to raise, collect and concentrate at, or as near the post of Copano, as convenience and safety will admit, all volunteer troops willing to enter into an expedition against Matamoras, wherever they may be found, at the mouth of the Brazos, city of Bexar, or elsewhere, whether in Texas, or arriving in Texas, and when thus collected and concentrated, to report, either to the Commanding General, or to the Governor or Council as he may prefer." The resolution that appointed him went on to say that after collecting the troops he was to "make a descent upon Matamoras, if he deems it practicable to take said place, or such other point or place, as the said agent may deem proper."[27]

Whereas at first sight the Advisory Council appears to have been deliberately meddling in military affairs in order to have a piece of the action, it is important to note that on December 30 Houston had himself ordered Fannin to take charge of the volunteers assembling at Velasco, down by the mouth of the Brazos, and to move them farther along the coast to Copano. It is unclear however whether Fannin was then expected to cooperate with or subordinate himself to Bowie, or whether, as seems rather more likely, his orders were actually prompted by Houston's realization that Bowie was by then no longer at Goliad and that Fannin would have to take charge in the meantime. It could certainly be argued, and probably was argued, that since Fannin's December 30 orders from Houston were of a later date, they superseded Bowie's December 17 instructions, hence the council's instruction that he was to report to a higher authority, although who that authority might be was purposely left to Fannin's discretion, for the council could already foresee trouble.

This is evident from the fact that just before close of business two days later, the council suddenly resolved to request Governor Smith to provide "a copy of all orders that he may have issued to the commander-in-chief of the army, or any other officer of the army," which certainly suggests that they were having doubts regarding to whom exactly Fannin should be reporting.[28] Unfortunately the resolution coincided with the arrival of a dramatic letter from Bexar that gave Smith more than ample ammunition with which to fight back. Although Grant was to get the principal blame for what happened, it was really Sam Houston's fault, and ironically the orders that precipitated the crisis had little direct connection with Matamoros.

Those who afterward defended the Alamo were fond of extolling Bexar's importance as the frontier piquet post of Texas, and so it might have been, but arguably the key to Texas during the revolution was the port of Copano, just north of Corpus Christi Bay. A Mexican army advancing from the Rio Grande, whether by Laredo or Matamoros, had to carry all its supplies. The only other alternative was to draw upon mule trains, and as James Grant had demonstrated long before, packing them overland from Mexico was far from easy. However if Copano and its entrance to the Gulf at Aransas Pass were in Mexican hands, supplies could be brought in by sea with relative ease. Meanwhile, the Texians were dependent upon the port for bringing their own supplies and reinforcements down from the Brazos and even directly from New Orleans. Houston for one was keenly aware of the importance of the place and, later in the campaign, would prove more concerned about fortifying and holding Copano than about going to the aid of Travis and his little garrison at the Alamo. For the moment though, Houston intended that Copano be held by the twenty-odd men of John Chenoweth's United States Invincibles, and it must have been the assignment of these volunteers to leave Bexar that proved the last straw as far as Colonel Neill was concerned.

Neill had already sent Lieutenant Blount to complain of Grant's marching off with the Federal Volunteer Army from Bexar, and now, five days later, he poured out his anger and frustration in a much quoted letter, which claimed in part:

> We have 104 men, and two distinct fortresses to garrison, and about 24 pieces of artillery. You will doubtless have learned that we have no Provisions nor clothing in this garrison Since Johnson and Grant left, If there has Ever been a dollar Since I have no knowledge of it. The clothing Sent here by the aid, and patriotic operations of the Honourable Council, was taken from us by the arbitrary Measures of Johnson and Grant. Taken from men who endured all the hardships of winter, and who were not even Sufficiently clad for Summer, many of them have but one blanket, and one Shirt, and what was intended for them given away to men Some of whom, who had not been in the Army more than 4 days, and many not exceeding two weeks. If a dividend had been made of them, the most needy of my men could have been made comfortable by the Stock of clothing and provisions taken from here. . . . The hospital is also in want of Stores, and Even the necessary provisions for well men was not left the wounded by Grant and Johnson.[29]

Just how much truth there was in these accusations is examined in the next chapter, but there can be little doubt that the letter was prompted not merely by these complaints but also by the news that Chenoweth had been ordered to Copano, thus leaving Neill with little more than eighty men to hold a post that in his estimation required some two to three hundred men. As always it took four or five days for the letter to reach San Felipe, and although January 10 was a Sunday, the council was immediately called into session by the governor to discuss both Neill's letter and an even more condemnatory epistle penned by Smith himself. Initially the session was to have been secret, but such was the violence of Smith's attack that on the following day the council resolved to publish a full disclosure of its proceedings.

Introducing Neill's letter, Smith admonished the council: "You will find there a detail of facts, calculated to call forth the indignant feelings of every honest man. Can your body say that they have not been cognizant of and connived at this predatory expedition? Are you not daily holding conference and planning co-operation both by sea and land? Acts speak louder than words, they are now before me, authorising a Generalissimo with plenary powers, to plan expeditions on the faith, the credit, and I may justly say, to the ruin of the country." The short answer was of course no. Since the principle of mounting an expedition against Matamoros had previously been endorsed by everyone concerned, including Henry Smith, the council was indeed very properly "planning co-operation by sea and land," but members had no foreknowledge of Grant's stripping Bexar of men and supplies—and nor, one suspects, did Frank Johnson. Moreover the council's orders to Fannin not only repeated those earlier given to him by Houston but, far from erecting him as a "Generalissimo with plenary powers," explicitly acknowledged his subordination to the official commander in chief and to the governor and council.

Unrestrained by anything so mundane as the truth, Smith then plunged on incoherently to denounce the council itself: "Instead of acting as becomes the counsellors and guardians of a free people," he raged, "you resolve yourselves into a low, intriguing, caucusing parties, pass resolutions without a quorum, predicated on false premises, and endeavour to ruin the country, by countenancing, aiding and abetting marauding parties, and if you could only deceive me enough, you would join with it a piratical co-operation." There was a lot more of this, thunderously culminating with the exhortation: "Look around your flock, your discernment will easily detect the scoundrels. The complaint; contraction of the eyes; the gape of the mouth; the vacant stare; the hung head; the restless fidgety disposition; the sneaking sycophantic look; a natural meanness of countenance; and unguarded shrug of the shoulders; a sympathetic tickling and contraction of the muscles of the neck anticipating the rope; a restless uneasiness to adjourn, dreading to face the storm themselves have raised." Having thus worked himself up into a literary frenzy, Smith concluded with a somewhat calmer ultimatum that unless the council publicly acknowledged its "error" and countermanded its orders by noon the following day, "your body will stand adjourned."

In the face of this violent tirade the council proceeded to express its "astonishment that this community could have been so miserably deceived in selecting for the high office of Governor, a man whose language and conduct prove his early habits of association to have been vulgar and depraved, and his present disposition, that of a tyrant."[30] In defiance of Smith's order to adjourn, the council resolved instead to order him "to cease the functions of his office," formulated articles of impeachment against him, and elected Robinson as acting governor. Realizing he had gone too far, Smith immediately penned an abject apology, but it was too late. And at that moment Frank Johnson returned to the fray with a most remarkable proclamation:

> Under sanction of the general council of Texas, they [the Federal Volunteer Army] have taken up the line of march for the country west of the Rio Grande. They march under the flag 1.8.2.4, as proclaimed by the government of Texas, and have for their object the restoration of the principles of the constitution, and the extermination of the last vestige of despotism from Mexican soil . . .[31]

That he was its author is questionable, for the proclamation bears James Grant's unmistakable imprint and in part intriguingly recalls a letter written to his cousin Glenelg by Palmerston, which celebrated the "glorious" overthrow of Louis Philippe by the French liberals:[32]

> [The volunteers] invite into their ranks all friends to freedom, of whatever name or nation. They invite them to unite in establishing on a firm and solid foundation, on Mexican soil, the banners of Morales and Hidalgo, inscribed with their own national mottoes.

Uninfluenced by views of individual interest, they desire that all true friends shall participate in the glory. Their names will be remembered in the bright pages of the historian, and in the ballad and song of the liberal Mexicans.

To arms! then, Americans, to aid in sustaining the principles of 1776, in this western hemisphere. To arms! native Mexicans, in driving tyranny from your homes, intolerance from your altars, and the tyrant from your country. In this very hour the crowned despots of Europe have met in unholy conclave, to devise the means of crushing liberal principles. Louis Philippe of France, faithless to his oath, now sits side by side with the monarchs of Russia, and Austria and Prussia, and Spain, and the minister of Santa Anna is seen among them. Before this, it is more than probable that the freedom of Mexicans has been sold to tyrants, and that a European force is to sustain the diadem on the head of the traitor Santa Anna. Not only Texas and Mexico, but the genius of liberty, demands that every man do his duty to his country, and leave the consequences to God. Our first attack will be on Matamoros; our next, if Heaven decrees, wherever tyranny shall raise its malignant form.

The council was of the same mind. On January 12 it issued a proclamation of its own, justifying itself and denouncing "the other department of the Provisional Government" and his various actions, including the commissioning of James Bowie. Rather enterprisingly the proclamation also tried to blame Smith for the troubles at Bexar and the "deplorable situation in which the troops of that garrison were left by Dr. Grant, who headed an expedition from that place to Matamoras," by asserting that the "only authority Dr. Grant ever had in the army was derived from Governor Smith." This also gave them the excuse to digress into a lengthy but tendentious explanation of how Smith had appointed Burleson to be commander in chief at Bexar "without the advice or consent of the Council," giving Burleson the authority to appoint Grant in turn as "his aid-de camp, who was thereby entitled to rank as Colonel."[33]

The council thus condemned and effectively repudiated Grant (rather than appointing him separately to command the expedition, as Houston afterward charged).[34] It was clear that someone now needed to take charge of the Bexar volunteers in the name of the council, and Frank Johnson presented himself as the obvious choice. He was duly authorized on January 14 to "conduct the volunteers who have entered upon the expedition to Matamoras . . . and that when the said volunteers are all concentrated as directed by the resolutions appointing J. W. Fannin, agent &c., a commander of the whole body be elected under the existing laws. Before which juncture, Col. Johnson should be authorized to hold an election by the volunteers from Bexar, of all the requisite officers, and have the same properly certified and reported to the General Council. And also that an election in the same manner be had, by J. W. Fannin, of the other volunteers, when assembled and in like manner reported."[35] In short, far from his being appointed to command the expedition, Johnson's authority was to be limited to the Bexar volunteers, and indeed it was expressly made clear to him that "nothing . . . shall be so taken, as to interfere with the agency granted to J. W. Fannin by the Provisional Government heretofore."

Whether Grant was prepared to acknowledge the authority of either of them remained to be seen.

5 • *High Noon at Goliad*

THE GARRISON LAY where the Atascosita Road crossed the San Antonio River at a point about ninety miles downstream from Bexar and forty miles inland from Copano Bay, and like many places in Mexico it had two names. To some it was known simply as La Bahía (or, as the Americans frequently wrote it, "Labadee"), but others knew it as Goliad. By either name it was currently one of the most important garrisons in Texas, for as Sam Houston pointed out, "Should Bexar remain a military post, Goliad must be maintained, or the former will be cut off from all supplies arriving by sea at the port of Copano."[1] Indeed, by doing just that, the Texian seizure of Goliad in October 1835 had been a major factor in forcing the surrender of Cos at Bexar (see map, next page).

Yet when Colonel James Grant rode in there on January 5, 1836, he found the little town weakly held and virtually abandoned. Nearly all its Tejano inhabitants, formerly numbering about one thousand, had long gone, leaving about seventy stone houses and squalid huts or *jacales* to just a few stray cattle and dogs. The only Texians in the place belonged to Captain Philip Dimitt's little garrison, forted up in the old Spanish *presidio,* and they had no intention of going anywhere near Matamoros. They simply wanted to go home. Only a week earlier Dimitt had been complaining to the council: "The volunteers are restless and did not expect such a long service in Goliad. It was difficult to persuade them to hold on during the month of November until the Siege of Bexar was over. Seeing their companions in arms returning to their families an anxiety prevailed to visit their own families at the same time declaring their readiness to service."[2] Now it was nearly a month since the siege had ended, but they were still holding on; thoroughly sick of soldiering, sick of Dimitt, and sick of the Mexican federation as well. They had also declared independence on December 20.

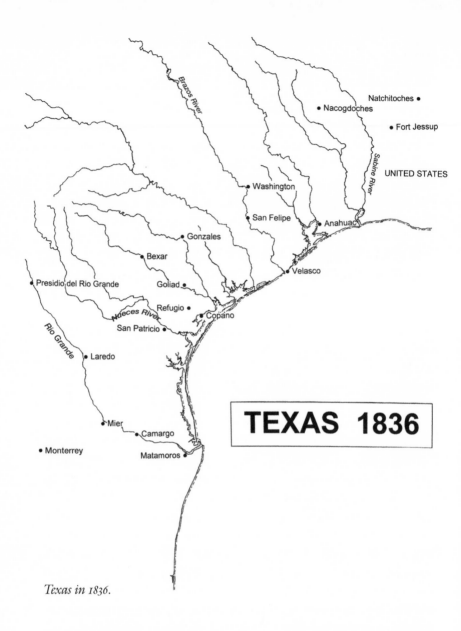

Texas in 1836.

Right up until that moment Dimitt was widely regarded as a federalist with strong family and personal ties to the Tejano community around
nearby Victoria and his home on Lavaca Bay. Through his wife María
Luisa Laso, her De León kinsmen, and his own brother in Zacatecas,
he was kept unusually well informed of what was happening in Mexico.
Notwithstanding his earlier falling out with Grant and Viesca he had

also been an enthusiastic promoter of the plan to take Matamoros and then spread the revolt through the other northern Mexican states, for this, as he said, "would be putting the war in the hands of its lawful and proper owners. . . . It originated in the interior of the country, in a contest for power, and there it belongs."[3]

All that changed, however, when the schooner *Hannah Elizabeth* ran aground on the bar at Matagorda Bay on November 18 and was captured by the Mexican Navy's *Montezuma*. The schooner was carrying supplies for the rebels, and its passengers included a handful of volunteers from New Orleans. About a month later one of the other passengers, Dimitt's father-in-law, Carlos Laso, escaped from Matamoros and brought word to him that "there was in circulation a Decree of the general Government That all Mexicans, foreigners, or Americans, without any distinction whatever taken as prisoners on this side of the Rio Grande should be immediately put to death."[4] Ominously, Laso and another escapee, Fernando de León, also claimed to have passed five dead "foreigners" on the road, executed in accordance with the decree. Not surprisingly, at this point Dimitt and his men suddenly began to feel very lonely, and two days later, on December 20, they mingled defiance and apprehension in a suitably ringing declaration of independence from Mexico. At first it may not have made much of an impact since the council promptly tried to suppress it, and most of the local Tejanos had already left town precisely because they were hostile to the Texians and their federalist friends. But now the declaration very nearly led to a stand-up fight between Grant and Dimitt. When the two men had first clashed in November, it was over the question of recognizing Viesca's authority as the legitimate governor of Coahuila *and* Texas; this time, although the initial cause of their falling out was the rather more urgent question of supplies, the original argument soon resurfaced and rapidly escalated into something altogether more serious.

In his famous jeremiad of January 6, Colonel Neill complained that Grant had not only stripped Bexar of men but had also taken away all the available provisions, clothing, medical supplies, and horses. Recall his protest that "the clothing Sent here by the aid, and patriotic operations of the Honourable Council, was taken from us by the arbitrary Measures of Johnson and Grant." Similarly Creed Taylor, perhaps taking his cue from Neill, declared that Grant, "without the shadow of authority, marched away from Bexar with 200 volunteers, after having despoiled the handful of men left under Colonel Neill of ammunition, blankets, medical stores, and everything else worth taking."

If these often repeated charges were true, there must have been precious little in the way of supplies at Bexar in the first place, for none of the clothing and stores requested by Frank Johnson on December 17 ever materialized. While forwarding Johnson's list of officers to Houston, Governor Smith turned the clothing and equipment requisitions straight over to the council for action, and the council in turn passed the requisitions on to the Military Committee. In retrospect this was probably a mistake, for a little over a week earlier that same committee had reported with disarming frankness that the appointment of a paymaster for the troops at Bexar was quite unnecessary because "there is no money in the Treasury to pay the soldiers." At length they now responded to Johnson's requests in true bureaucratic style by ruling that the officers at Bexar should first be required to make proper returns of their existing men and equipment, "because it is impossible for the General Council to order supplies, or make provision for a garrison or any military post, without knowing its situation and condition in every respect."[5]

This paper-shuffling exercise took them right up to the end of December, and consequently Johnson once again angrily refuted the charges, insisting that "we only have to say that he [Grant] took, by authority of the proper officer, one six pounder gun, and one 6 or 8 inch mortar, with suitable ammunition for the same.[6] As to supplies and comforts, there were none to take, the quartermaster's department being as empty as the treasury of Texas. . . . Not a thing was taken from Col. Neill in the shape of supplies. He was left in possession of a full proportion of what had been surrendered by the enemy."[7] The identity of the "proper officer" who authorized Grant to take the six-pounder and the howitzer (not a mortar) poses an intriguing question in itself, but more particularly Johnson went on to declare that "it is only necessary to say that there was no supply of clothing, and that provisions were obtained from the surrounding country." The latter point was at least obliquely acknowledged by Neill in his catalogue of woe when he alluded to the complaints arising from the "extent to which the impressments of Cattle and Horses, has been carried by Johnson and Grant." Creed Taylor noted that "each day a detail was sent out to round up beeves and fat cows for food for the garrison, and when a Mexican appeared in town with a good horse, ownership to the animal was promptly transferred to a needy Americano. Reliable Mexican citizens have told me of many of the practices of the volunteers while in San Antonio, all of which were a shame and a disgrace to the American name."

Even Sam Houston agreed that when he himself arrived at Goliad he found the volunteers "destitute of many supplies necessary to their comfort on a campaign."[8] Neill's complaints notwithstanding, the plain fact of the matter was that right from the beginning there had been far too few horses to go around, and this shortage only worsened during what all concerned agreed to be an unusually hard winter. On top of that, after just four days on the road Grant and his men were very short of food and coffee, which hardly supports their having taken much in the way of supplies in the first place. Displaying the same ruthlessness that had carried the army out of Bexar, Grant now proceeded to seize all the horses he could lay hands on, irrespective of whether they were "public" (i.e., government) property or privately owned.[9] Flour and coffee were a different matter, however, and according to Captain William Cooke of the San Antonio Greys, "Dimitt refused to furnish us with provisions, of which he had a large store, upon the grounds that we were acting contrary to the wishes of the people of Texas, in uniting with the Mexicans west of the Rio Grande."[10] This was probably true enough, although a young Georgian named Reuben Brown may have been equally near the mark when he reckoned that the refusal was simply "in consequence of personal animosity against Col Grant."[11] Either way, what happened next is revealed in a fascinating affidavit by one of Dimitt's men, who for some unexplained reason found himself at Grant's headquarters:

Volunteer James H. Bowman states that whilst at Headquarters yesterday evening or afternoon [7 January] in the camp of the Volunteers on the San Antonio River, a short distance above Goliad, Captain Burk of the Mobile Greys came into the camp of the Commander of the said Volunteers, Dr. Grant, and asked him, Grant "What was the reason they had no bread?" Grant replied, "I intend to go up and see that fellow (meaning Dimitt) and tell him that he might as well let us have the flour, for it would be taken anyhow." Captain Burk then replied "detail me, and I will go and rattle the house down on his head." To this Grant responded, "I will go myself after a while, and tell him if he don't give it up, we will have it by force." Burk then asked if Dimitt did not come under him (Grant) to which Grant replied "certainly he does."[12]

Angrily repudiating Grant's assertion that as self-proclaimed acting commander in chief of the Federal Volunteer Army, he had any authority over Dimitt—the Goliad garrison had always been a separate command—Dimitt tried to raise the stakes by provocatively hoisting what he called the flag of independence on the walls of the presidio. This may have been a design he devised himself, displaying a piratical bloody arm and sword on a white ground, but calling it a flag of "independence" suggests it may actually have been a blue flag bearing a lone star and the word *independence*, which had been left at the presidio by a member of William Scott's Lynchburg Volunteers. At any rate Grant, who had marched in under the famous 1824 tricolor, promptly ordered the other flag hauled down, declaring that he and his men "ware federalists and would Stand to the Constitution of 1824."[13] Indeed Reuben Brown commented that there "was not then probably a dozen in our expedition in favor" (of independence).[14] Things were starting to get out of hand, and Captain Cooke wrote that "we all expected to have a fight with his force. . . . During the time of the altercation both parties were kept in readiness for a fight."

Happily it never came to that. Dimitt had already made himself thoroughly unpopular with his own men, and now they suddenly found themselves even more urgently preoccupied than before with the need to get home and "plant corn." Consequently, as the confrontation with Grant's federalist volunteers escalated, Dimitt became uncomfortably aware that if it came to a fight he was probably going to be seriously outnumbered; accordingly, he backed down. Judging by Houston's later report there must have been little flour at Goliad after all, but Cooke recorded that the next day Dimitt "consented to furnish us with Coffee, Sugar &c &c for a three months campaign." Notwithstanding the widespread complaints about drunkenness, it is sometimes hard to avoid the impression that coffee rather than whiskey was the mainspring of the rebel forces. They might be unpaid, poorly supplied, sometimes half naked, and reduced to eating an unrelieved diet of freshly killed beef, but war without heavily sweetened coffee was simply too awful to contemplate.

Once the precious coffee had been handed over, an uneasy truce descended and "we were permitted to exchange civilities" as two more companies of volunteers turned up at Goliad under Captain Peyton Wyatt: his own Huntsville Volunteers armed with those "fifty first rate

U.S. muskets" and Captain Amon B. King's rifle-armed Paducah Volunteers. Since both companies had been sent forward by Sam Houston to garrison Copano and therefore did not form part of Grant's little army, Dimitt seized the opportunity to get out of the hole he had dug for himself. Furloughing both his men and himself, he dashed off a letter of complaint to Governor Smith on January 10 and then turned over command of the presidio to Captain Wyatt. Somewhere along the road the messenger carrying his letter must then fortuitously have run into James Bowie, who was hurrying to Goliad in obedience to Smith's orders. Once the situation was explained to him, Bowie in turn penned a hasty letter to Sam Houston, breathlessly advising him: "Some dark scheme has been set on foot to disgrace our noble cause. I shall leave with Captain Blount in an hour, and shall reach Goliad by daylight, and put a stop to Grant's movements."[15]

Given their previous association it could have been an interesting confrontation, but a few hours before Bowie arrived, Grant rode off down into Tamaulipas in search of Colonel Gonzales and his federalist cavalrymen.[16] In Grant's absence the volunteers were temporarily left under the command of Robert Morris, who flatly declined to recognize Bowie's authority. Curiously, although Bowie still had orders to go to Matamoros, William Cooke remembered that "Bowie's object appeared to be to induce our men to return to San Antonio—He used every means in his power to effect this object—They however at length determined to recognise the order of Genl Houston, and marched to Refugio."[17] At first reading, Cooke's slightly shaky chronology might suggest some kind of secondary conflict between Bowie and Houston. In fact, since Bowie preceded Houston to Goliad by some days, Cooke must actually have meant that Bowie tried "to stop Grant's movements" as soon as he arrived, by persuading the volunteers to return to Bexar, but that they instead resolved to continue toward Matamoros in the belief that Houston's original orders still applied, for as will become clear, most assumed or may have been led to believe that Grant was acting in Houston's name in leading the expedition.

Be that as it may, Houston's own characteristic dilatoriness did not help. On December 30 he had assured Governor Smith that he would be ready to "set out with a staff of the army in three days for Copano or Matamoros."[18] Yet he was still in Washington when Smith's messenger arrived with the news that Grant had marched from Bexar. What happened next was outlined in his subsequent report to Smith, in which he claimed:

In obedience to your order under the date of the 6th, I left Washington on the 8th and reached Goliad on the night of the 14th. On the morning of that day I met Captain Dimit, on his return home with his command, who reported to me the fact that his *caballada* of horses (the most of them private property) had been pressed by Dr. Grant, who styled himself acting commander-in-chief of the federal army, and that he had under his command about two hundred men. Captain Dimit had been relieved by Captain P. S. Wyatt, of the volunteers from Huntsville, Alabama. I was also informed by Major R. C. Morris that breadstuff was wanting in camp; and he suggested his wish to remove the volunteers further west. By express, I had advised the stay of the troops at Goliad until I could reach that point.[19]

The historian Henderson Yoakum, on the other hand, asserted that his friend Houston did not arrive there until two days later and, "having reached Goliad on the 16th of January, ordered the command of Major R. C. Morris to take up the line of march for the mission of Refugio on the next day at ten o'clock."[20] This makes rather more sense, for Morris's reported "wish" to move farther west was in part prompted by a message from Colonel Fannin, "informing us he had embarked at Velasco and would meet us with five Hundred men at Copono."[21] Houston may simply have made an error as to the date, when he got around to writing his January 30 report—or perhaps more likely, he may have been deliberately concealing the same lack of urgency he would later display in taking command of the Alamo relief force at Gonzales.

At any rate, the next morning a fresh crisis arose with the arrival of yet another letter from Neill. Dated as recently as January 14, it reiterated his complaints to Houston about the shortage of provisions at Bexar and above all the shortage of men. "Not less than twenty will leave tomorrow," he protested, presumably referring to Chenoweth's United States Invincibles, "and leave here only about eighty efficient men under my command, there are at Laredo now 3,000 men under the command of Genl Ramirez [y Sesma], and as it appears from a letter received here last night, 1,000 of them are destined for this place, and two thousand for matamoros."[22] Ironically enough, Neill's letter may even have been delivered by Chenoweth's men, en route to Copano, for at least four of those who rode back to die with James Bowie at the Alamo were former members of the Invincibles.

Houston had already ordered Dimitt to raise a fresh company for service at Bexar, and in the light of this latest news he told Governor Smith that he was also sending Bowie "with a detachment of from twenty to fifty men." He made clear that he was far from happy about it: "I have ordered the fortifications in the town of Bexar to be demolished, and, if you think fit of it, I will remove all the cannon and other munitions of war to Gonzales and Copano, blow up the Alamo and abandon the place, as it will be impossible to keep up the Station with volunteers, the sooner it can be authorised the better it will be for the country."

If Bexar was to be evacuated there was really no need for any of those reinforcements accompanying Bowie, but perhaps Houston thought they might lend the colonel some authority for what he had to do. In the meantime, he was having serious second thoughts about the whole Matamoros business, even without taking into account the rumored two thousand Centralista troops Neill reported to be heading toward the place: "In an hour," he declared, "I will take up the line of march for Refugio Mission with about 209 efficient men, where I will await orders from your Excellency, believing that the army should not advance with a small force on Matamoros in the hope or belief that the Mexicans will cooperate with us. . . . I would myself have marched to Bexar but the Matamoros rage is up so high that I must see Colonel Ward's men. You have no idea of the difficulties I have encountered."[23]

William Ward and his Georgia Rattlers were due to arrive shortly at Copano by steamer with Colonel Fannin and were then expected to march the short distance inland to Refugio; but after two days on the road, Houston and Morris arrived there to find no sign of them. The only troops occupying the old mission were a little contingent of genuine Texian regulars commanded by Captain Ira J. Westover. They were supposed to be garrisoning Copano but had instead decided unilaterally to move themselves up to Refugio since there was no decent water supply at the landing.

While they all waited for Fannin and Ward, Houston went to work. At the outset when it was requested to determine how the regular army should be organized, the provisional government's Military Committee recommended that it should comprise a regiment of infantry and a regiment of artillery and that "each regiment will consist of two battalions, each battalion of five companies, and each company of fifty-six rank and file." In addition, each of the five companies was to have a total of eleven officers—a captain, two lieutenants, four sergeants, and four corporals—all ranked according to precedence. Although these recommendations were specifically embodied in an Act to Raise a Regular Army, passed on November 24, 1835, the same organizational matrix was intended to be applied to the volunteers. They were to fall into two classes: "Permanent Volunteers," who were to be enlisted in the service of Texas for a period of not less than six months in return for the promise of 640 acres of land, and "Auxiliary Volunteers," who signed up for only three months and 320 acres. Unlike the handful of regulars, whose officers were directly appointed by the provisional government, all the volunteers could elect their own officers at the outset, from the captain all the way down to the fourth corporal, and once elected those captains and lieutenants were to receive commissions from the government, confirming them in their rank until they resigned or were killed or dismissed.

Grant's Federal Volunteer Army now encamped at Refugio had indeed elected its officers and was properly organized on something like those lines. It consisted of a complete infantry battalion of five companies under Major Robert Morris, together with an independent company of cavalry under Captain Benjamin L. Lawrence, but none of the officers except Morris had a proper commission. When Houston received Frank Johnson's request for those commissions in December, he had declined to act, not only because he had his own agenda but also for the entirely legitimate reason that neither the Bexar men nor their officers were properly enlisted in the service of Texas. Even the council disapproved of this omission and took Johnson to task on that very point when he turned up at San Felipe in the first week of January.[24] While diplomatically acknowledging that "some misconception of rights, had arisen among the volunteers, from the want of a proper knowledge of the existing laws upon the army organization," they were rightly concerned that until this was rectified, the volunteers were not acting under any lawful authority. Grant had of course claimed them for what he called the Federal Service of Mexico, but since there was no properly constituted federal government in Mexico (the motley group of exiles in New Orleans hardly counted), they were in effect Grant's private army.

Nobody was particularly happy about that, and having caught up with them, Houston was now determined to do something about it.

Ever since joining the army, claimed Reuben Brown, Houston "addicted himself to the most shameful dissipation carousing and drinking continually with the soldiers."[25] It was a classic Houston performance, and having convivially prepared the ground, he now intended to cut the army out from under Grant by the simple expedient of properly mustering all of them as Auxiliary Volunteers in the service of Texas. Once that was done he would then have the legal authority, as commander in chief, to order them to stand fast at Copano or fall back to Goliad, the Guadalupe, or even the Colorado, as the situation required.

His task was made all the easier by Grant's fortuitous absence. Although Creed Taylor claimed in later years that Grant "was not popular with the officers and men," he himself was never a member of the expedition; in contrast, the admiring Ehrenberg frequently asserted that Grant was "universally popular." Grant, after all, had promoted the expedition in the first place; back in Bexar, according to Yoakum, he "was incessantly painting in lively colors the rich spoils of Tamaulipas, New Leon, Coahuila, and San Luis Potosi, the facility of the descent, the cowardly nature of the inhabitants, and the charming and beautiful valleys of the San Juan, the Sabinas, and the Santander."[26] It was also Grant who had led them south to Goliad and faced down Dimitt, virtually at gunpoint, to get his men the horses and supplies they so badly needed. But—crucially—a great many of them appear to have believed that he did so in Houston's name.

Houston's first act, surprisingly enough, was to try and get rid of the regulars by ordering them back to Goliad to replace Wyatt's men, who were then to be called forward to Refugio. In his January 30 report he stated that this was necessary for the security of Goliad, yet while he had always intended that Wyatt's men should join with the other volunteers, Houston rather contrarily told Smith in his earlier letter of January 17 that he also wanted all of the regulars concentrated at Copano. Sending away those already at Refugio therefore made little sense, particularly as he complained to Smith, "I found much difficulty in prevailing on the regulars to march, until they had received either money or clothing."

At first sight both his keenness to send them away, and their own reluctance to go, "truly destitute" as they were, appears puzzling, for being regulars they were unquestionably his to command. In fairness, however, he probably had good reason for regarding this company of about 40 regulars with some suspicion. They belonged to two different groups, both of which to his mind had a dubious history. Westover had recruited his own fourteen men from among the Irish settlers at San Patricio and Refugio itself. Significantly, like Grant, they were not and never had been Americans and so were probably seen by Houston as too closely aligned with the Tejano federalists. What was more, at least some of them were the same men who had joined with Grant and Viesca when the two passed through San Patricio after their escape in November, and then backed Grant in his original dispute with Dimitt. The others, currently commanded by Lieutenant Francis W. Thornton, were equally suspect in Houston's eyes, for they were none other than some of the tattered survivors of Mexía's ill-fated Tampico expedition, still wearing what was left of their Mexican uniforms and defiantly calling themselves the Tampico Blues. The services of these unemployed mercenaries had been offered to the council by Captain John M. Allen and accepted with some alacrity, thus making them what Thornton called the first company of regulars "that ever marched to the tap of a drum under the provisional government of Texas."[27]

As it happens, Allen himself was currently away trying to raise more recruits on the cosmopolitan New Orleans waterfront, but given the mercenaries' equivocal past, Houston probably thought it safer to get them all out of the way, and his suspicions cannot have been eased by their professed reluctance to go. At length however, go they did, and then he turned to the Bexar volunteers, inviting Major Morris to see him at Ira Westover's quarters "whenever it will suit his convenience," as Houston wished to "make some communications through him to the volunteers at this post."[28] The summons was presumably to apprise Morris of the orders Houston was about to issue for organizing the troops "agreeably to the ordinance for raising an auxiliary corps to the army," published by the provisional government. Given a few more hours, the general might have succeeded, but unbeknownst to him, Frank Johnson had also caught up with the army that night and confronted Houston on the morning of January 21, just before the men were called to "a general parade, for the purpose (as was stated) to reorganise the troops and explain to them the desire of the Provisional Govt."

At that point it all turned very messy indeed. "It was understood that he [Johnson] was empowered, by the general council of Texas, to interfere in my command," complained Houston huffily. "So soon as I was made acquainted with the nature of his mission, and the powers granted to J. W. Fannin, jr., I could not remain mistaken as to the object of the council, or the wishes of individuals."[29] In reality Fannin's orders directed him only to assemble and outfit the troops for the expedition and arguably still subordinated him to Houston, while Johnson's own January 14 orders similarly limited *his* authority. Indeed, by any sensible reading of those orders, Johnson was himself required by the council to remuster the Bexar contingent properly as Auxiliary Volunteers and attach them to Fannin's command.

That Fannin, for his part, was enjoined to report "either to the Commanding General, or to the Governor or Council as he may prefer" was certainly unfortunate but surely reflects a sensible if misguided intention to allow for all eventualities. Otherwise why give him the choice rather than simply cutting both general and governor out of the loop?

Taken by themselves therefore, the instructions did not necessarily conflict with Houston's own orders to Bowie and Fannin. But Johnson had never concealed his intense dislike of Houston, and in his January 3 letter to the council he made a point of assuring its members: "You may rely on all going well, if we are not interfered with by officers of the regular army." In the present circumstances there was little prospect of his cooperating with Houston, let alone taking any orders from him. Emboldened by the recent events in San Felipe, Johnson undoubtedly made that clear to the beleaguered commander in chief and underlined the point by presenting him with a copy of the "resolutions of the general council, dated 14th of January." Thus Houston learned for the first time that Henry Smith had been deposed and impeached.

This spelled possible disaster, for thus far, surprisingly enough, the general had not heard a single shot fired in anger in the defense of Texas. Indeed he had consistently argued against any military action at all until sufficient numbers of volunteers arrived from the United States. With few friends on the council, he was almost entirely dependent on the support of Henry Smith, and now the governor's overthrow, coupled with the council's positive orders to move on Matamoros and with Johnson's active hostility, not only left him politically isolated but also completely undermined his authority. Unsurprisingly, by the time some notion of all of this filtered down to the ordinary soldiers, many, including Reuben Brown, got the idea that Houston "did not disapprove of the expedition until he learned that Fannin was the choice of the volunteers to Command them—his jealous feelings towards Colonel Fannin prompted him to put down the expedition if possible"; Brown's jaundiced view may have been colored by the fact that he and Fannin were old friends.[30] But Houston, as we have seen, had already been expressing some doubts about the expedition in his January 17 letter to Smith. Nevertheless the waters were sufficiently muddied by Johnson's intemperate meddling that the charge was believed by at least some of the volunteers. Either way, instead of simply mustering them into the Texian Army and taking formal command, as he might easily have done before Johnson turned up like the Devil at prayers, Houston was now going to have to appeal to them.

The only real account of that appeal comes from Herman Ehrenberg, who recorded it some time later from memory and no doubt considerably embellished it as he went along, although the gist of it is plainly there.[31] Houston, he said, began by praising the volunteers' patriotism and expressing a hope that the decisive battle would be fought on the "foaming Guadalupe," which ran somewhat to the east of both Bexar and Goliad. Then he turned closer to hand, praising their courage, but warning that they would gain nothing by taking Matamoros, "a town that can have no value for us and that lies beyond the border of our territory." Far better, he continued, to let the enemy come to them, "fatigued by long marches and privations." However, finding them unmoved by this prospect, he changed tack and urged that if they insisted on going to Matamoros, they should at least wait a short time longer until the expected contingents from Georgia and Alabama arrived.

If Ehrenberg remembered Houston's speech correctly, this was hardly going to get him anywhere, and Captain Thomas Pearson immediately strode out to offer a brisk rebuttal, asserting that they had already waited too long and that neither the reinforcements nor any of the supplies had turned up. As for those "long marches and privations," he complained, they themselves were already "enduring the hardships of a campaign," and that being so, they would be better off trying to achieve something rather than waiting idly at Refugio. A practiced orator, he then rounded off his harangue with a straightforward appeal to "all who are in favor of an immediate departure for Matamoras. Colonels Johnson and Grant and Major Morris are in favor of the expedition and will participate in it. Once more, let us not hesitate longer, and, all who endorse my position, be ready at noon—to leave for Matamoras!"

After Houston's wavering and uninspiring start, Tom Pearson's rousing reply was almost enough to swing the debate, but then the general, still profiting by Grant's absence, stepped up again. This time he argued: "Our proclamations to the other states of the Mexican confederation, asking them to support us in our struggle for the restoration of our former rights and for the protection of the Constitution of 1824, have, as you know, been without results." In reality of course, it was those other states that were looking to the Texians for aid, and the Matamoros expedition was supposedly aimed at providing it. Nevertheless Houston, having hit his stride, plunged on with a fine disregard for the truth: "Even many of the Mexicans who live between the Sabine and the Rio Grande have disdainfully forsaken the cause of freedom. . . . Also from the otherwise liberal inhabitants of Zacatecas we have observed no movement in our favor." The fact that the Zacatecans had already been defeated, and then thoroughly worked over by the Centralistas, was obviously of no consequence, and Houston rounded off this remarkable bit of rhetoric with a tub-thumping conclusion: "Since it is impossible to call forth any sympathy from our fellow Mexican citizens and no support is to be expected from this side and as they let us, the smallest of the provinces, struggle without any aid, let us then, comrades, sever that link that binds us to that rusty chain of the Mexican federation."

This time, said Ehrenberg, "cheers of joy greeted his eloquent appeal," and Cooke also declared that his address "completely defeated the object of Col. Grant." Houston's victory was nevertheless a hollow one, for he had still failed to win control of the army for himself. Instead, washing his hands of the whole business for the present, he almost immediately afterward left the army and took himself off on a pointless diplomatic mission to the Cherokee of East Texas, remaining safely out of the way until the Consultation reconvened at San Felipe on March 1.

Indeed the whole affair was far from being as straightforward as Cooke and Ehrenberg suggest. For a start, Lawrence and his cavalrymen were probably on outpost duty when Houston made his appeal (and some of them may even have been out with Grant), for Reuben Brown was curiously vague about the whole business and said nothing at all about the parade ground confrontation. Instead he wrote that the general merely told the volunteers "an express had been sent him requiring him to go immediately to San Phillipe at that time the seat of Government and we afterwards learned that the express contained the information of the arrest of Govr Smith by the council. He remained twenty four hours after he got the express and was constantly engaged in private conversations with the volunteers endeavoring to influence them to abandon the enterprise in which they were engaged and succeeded with our Company. Captain Lawrence resigning and accompanying Gen Houston."[33]

At first sight this is very much at odds not only with Ehrenberg's highly dramatized version but also with Cooke's rather more laconic account, for although the chronology of the captain's notes covering this period is as muddled as ever, he quite unambiguously wrote that after the appeal, "it occupied several days to arrange matters between Houston & Grant" before the general headed east. Nevertheless, both versions may still be correct, for Brown went on to say that "a few days after he [Houston] left and subsequent to the time Fannin was to have joined us, the muster roll was called and only sixty men out of two hundred found willing to proceed to Matamoras, the rest being dissuaded by Houston." Clearly then, Grant, who had been conspicuous by his absence during these proceedings, was now back again, and after some kind of confrontation of his own with Houston, had succeeded in coming to an understanding with the general that if Fannin did not turn up by the appointed time he would be free to go forward to the Nueces with as many of the volunteers as would follow him.

Of the original six companies mustered by Johnson and Grant at Bexar on December 17, two—Thomas Breece's company of New Orleans Greys and James Neill's artillery company—had elected to stay there, together with about half of Lewellen's company under John Chenoweth. Lewellen himself and the rest of his men followed Grant, as did Cooke's company of New Orleans Greys, which had now rechristened themselves the San Antonio Greys; Burke's Mobile Greys; Pearson's company; and two newly organized ones led by Henry Wigginton and Benjamin Lawrence. All in all, as we have seen, Houston reckoned that after sending Baker and his men back to Bexar under Jim Bowie, they numbered "209 effective men" when they marched from Goliad.[34]

Now about half of them elected to wait at Refugio for the arrival of Colonel Fannin. William Cooke's San Antonio Greys, once the 2nd Company of New Orleans Greys, had fought alongside Grant at Bexar and afterward nearly all of them engaged to go with him to Matamoros, but after Houston's January 21 appeal most of them changed their minds and enlisted as Auxiliary Volunteers. Neither Cooke nor Ehrenberg adequately explained this *volte face,* but the simplest answer is that they had until now believed that the expedition was ultimately to be led by Sam Houston. It may also be significant that Cooke was already on the waiting list for a regular commission and would later go on to enjoy a distinguished career in the Texan Army under the republic. He may therefore have been more susceptible to Houston's blandishments than he later admitted and therefore exercised his considerable personal influence in swaying not only his own company but probably Captain Burke's as well. The Mobile Greys arrived at Bexar too late to participate in the fighting, but afterward they absorbed a fair number of men from Tom Breece's 1st Company of New Orleans Greys, when it voted to stay there. Consequently the San Antonio Greys and the Mobile Greys were thereafter closely associated. Once Cooke persuaded his own men to take the oath of allegiance to the provisional government, it was probably only natural that Burke's men should follow suit.

The outcome was much less clear-cut when it came to Henry Wigginton's and Benjamin Lawrence's companies, but there may have been other, unconnected factors at work here, including more than just a suspicion of poor leadership. They too were in some degree composite formations, although a significant number of men in both companies originally came to Texas as Captain James Tarleton's Louisville Volunteers. Like the Mobile Greys, they arrived at Bexar after Cos's surrender but were almost immediately reorganized. The infantry, still retaining their original title, formed the nucleus of a new company commanded by Wigginton, while those possessing horses were transferred to Lawrence's company, which originally came from Tennessee and was now renamed the United States Independent Cavalry Company. A number of other assorted strays, such as Reuben Brown and the Love brothers, had also joined these companies at Bexar, but while a similar process of recruitment and assimilation strengthened both the San Antonio and Mobile Greys, neither Wigginton's nor Lawrence's unit seems to have settled down properly. At Goliad a few men even returned to Bexar with James Bowie, and then at Refugio both commanding officers resigned, and the companies effectively broke up. Some men, including Henry Wigginton himself, decided to quit while they were ahead and returned to the United States, although a rump of both companies did enlist as Auxiliary Volunteers and after Fannin eventually arrived were absorbed into other units. A third group however, including Brown, determined to follow Grant and so transferred to either Pearson's or Lewellen's companies.

Tom Pearson's company, recruited like Cooke's in New Orleans, had arrived in Texas by way of Paso Cavallo back in November but was so delayed by getting an eighteen-pounder cannon brought up from Dimitt's Landing that the fighting in Bexar was over by the time they arrived there. Being so closely associated with this big gun, which was later to figure so famously in the defense of the Alamo, may account for their designation as an artillery company in Johnson's December 17 list, and at least one of the men who joined at Bexar; a German immigrant named William Langenheim, had certainly been a gunner in Captain Nidland Frank's company during the siege. Presumably some of them were now charged with looking after Grant's two guns, but otherwise there is no real evidence that Pearson and his men ever served as anything other than an ordinary infantry company in Morris's battalion. Tom Pearson himself was clearly a combative and downright pugnacious character, originally from Philadelphia, although Reuben Brown remembered he was connected with a theatre in New Orleans when he raised or was elected to lead the company there. Few of his original men can now be identified. About half of them, including his lieutenant, Henry Cooney, seem to have come either from Pennsylvania or from New York, or were foreign immigrants, reflecting the origins of both the New Orleans Greys and the Tampico Blues; but the others, nearly all of whom joined the company after its arrival at Bexar in December or at Refugio in January, appear to have been a fairly promiscuous mixture of Texians and men who later transferred in from either Peacock's Mississippians or Lawrence's Tennesseans.

Tom Lewellen's company was yet another composite formation patched together in the aftermath of the fighting at Bexar. Some of the men, like Lewellen himself, were Texians from near San Augustine, who had served at the battle in Ben Milam's division. Most of the others apparently came from Mississippi and had previously belonged to Peacock's United States Invincibles. According to Johnson's December 17 list, John Chenoweth was Lewellen's lieutenant for a time, before deciding to stay on in Bexar with Neill and reform the Invincibles. All in all, of those men eventually listed on Sergeant Hutchins Pittman's roll, about a third came from the Redlands of East Texas while the rest were from New York, Tennessee, Mississippi, Kentucky, and even from Poland, and it was this company that Reuben Brown and John Love chose to join at Refugio.

Just why these companies and various other individuals, such as Brown, decided to follow Grant is a moot point. The fact that both included comparatively large numbers of foreigners and men from the northern states, such as New York and Pennsylvania, may mark them out to some extent as different from those units coming to Texas from various southern states in the spirit of manifest destiny—whether or not that destiny included buttressing the slave-owning section. Arguably of course the New Orleans Greys turned San Antonio Greys were just as cosmopolitan in their composition, but while the meeting in Banks' Arcade certainly imbued that particular group of volunteers with an enthusiasm for the Texian cause, it was perhaps only the personal influence of leaders such as Cooke that kept them there.

The probable truth of the matter is that Santa Anna was right—those who followed Grant were simply adventurers and filibusters; the successors of those who had gone to Texas in Spanish days with Long and Magee, and the forerunners of those other desperados who would soon fight under Walker in Nicaragua or Wheat in Cuba. In total, by Reuben Brown's 1858 accounting there were now sixty-four of them, including Major Robert Morris, forming what has become known to historians as the Johnson and Grant party, although which of the two men was actually in command poses another interesting question.

Johnson's January 14 orders from the council certainly confirmed him in command of all the Bexar volunteers and just as explicitly denied that James Grant had any authority over them or anybody else. Yet despite Johnson's dramatic intervention with written orders from the council, Houston still continued to recognize Grant as their de facto commander, as evidenced by Cooke's reference to the time needed to "arrange matters" between them, with no mention made of poor Johnson except as an afterthought: "I neglected to state," Cooke rather casually noted in his narrative, "that Col F. W. Johnston had rejoined us at Refugio and united with Grant"—which hardly argues for Johnson playing a leading role in the proceedings. Since Houston would later be characterized as Grant's "bitter enemy" and so had no reason to favor him over Johnson—clearly regarding him as by far the more dangerous of the two—the only sensible explanation is that the Scotsman had successfully argued that he and his men were indeed in the federal service of Mexico, not of Texas. As for Johnson, instead of remaining at Refugio with the greater part of his disintegrating command, he chose to ride south with Grant and the filibusters, thus preserving the illusion, at least in his own mind, that he was still in control and that Grant was merely his second in command.

And so they set off; James Grant, the rogue British agent still trying to drag Texas irrevocably into a Mexican civil war that would keep it out of American hands; Frank Johnson, his notional commanding officer, whose real preoccupation by now was probably to prevent Grant from "stealing" his men, and those sixty-four assorted adventurers "ready for anything or any enterprise that afforded a reasonable prospect of excitement and plunder."

6 · *Rio Grande*

WILLIAM COOKE may have thought that Houston had "completely defeated the object of Col. Grant" at Refugio, but James Grant himself may not have seen it quite that way. On the contrary, despite all the setbacks and troubles of the past three months, the plan to "revolutionize" Mexico at last seemed to be at the point of coming to fruition. Amid the chaos of the Texian revolt he had assembled a Federal Volunteer Army and in the process had engineered the capture of Bexar; peremptorily faced down (for the moment at least) the threat to federal unity posed by Dimitt's declaration of independence; personally fought off one attempt by Colonel Neill to prevent the army from marching; and better still, had just seen Sam Houston retire humiliated after a second such attempt. Now the army was poised at Refugio, seemingly only awaiting the arrival of the main body under Fannin before marching on Matamoros (map, next page).

However, Colonel James Walker Fannin was late. There was nothing in the least unusual in this, and over the next two months the former slave trader from Georgia would succeed in elevating procrastination to something not unlike a fine art. To be fair to him, the immediate cause of the present delay was something entirely unexpected—nothing less than direct and all too effective British intervention, at a very undiplomatic level.

Whatever his personal motives and ultimate failings, the hapless Fannin had successively been given clear orders from both Sam Houston and the council to take charge of the various American volunteer groups gathering at Velasco. From there he was to ship them farther along the coast to Copano and rendezvous with those contingents coming overland from Bexar and everywhere else west of the Brazos. In January 1836, it seemed that just about every fighting man in Texas was intent on going to Matamoros and the Rio Grande, including William Barret Travis and a newly arrived ex-congressman from Tennessee named David Crockett.

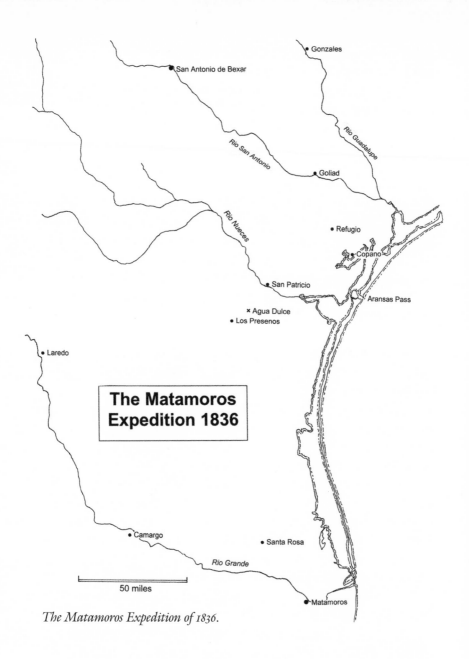

The Matamoros Expedition of 1836.

They all marched south and west in companies, in little groups, and even as individuals. Yet although Fannin duly found Major William Ward and the Georgia Rattlers patiently waiting for him at Velasco, hardly anybody else had turned up. Apart from the Georgians there was just a small company of riflemen from Kentucky commanded by Captain Burr

Duval, and bizarrely enough, Captain Luis Guerra's artillery company, which had escaped from Tampico with General Mexía. All in all they mustered little more than two hundred men rather than the five to six hundred he was expecting.

Other units, such as the dashingly named Red Rovers from Alabama, were confidently reported to be close at hand, and two companies of regulars under Amasa Turner were also daily expected from New Orleans, but worryingly, there was no sign at all of the largest contingent; an eagerly awaited battalion of volunteers from New York. As late as January 23 the acting governor of Texas, James Robinson, was still hopefully writing that "we have advices that two vessels with 200 soldiers each from New York are looked for hourly having been spoken off Bahamas Island."[1] Yet this particular contingent, sponsored by a Friends of Texas committee in New York City headed by none other than James Grant's speculating colleague Samuel M. Williams, was long overdue. Despite the furious protests of the city's Mexican vice consul, Don Pedro Gonzáles, they had sailed for Texas on the *Mattawamkeag* on November 21 and by all reasonable expectation should already have arrived. What had gone wrong?

Robinson's optimism was misplaced. The Bahamas sighting was out of date and the information was incomplete, for Colonel Edwin Morehouse and his volunteers did indeed get as far as the British colony—but no further. On December 2, after nearly two weeks at sea, a small party of New Yorkers went ashore on the eastern island of Eleuthra, ostensibly in order to purchase some fresh provisions. Instead, finding the owner away, they casually helped themselves (without payment) to four or five hogs and some poultry from the plantation of a Mr. Williams. Worse, they were alleged to have drunk all his wine, which if literally true would have been remarkable. By chance a Royal Navy vessel, HMS *Serpent,* was then in harbor at Nassau, and as soon as word of this appalling criminal rampage reached the colony's lieutenant governor, Colonel William Colebrooke, he requested her captain to put to sea at once and apprehend the "pirate."

Commander Evan Nepean was properly eager to be of assistance to the colonel but had to confess that "the state of the wind" was going to prevent his ship from getting out of the port. Nothing daunted, Colebrooke took the opportunity to remind his superiors tartly that he had repeatedly asked to have a steam tug stationed at Nassau for just such an emergency, and in the meantime he commandeered a smaller and handier local schooner named the *Anna*. With a detachment of the 2nd West India Regiment stuffed on board, but apparently no cannon (suggesting that little credence was given to another report of the "pirate" carrying as many as eight guns and a crew of 250), the gallant Nepean eventually managed to warp the schooner out of the harbor and set off after the invaders. For the sake of some wine and a few hogs, such an urgent and determined display of activity might be interpreted by officialdom as something of an overreaction, so while waiting to see what happened next, Colebrooke sat down to dash off a dispatch to the Colonial Office in London, reporting the alleged outrage and carefully justifying his actions by dramatically warning Lord Glenelg "that the existence of the slave trade to such an extent and the unsettled conditions of the neighbouring countries have led to a revival of Piracy in these seas."[2]

No one at the Colonial Office can have been in any doubt at all that he was referring to Mexico, and in particular to Texas, when he spoke of the "unsettled conditions of the neighbouring countries." Although the Caribbean Basin was otherwise quiet and untroubled, the fighting in Texas and northern Mexico had indeed spilled out into the waters of the Gulf. The Tampico debacle aside, rebel privateers and blockade runners began skirmishing with Mexican vessels in the first days of September, and it would not be until over a year later on December 15, 1836, that the Foreign Office belatedly obtained a legal opinion that the Texian vessels then blockading Matamoros were *not* pirates after all, but legitimate belligerents![3] Nor was anyone in the least surprised therefore when Commander Nepean duly caught up with the mysterious brigantine and found her to be "the Matawamkeag from New York bound to Belize & New Orleans with 170 Men on board who gave themselves out as Emigrants, but who were in fact a band of soldiers of fortune composed of all Nations, having Arms and Ammunition on board (the Arms we have since ascertained were all loaded) forming part of an expedition fitting out by a Committee in New York, not indeed under the open sanction of the United States Government, but there are many reasons to suppose connived at by that power."[4]

There were indeed reasons enough to justify those suspicions, for in a letter of protest addressed to William Price, one of the New York district attorneys, Don Pedro Gonzáles had vainly complained of public meetings at the Shakespeare Hotel and in Tammany Hall itself, where financial and political support was solicited for the rebels; he also complained of the committee's yet more blatant establishment of an official recruiting office at no. 62 Front Street in the city.[5] On closer inspection, however, the "soldiers of fortune" turned out to be a fairly unprepossessing bunch. The ship's hold was full of swords, and curiously enough a quantity of lance and pike heads, but the would-be filibusters had only twenty-seven muskets and rifles and fifty-two pistols among them.[6] It would seem that they had already fallen out among themselves, for on arriving at Nassau "the Europeans, who are Poles, French and Germans applied to be separated from the Americans." Segregated or not, all of them were committed for trial "on a charge of felony and Piracy," and there they remained, guarded by the black soldiers of the 2nd West India Regiment for two long months—which for some of them may have been a deeply humiliating experience in itself.

Although the British officials and agents actually on the ground— such as the Tampico consul Crawford, Colebrooke and Nepean, and of course Grant—were doing all they could to frustrate the Americans, they were doing so without any official sanction, encouragement, or coordination. Like Palmerston, Lord Glenelg, the colonial secretary, turned out to be surprisingly indifferent to the whole business and offered Colebrooke no guidance on the disposal of the prisoners. Indeed at one point his sole comment on the affair was to reprimand the colonel fussily for discussing two quite separate matters in one dispatch![7] Not having the wholehearted support of his own superiors, Colebrooke rather reluctantly decided that despite his having obtained confessions from those who had stolen the hogs, there was insufficient evidence to try any of the adventurers—or rather to justify turning the affair into a full-blown diplomatic incident involving the American government. Disgustedly ordering the prisoners' release on January 23, he reported to London with some satisfaction "the destitute situation of two officers and thirteen men, Polish Exiles, who had withdrawn from the party in consequence of ill-usage and had thrown themselves under the protection of the British Government." As a result of his action, it was not until February 12 that the *Mattawamkeag* volunteers reached New Orleans, and they never would play an effective role in the battle for Texas.

On the contrary, their lengthy detention in British custody contributed to Fannin's delayed departure, for in the vain hope that they and the other reinforcements would eventually turn up, he waited until January 24 before finally setting sail from Velasco. With the wind against him he did not make landfall at Aransas Pass until January 28, and it took another week to get all his men ashore and move them the fifteen miles inland to the mission at Refugio. The volunteers waiting for him there had been requested to have carts and teams ready, but either these were not to be had or no one bothered to assemble them. February 4 found Fannin still waiting for his heavy baggage and looking out hopefully for another schooner, the *Liberty,* which was bringing another eighty men under Captain Jack Shackleford.

Oblivious to Colebrooke's unexpected intervention and its consequences, Grant had by now moved his own men from Refugio down to the other Irish colony at San Patricio, where he still expected in due course to be joined by Fannin and the rest of the volunteers. Small though it was, the little village lay on the border between Texas and Tamaulipas, just to the east of the point where the Atascosita Road crossed the Nueces River. The Mexicans had long recognized the strategic importance of the crossing by establishing a military way station a few miles away to the west. Fort Lipantitlán (which took its name from an old Lipan Indian camp that once stood on the site) was a far from impressive post. John Linn, who had helped capture it in early November, recalled it as nothing more formidable than a few *jacales* surrounded by "a single embankment of earth, lined within by fence rails to hold the dirt in place." He judged it "would have answered tolerably well, perhaps, for a second-rate hog pen."[8]

At the time of its capture the post had been held by a *presidial* company commanded by Captain Nicolás Rodríguez. In one of those farcical little episodes that characterized the early days of the Texian revolt, Rodríguez set off from the post at the very end of October with a mixed force of about eighty presidial troopers and Irish volunteers, intending to raid the newly established Texian garrison at Goliad. Riding straight up the Atascosita Road, he and his men completely missed bumping into a Texian force of some thirty men led by Ira Westover, who were simultaneously heading south out of Goliad along the "low road" to attack Lipantitlán! By the time Rodríguez realized what was happening, Westover and his men had crossed the Nueces and bluffed the remaining garrison (which included five Irishmen and an Englishman) into surrendering on November 3. The next day, however, while the Texians were struggling to return across the rain-swollen river, Rodríguez came hastening back, only be driven off by depressingly accurate rifle fire in a thirty-minute skirmish known as the battle of the Nueces Crossing.

After the fighting was over, Westover and his men moved into San Patricio to rest up and to attend to Rodríguez's wounded. Having found themselves fighting against a number of the Irish settlers, including the colony's *alcalde,* judge, and sheriff, the Texians probably expected a hostile reception but instead were made unexpectedly welcome in the village. On the whole at this time the majority of the inhabitants were ostentatiously neutral; whatever their true sympathies, they simply could not afford to antagonize any of the armed bands swaggering about the countryside. Westover was still occupying the place when Grant, Viesca, and Gonzáles arrived on November 8, but then they all moved on to Goliad together. There, besides Dimitt's contretemps with Grant already detailed, Dimitt also had a falling out with Westover, whom he accused of failing to carry out his orders.

What was more, Westover's decision to pull out of San Patricio was reckoned to be a big mistake, as Dimitt was still irritably pointing out at the end of December. "It is certainly of great importance to occupy that post," he insisted to Robinson. "We owe it to the people to protect them, from insult and liability to insult by the enemy, and we ought, if possible, to screen them from even the suspicion of a willingness to give countenance to the military in any way whatever. And we owe it to ourselves, so to cover the border settlements, as to challenge the predatory visitations of the foe. By doing this, we shall multiply our friends and make a salutary impression on our enemy."[9]

There was much to be said for establishing a permanent garrison in the village in order to serve as a listening post for news from Tamaulipas and as a tripwire for any centralist troops advancing up the Atascosita Road, but the immediate cause of Dimitt's concern was the still uncertain allegiances of the Irish colonists who made up the greater part of the town's inhabitants. Although a predominantly English-speaking little settlement, it was a frontier town in every sense of the word and needed to be treated accordingly. Thus Dimitt recommended:

The force sent to occupy that post ought to be provided with a good supply of provisions, suitable tools to be able to mount a cannon and to repair guns. This will give active employment to the volunteers—will place them in view of the enemy—and show that we seek rather than avoid them. This will give protection to our frontier—a hundred men well equipped, mounted and armed—could greatly retard the enemy before it would be brought to bear on Texas in a general engagement—with a three gun battery at El Copano and another at Corpus Christi both garrisoned by small force, the whole south-western frontier of Texas would be placed, even without an expedition to Matamoros, in as good a condition, perhaps, to hold the enemy in check till a regular force can be brought into the field.[10]

Arguably this was exactly what Colonel Grant was now doing, and in fact when he came down to San Patricio at the end of January, 1836, he did indeed bring three brass guns.[11] These may have been intended to be placed in the abandoned fort, although there is no evidence that they ever were. But Grant had no intention of waiting long in the village, for he urgently needed to cross the river and coordinate operations with the Tamaulipas Federalistas, which meant finding either José María Gonzáles or Don Plácido Benavides.

A prominent landowner from Victoria, Benavides commanded a Tejano company at the storming of Bexar and like, Juan Seguin, was offered but turned down a regular commission in Travis's Legion of Cavalry. Instead he joined Grant and rode south from Bexar in late December as part of Colonel Gonzáles's "division of observation." Exactly when Grant reestablished contact with him is unclear. He may have done so while Houston was making his fateful appeal to the army at Refugio, but it is probably more likely to have been soon after he and his men established themselves at San Patricio. At any rate by the time Grant did catch up with Benavides at Camargo, he and Gonzáles had separated, and the colonel was now somewhere south of the Rio Grande with about 240 troopers. Benavides still had forty-seven of his own men, but another hundred or so locally raised Federalistas were riding under a rather slippery lawyer turned revolutionary from Laredo named Captain Antonio Canales, who intriguingly enough would later earn himself the nickname El Zorro—the Chaparral Fox. It all looked very promising and although there was as yet no general uprising, Benavides was also in contact with the principal alcalde of Matamoros, who was in turn acting as a go-between for General Vital Fernández, the commanding general of Tamaulipas. It was Fernández, according to Jorge Fisher, who had first proposed an "intire separation of the northern Confederated States from Mexico" to form a new republic. Now he and his four-hundred-strong garrison in Matamoros were confidently expected to declare for the Constitution of 1824 just as soon as the Texians appeared.

First, however, Grant also needed to deal with Captain Nicolás Rodríguez, the former commander of the Fort Lipantitlán garrison, who was said to be camped nearby. Rodríguez still had many friends among the San Patricio Irish, and ever since the fight at the Nueces Crossing he and an intelligence officer named Manuel Sabriego—who had been one of the principal targets of Westover's earlier expedition—had both hung around in the area, visiting the town with impunity and regularly picking up intelligence of the Texians' movements. "A rumor is in circulation here," complained an annoyed Dimitt on December 28, "that Rodríguez, the Commandant of Lipantitlán, is in daily habits of personal intercourse with the population of that place, coming to and returning from the town at pleasure." Rodríguez would certainly have learned of the Goliad declaration of independence during those visits, and in early February Grant's second in command, Major Robert Morris, ominously observed: "The people of Tamaulipas as well as those of the Rio Grande complain much of Dimmitt's Proclamation, and would have acted with more decision were it not for that act, but they fear it is now almost impossible."[12] Dealing with Rodríguez was therefore an immediate priority for Grant and his filibusters, and according to a San Patricio colonist named John McMullen, no sooner had they arrived in the Irish village than "Col Grant Prepared and started with twenty five men to surprise him taking with him the Person who Gave the information which was one of Rodrigues own men."[13]

It was almost certainly Captain Tom Lewellen's company that went with Grant, for one of the party was the young Georgian Reuben Brown, who equally laconically told President Lamar that "we received intelligence of an advance guard of the lower division of the Mexican Army amounting to about twenty four: A detachment of us, nineteen in number, immediately left San Patricio in search of them, and came upon them about 20 miles from that place; we captured them without resistance, and returned to San Patricio."[14] In 1858 he wrote a rather more spirited account of the episode for the *Texas Almanac*, revealing that the expedition had also had a more prosaic purpose: "We received information from Fannin that he would be at Copano as soon as possible," remembered Brown, "but [he] had been unavoidably detained in Matagorda Bay; and he wished us to collect together as many horses as possible to enable him to mount his men." Securing those horses was going to be absolutely vital to the success of the expedition.

As we have seen, according to Creed Taylor, Grant had blithely assured the volunteers at Bexar that "grass, game and wild cattle and horses abounded, and the march to the Rio Grande would not be difficult, but rather a journey of pleasure." Yet from his earlier journeying and his experience of packing mule trains through the area in the 1820s, Grant knew only too well that the country between the Nueces and the Rio Grande, which would later become known as the "Nueces Strip," was actually an arid semidesert. Captain William S. Henry, who led an infantry company down the Atascosita Road almost exactly ten years later in March 1846, noted in his diary that under the hot sun the road turned into loose sand that was "like hot ashes, and when you stepped upon it you sank up to your ankles." In the cold February of 1836 the volunteers were much more likely to encounter mud than burning sands, but it most emphatically was not going to be a "journey of pleasure."

Nor were conditions off the road much better, for the otherwise open prairie gave way from time to time to dense masses or mottes of oak, mesquite, thornbush and cactus, and about thirty miles north of the Rio Grande was the Arroyo Colorado (Brown's "Sal Colorado"), a four-foot-deep tidal stream about one hundred yards across with steep banks on either side, which in turn were flanked by large areas of salt pan. The plain fact was that if James Grant or anyone else was going to take the volunteers all the way down the Atascosita Road and across the Rio Grande, those horses would indeed be badly needed. As Brown related in his 1858 account:

> For this purpose and in order to scout the country, we divided our men into two parties, one of which remained in San Patricio under Colonel Johnson, while the other proceeded westward in search of horses, etc., under Col. Grant. I went out with this party. Having reached the Sal Colorado, about sixty miles from San Patricio, we fell in with some half a dozen Mexicans guarding three or four hundred head of horses that had been sent out there to be recruited for the service of Urrea's division of the invading army, then preparing to set out. We ascertained that Rodrigues, their Captain, was encamped

near by with a small force, and we made the men guarding the horses (whom we took prisoners) guide us to the camp of Rodrigues, which we reached by going in single file by a narrow pathway through a dense thicket of chaparral, and finally found the encampment in a small open space surrounded on all sides by this chaparral. The tents were enclosed by brush thrown up, and guarded by a sentinel. The sentinel, on seeing us, fired his scopet at me, as I was in the lead, but missed me, and I then shot him. We jumped over the brush at once, and, making for the tents, we took them all prisoners without firing another gun. This was just at daybreak. I took Rodrigues myself, although he surrendered only after much resistance.

Continuing in the finest tradition of Texan storytelling, Brown went on to claim that Grant and his men returned to San Patricio with sixty-seven prisoners and "several hundred horses." Johnson told a slightly different story. Maintaining the fiction that Grant was under his command, he somewhat less ambitiously reported that "a small detachment of my Division (20 men) under Col. Grant took on the night of the 30th ult, Capt. Rodriguez & his compy (26 men) with all their horses (50) arms etc without the loss of a man."[15] Whatever the real numbers of horses and men involved, this was a useful little victory that dealt with a long-standing nuisance, and more important in Johnson's estimation, this left "the road clear from Nueces to Rio Grande."

Johnson then rather enthusiastically went on to assure his fellow agent, Fannin, at last safely landed at Copano, that "our friends, the liberals of Tamaulipas, are arriving in all quarters, and will form a most respectable addition to our force. Every thing looks most propitious, and unless our head strong countrymen, by a premature Declaration of Independence, rouse the jealousy of the Federal party victory is secured and by one blow, we may calculate over throwing the Tyrant Santa Anna & his minions." Scarcely pausing to draw breath, he proceeded to declare: "The forces you have and these here and about 350 under Gonzales & Canales together with the certain assistance we will receive from all parts of Tamaulipas and Nuevo Leon, will prove amply sufficient to give the most important blow that has ever been struck in the Republic—and place Texas in a situation to dictate to the neighbouring states." Suitably impressed, Fannin promptly forwarded this optimistic intelligence to Acting Governor Robinson at San Felipe, confidently adding: "Matamoras is poorly supplied with troops—our friends are in power—I have reason to believe, that if a quick movement is made, not a shot will be fired. . . . I shall proceed west—and must beg of you to order the naval force to co-operate with me before Matamoras, between 20th & 28th inst."[16]

Not all the news from the south was good, however, for despite Johnson's assurances, the road was emphatically not clear. Brown in both his narratives unambiguously referred to Rodríguez and his men acting as an advance party of Urrea's division. If Brown was not speaking from hindsight, this indicates that Grant at least was aware of Santa Anna already being on the move—and long before anyone in Texas had anticipated. "By advices from Monterey of the 18th. Ult [January] and from Matamoros of the 20th, ult," wrote Johnson, in contradiction to his other cheerier news, "I learn that Santa Anna was in Saltillo with 2300 men, and a good train of artly."[17] In fact the grandly titled "Army of Operations" marching north out of San Luis Potosí was a good deal larger than these "advices" suggested, certainly much more formidable than the scratch force with which General Cos had been expected to subdue the province the year before. The advance guard alone, led by Brigadier General Joaquín Ramírez y Sesma, comprised three battalions and a reinforced cavalry regiment totaling some 1,100 infantry and 300 cavalry—all of them regulars—while the main body under Santa Anna himself was even larger, mustering a further twelve battalions with a notional combined strength of about 3,600 men, together with various cavalry units numbering around 680 troopers. He also had a substantial train of artillery, and an uncounted horde of camp followers, but a scanty supply of provisions and next to nothing in the way of medical staff.

The timing of the army's appearance in the north was hardly accidental, for Santa Anna too was well aware that the Federalistas' "general plan of revolutionising all over Mexico" was scheduled to begin sometime in February and that he therefore had to move quickly to prevent it. Exactly how much he knew at the time of what was intended is open to question, but it is more than likely that the entire plan had already been betrayed to him by one or other of the many conspirators. There is even a school of thought holding that the whole notion of the Matamoros expedition was planted by Santa Anna in the first place, simply as a means of drawing the Texians down to their destruction on the Rio Grande.[18] Don Pedro Miracle, who briefed the General Council on the plan in

December, afterward turned out to be a double agent, and certainly the intelligence being supplied to Grant at this time, and through him to Johnson and the other Texian leaders, was badly tainted. In a curious echo of both Grant's November 13 letter to Austin and Miracle's briefing of a month later, Johnson breathlessly tempered the news of Santa Anna's movements with spurious reports that "the states of Zacatecas and Guadalaxara en mass, had taken to arms in his [Santa Anna's] rear, and that the movement agt. the General Govt. was likely to form general throughout the nation. The troops which occupied Laredo have retired to Saltillo & Monclova—those at Rio Grande (town) it is supposed will likewise make a retrograde movement, and their numbers are by no means important in any case. Disaffection has crept into the arch tyrants ranks—20 to 30 men desert daily & tho Matamoros is almost entirely without a Garrison, he is afraid to send off assistance, least they should revolt on leaving his camp."[19]

Untroubled by these phantom uprisings, Santa Anna had reached Saltillo, from where he intended to push north to Monclova and then east along the old Spanish Camino Real or King's Highway to Bexar and so into the heart of the American colonies. What was more, contrary to Johnson's overconfident assertion that he dared not send any assistance to Matamoros, Santa Anna had already done just that. On January 15 Brigadier General Juan José de Urrea was ordered to secure the city with his Independent Division and then, having done so, to clear the Atascosita Road and demonstrate against the Texian position at Goliad. Given that the bulk of the Texian forces were known to be concentrating in this area, Urrea was given precious few troops to do the job. At first his so-called division consisted of nothing more than a reinforced cavalry regiment, made up of a mere 180 troopers of his own Cuautla Permanente under Colonel Rafael de la Vara and another seventy from the San Luis Potosí and Bajía Activo companies. At least they were not the usual scrappy collection of presidiales the Texians had come up against so far; these were "choice troops from the interior . . . armed, every one, with lance musket, pistols and sword."[20] The same could not be said of his infantry, who were to join him at Matamoros. Leaving aside Vital Fernández and his potentially dubious garrison, all he would find there were three hundred men of the Yucatán Activo Battallon, ordered up from Tampico. This was a newly conscripted battalion of Maya Indians, who for the most part could not speak Spanish and were barely trained, poorly equipped, and altogether physically ill-suited to face the rigors of a Texas winter. Santa Anna was reluctant to let Urrea have a veteran infantry regiment, for the forty-year-old general was not only a very capable career soldier—he was also a committed federalist.

Born in Tucson, Arizona, in 1795, Juan José de Urrea began his career in the Spanish Army and made his subsequent reputation as an Indian fighter in Durango. He served briefly as the Mexican minister in Colombia and largely owed his present appointment to having raised Durango for Santa Anna in 1832. At that time of course, they were both avowedly Federalistas, but Santa Anna had in the meantime changed sides and may have feared that if Urrea were given better trained and more politically sophisticated troops, he might indeed be tempted to "revolt on leaving his camp" and declare for the Constitution of 1824. In the event, any suspicions proved groundless. Urrea's Colombian experience had left him with a healthy suspicion of American motives, and in the face of the Texians' overt moves toward seceding from the Mexican republic, the general found little difficulty in temporarily reconciling himself with the Centralistas. On his march he found in "the towns of the north, from Matamoros to Guerrero, great adherence to the constitution of 1824, and the people, believing that the [Texian] colonists were upholding it, kept in touch with them, being disposed to take up arms and join their cause." He lost no opportunity to convince the would-be federalists of their error and to highlight the fact that the Americans' intention was to secede from Mexico—thus appealing to their patriotism and simultaneously raising an understandable suspicion that if this did happen, they would be left in the lurch by their supposed Texian allies. Gonzáles's men were surprised and scattered in a neat little action at Guerrero on January 25, and Urrea arrived in Matamoros on January 31, ready to do battle with the rebels on behalf of the dictator.

How much of this Grant knew or suspected at this stage is uncertain, but with Rodríguez now safely out of the way and Fannin at last on hand, he and Johnson set off across the Nueces on February 4. As already noted, while their first and most urgent need was to reestablish contact with the Federalistas, securing more horses was nearly as important. As Creed Taylor recalled:

The winter had been unusually severe on stock and the army found itself in great need of mounts. In the valley of the Rio Grande on the

Texas side roamed vast caballadas of horses, the property of Mexican citizens in Matamoros. Grant determined to secure a sufficient number of these animals to supply his army, and to that end set out in February with forty-five picked men for the Rio Grande, Col. Frank Johnson accompanying the expedition as second in command. They crossed the Arroyo Colorado and approached within eight or ten miles of Matamoros. They soon secured all the horses they wanted—the tactics of the Comanches being largely employed in the hasty round-up and swift retreat northward. When they had crossed the Arroyo Colorado, a furious "norther" accompanied by rain and sleet beat down upon them, and during the night two of the men and a number of the horses died from the effects of the extreme cold. Grant reached San Patricio on the twelfth of February [*sic*] with only about one hundred animals, having lost a large number along the route.[21]

As usual, Taylor's heavily ghosted narrative was out by a few days in its reckoning, for the evidence points to Grant returning to the Irish village on February 8. At any rate, just two days after he had turned around and gone out again, Benavides, who had obviously missed him on the road, hastened up from Camargo with unwelcome news that amply confirmed the earlier rumors.[22] "Don Placido Benavides has just arrived, & brings disagreeable intelligence," wrote a worried Major Morris. "Gonzáles command is entirely dispersed, and twenty two men taken prisoners. Three hundred Cavalry and three hundred infantry have arrived at Matamoros, which in addition to the Garrison makes the effective force now there 1000 men, and more are expected shortly. Cos and all his officers from Bejar are raising troops to march on Texas. One thousand men are already on the Rio Frio. One thousand more on the march near the Rio Grande destined for some point of Texas; and forces are gathering rapidly in all directions for the same object. It is believed that an attack is intended on Goliad and Bejar simultaneously."[23]

Matters were coming to a head rather more rapidly than expected, and now the whole plan was suddenly in danger of unraveling, for as Benavides explained to Morris:

The inhabitants of Tamaulipas are generally in favour of (1824) but are so much oppressed by the military, many of the principal men having been arrested they are completely fettered. Santa Anna caused a report to be set afloat he was with the troops at Matamoros, but it is ascertained beyond all doubt that he is on the way to the Rio Grande for the purpose of pushing on those forces. Don Placido deems it of the utmost importance that troops be sent to Bejar as well as others retained in this direction and also assures me that Santa Anna wishes to draw the Troops of Texas out to Matamoros in hopes to throw a strong force in their rear while he makes his attack on the upper part of the Colonies. This information he received from the first alcalde of Matamoros. He has been within 20 leagues of the town and corresponded with him. . . . Santa Anna has sworn to Take Texas or lose Mexico.

Morris, clearly rattled by this news, also informed Fannin that "Roderigus has broken his parole since 5 o'clock this evening and as I have but 18 effective men here and no horses, I could not pursue him." Allowing Rodríguez to escape, no doubt with the aid of his Irish friends, was eventually to prove a fatal mistake, as Morris probably realized when he added that "Doct. Grant has been out two days with thirty men. I feel very anxious about him."

He therefore sent Benavides straight out again to find Grant, while Fannin, having somehow gotten the impression that Morris was in imminent danger of attack, for once in his life acted promptly and responded by dispatching Captain William Cooke with both the San Antonio and the Mobile Greys as a "reinforcement" to San Patricio on the morning of February 8. "About the 5th of February," wrote Cooke. "Maj. Morris whom Grant had left in command at San Patricio whilst he was on an expedition after horses, sent an express to Col Fannin stating that he had received certain information that a force of Mexican troops amtg to 1500 were within a few hours march of him and requesting reinforcements." Morris's letter had in fact said nothing of the sort, but a verbal appeal to that effect may have been carried by his messenger, Dr. Hoyt. "Col. F. ordered me to take my compy & Capt Burkes & make a forced march to his assistance," continued Cooke with some pride. "We did so—marching the distance of forty eight miles in one day—On our arrival we found that Morris had been misinformed Col Grant and party returned the same day."[24]

Any optimism Grant may have felt on finding Cooke and his men had arrived was soon dashed, for Reuben Brown recorded unambiguously that "shortly after our return to San Patricio, another letter was received from Col. Fannin, (then at Refugio) stating that he, had received Orders from Houston to decamp for Goliad, and there remain for further orders. On the reception of Fannin's letter we abandoned the idea of an expedition to Matemoras."[25] Unnerved by the news of Santa Anna's advance, Fannin was indeed planning to fall back and concentrate his forces at Goliad and was even considering retiring behind the Guadalupe. As he had explained in a letter to Robinson, "unless a turn out in mass be made, and that speedily, the force now in the field cannot keep the invaders in check long enough to prevent the fury of the war being felt in the heart of the country—if ever Santa Anna crosses the Guadaloupe with 5,000 men, we have to fight west of the Brazos, if not the Trinity! I feel certain that, even in that event, this army would inevitably perish or surrender."[26] At first sight, Brown's reference to Sam Houston's involvement seems puzzling, since the general was temporarily out of the picture at this juncture. But ultimately of course Fannin had always been subject to Houston's authority and may have invoked it now, for he told Robinson that he had ordered all of the men and the three guns brought back from San Patricio.

In the circumstances this was understandable enough. All things considered, Fannin was having a difficult time, and it made obvious sense to concentrate all the available forces. Not only was there alarming news from the south, and still no sign of either of the two companies expected from New Orleans under Captain Amasa Turner or the wayward New York battalion, but, as he bitterly complained, he was also getting precious little support from his fellow Texians: "Out of more than four hundred men at and near this post, I doubt if twenty-five citizens of Texas can be mustered in the ranks—nay, I am informed, whilst writing the above, that there is not half that number;—does not this fact bespeak all indifference, and criminal apathy, truly alarming?" He begged Robinson to call out the "civic militia" and gloomily warned: "It is useless to controvert the fact that that our true strength and geographical situation are well known to Santa Anna."[27]

Alarmed by Fannin's all too obvious despondency, Robinson tried to encourage him by promising that the militia would immediately be ordered out to his support, only to have to admit in the next line that there was no longer a quorum in the council and that to all intents and purposes Texas was leaderless! The earlier falling out between Smith and the council had proved fatal to the provisional government, which effectively dissolved within days of Smith's attempted impeachment amid a continued welter of accusation and counteraccusation. Smith still enjoyed the loyalty of Sam Houston, for what that was worth, but neither he nor the new governor, Robinson, could exert any meaningful authority over anyone else. Until the Consultation reconvened at San Felipe on March 1 there was literally no one in charge and so no way of ensuring that the militia actually turned out or that those desperately needed supplies were forwarded to the troops. For better or worse, at this moment the fate of Texas rested with a handful of volunteers and filibusters answerable to no one but themselves. Robinson closed therefore by advising Fannin to "occupy such points as you may in your opinion deem most advantageous . . . but do not hazard much until you are reinforced [as] a defeat of your command would prove our ruin—all former orders given by my predecessor, Genl Houston or myself, are so far countermanded to render it compatible to now obey any orders you may deem Expedient."

That officially marked the end of the Matamoros expedition, for Fannin was thereby formally released from all the multitude of orders previously issued by Henry Smith, by Sam Houston, and indeed by the council and Robinson himself, directing him to march on the town.[28] Instead the colonel was now authorized to act according to his own discretion in the defense of Texas against the imminent attack. Ordering the concentration at Goliad was a useful first step, but unfortunately it would soon become clear that he was quite incapable of exercising that discretion much further.

Grant and Johnson, on the other hand, although equally dismayed by Fannin's pessimistic assessment of the situation (and no doubt cursing Morris for his ill-starred intervention), argued that instead of simply giving up at this point and effectively running away, they should press on regardless and that instead of going on the defensive, Fannin should bring all his men forward to San Patricio without delay.

"It is of importance that you should be aware of the actual state of Matamoros more clearly than I can state in a public letter to avoid mens names being bandied about while they are still in the power of the enemy," Johnson pleaded on February 9, with Grant obviously sitting at his shoulder. "If a force of 3–400 men is sent agst Matamoros,

Vital Fernández, who commands with 800 Tamaulipas troops, will immediately join you—and the whole of the frontier towns will immediately follow—Lemas continues fine & for the purpose of both acquiring essential information & not incurring suspicion he has gone for a few days to Saltillo to visit Santa Anna." This latest news accounts for Grant's Comanche-like haste in returning from his foray, for having "approached within eight or ten miles of Matamoros," he had indeed reestablished contact not only with General Fernández but also with Don Pedro Lemus, the governor of neighboring Nuevo León, and still hoped to bring both states out in revolt. Consequently Johnson went on to insist:

> Fear nothing for Bexar or Goliad or any point of Texas if an attack is made on Matamoros. The enemy will be compelled to change his place of attack & we will maintain the war in his own Country & with his own means with every advantage on our side. The true policy is to unite all your forces here, leaving small garrisons in Bexar & Goliad & proceed without delay into the interior. With 150–200 men I will engage to keep Santa Annas partizans in play from the town of Riogrande to Reynosa, cut off any reinforcements he may wish to send to the coast & leave you thus to take possession of Matemoras & even Tampico if necessary without his being able to send aid to these points—I can raise the whole country agst Him & then the interior must move so as to compel him to a retrograde movement. . . . Quickness in your present movements will prove the salvation of Texas."[29]

Once again Johnson conjured those illusory uprisings in the interior, enthusiastically continuing: "By a letter recd in Mier on the [?] ult. from a person of credit in Saltillo it appears that very serious movements in the states of Zacatecas & Guadalaxara agst. Santa Anna were likely to induce him to return incognito to the interior leaving the command of the Army to Genl. Felisola—If this proves Correct & from collateral evidence it appears probable, it will be equal to a victory to us as Felisola is an old woman—& Santa Anna will not retire unless the Wigwam is in a serious uproar."

Johnson would eventually turn out to be dead right in his assessment of Santa Anna's second in command, Vincente Filisola, as an "old woman"; had it ever occurred, a federalist uprising in Tamaulipas and Nuevo León might indeed have compelled that "retrograde movement." But he and Grant were disastrously wrong about everything else. In the first place, in this overly optimistic assessment of the situation they were ignoring General Urrea's presence, and they were so far unaware of the consequences of his easy scattering of Gonzáles's forces. Not only had the colonel's men all either been dispersed or been captured by now, but as a well-known and respected federalist himself, Urrea had found little difficulty in persuading his prisoners to change sides and serve under him instead—which may explain why Captain Manuel Barragan's Rio Grande company, specifically identified by General Cos as one of those joining with the rebels back in December—was now part of Santa Anna's army marching on Bexar. At Matamoros itself, General Fernández also stood aside and instead of joining the planned revolt hastened to provide Urrea with biscuit and other badly needed supplies, although his opportunistic generosity would not save him from being relieved of his command a few months later. As for Don Pedro Lemus, the governor of Nuevo León; he had indeed ridden off to Saltillo, not to divert suspicion from himself and establish an alibi when the uprising began but to make his peace with Santa Anna and argue for an invasion of Texas by way of Monterrey, crossing the Rio Grande at Mier in order to march directly on Goliad—and Grant's Federal Volunteer Army!

The once promising general plan of revolutionizing, aimed at creating a new republic of northern Mexico, was effectively foundering on mutual distrust, just as Stephen Austin had predicted it would. Instead, Federalistas and Centralistas were sinking their differences and temporarily uniting behind Santa Anna against the Texians, in the name of Mexico, and so bringing about the complete breach that James Grant had fought so long to prevent.

7 • *"Go in and Die with the Boys"*

AND SO, UNAWARE that it was already too late, Grant decided to go out again immediately, without waiting for a reply from Fannin to Johnson's plea, in case it might bring more positive orders for Cooke and the others to fall back to Goliad. Although this foray was seemingly represented as such both at the time and later, the "secret expedition" was not to be a mere horse-gathering foray, let alone a "mustanging" expedition, but was rather a last attempt to link up with his federalist friends, with or without the aid of the Texians. "Col. Grant and Johnson prepared then to go to Matamoros," remembered the San Patricio colonist, John McMullen, "from Information the[y] rec. from them that if they would go the[y] would get a great majority to join them, and that ther was two hundred men ready in wait for them out in the Country under the command of Capt. Canales [at] Comargo; and by going to that place the[y] would get all the people of the towns on the rio Grande to Join them Grant imediately Proposed to go on."[1]

He really had little choice, for at this point he badly needed some tangible demonstration of Mexican support if Fannin were ever to be coaxed or cajoled into coming forward after all. Fernández and Lemus had told Grant they would not commit themselves until the Texians appeared on the Rio Grande, but Antonio Canales might be a different matter. El Zorro was indeed waiting at Camargo, but like most of Grant's other erstwhile colleagues, he too was carefully repositioning himself.

It was probably sometime either on February 9 or more likely February 10, 1836, when the British agent, unwilling to acknowledge these shifting allegiances, rode out of San Patricio at the head of more than one hundred cavalry for what would turn out to be the last time.[2] As before the majority of them belonged to Lewellen's and Pearson's companies, but now they also included some volunteers from among the recent arrivals, such as Stephen Dennison, a former New Orleans Grey who came down to the village with Burke's company.[3] There is broad agreement that the Americans mustered some sixty or seventy men in total, but this did not include Plácido Benavides's men, who must have accounted for another thirty or so. To get them all mounted Grant must have taken every horse in the place, whatever its condition, and even then he still left behind a number of his original men as well as the greater part of the two companies brought down by Cooke.

Only a few hours after Grant had gone, Cooke was astonished by the arrival of a Mexican officer in full uniform. While Cooke did not identify him, this rather startling apparition was none other than Lieutenant Jesús "Comanche" Cuéllar, the same officer who had been the first to defect from Cos's army at Bexar and had helped guide Johnson and Grant's column when the assault on the town began. Professing himself a committed federalist, he had gone south with Colonel Gonzáles, but now apparently he was back again and carrying "a passport and letters from Grant & Morris to me—The amt of Grants letter to me was that he had recd through this officer information from Vital Fernández, Comdg Genl. of Tamaulipas who offered to unite with him (the moment he reached the Rio Grande), with 1800 men—Morris letter stated that he no longer intended to serve the Govt. of Texas that he had received the appointment to the command of a Regiment in the Federal service of Mexico."[4]

Here then was Grant's real justification for going down to the Rio Grande one more time, although exactly where Frank Johnson fitted into all this was unclear—for while urging that the troops should be brought forward, he had conspicuously not joined Morris in repudiating the provisional government's authority. No one but Johnson, however, was in any doubt that Grant was in command of the expedition, and Cooke very properly forwarded copies of both letters straight to Fannin. At Goliad, Fannin can hardly have been pleased by this latest news, for once again it thoroughly upset his plans. Not only were Grant and his men completely ignoring Fannin by heading off toward the Rio Grande, but one of the reasons for sending the San Antonio Greys and Mobile Greys down to San Patricio was to try to reunite Johnson's Bexar Battalion. Exasperated, Fannin immediately responded by sending yet a third company down to San Patricio, under Captain Burr Duval, with orders to recover the guns and ammunition. Within a few days all three companies were on their way back, leaving the village guarded only by a small party under Sergeant Pittman.

In the meantime, Grant pressed on hard for the promised rendezvous with the Federalistas. "On crossing the Rio Nueces," said McMullen, "there come an other Spie of the enemys to them Stating as heretofore that the[y] Could with Safety take Matamoros." Brown confirms this, remembering that "on the second day out a Mexican fell in with us, pretending that he wished to join us, and that he would bring with him a small Mexican company of mounted men. We suspected him for a spy," he said, "and our suspicions were confirmed in the morning when we found he had left during the night." Nevertheless, continued McMullen, they proceeded until they got to a ranch called Santa Rosa, about midway between where Raymondville and Brownsville are today, and just thirty miles northwest of Matamoros. Brown underestimated the distance they had traveled, but recorded that after "getting about seventy five miles from San Patricio nearly half our horses gave out, consequently Col Johnson with about thirty others were compelled to remain."[5] Although the halt was an enforced one, it may also have been a fortunate one, for according to McMullen it was at Santa Rosa that Grant was at last warned, "through the interfarence of his friends," who told him, Colonel Johnson, Major Morris, and another officer that if they went, they need never look to return, that "it was only a plan of the enemy to get them [there and] to destroy them," and at the same time that they were "placing to much confidence" in Mexicans who were acting as spies. The officers were told that it would be better for them to return to the main army or to remain where they were, McMullen recounted.[6]

Falling back to the Nueces after receiving this warning would certainly have been sensible, but the exhaustion of their horses made that impossible, and instead Grant went out looking for fresh ones. Johnson afterward angrily asserted: "The expedition, west of the Nueces, for horses and mules was not, as is insinuated [by Houston's apologist, Henderson Yoakum] for their own emolument and profit, but to supply a want in the service—a cavalry force." This shortage was starkly obvious from the fact that it was only by pooling all the usable horses that Grant was able to find sufficient to mount Lewellen's company, while leaving Johnson at Santa Rosa with Pearson's men. Unfortunately Brown's two narratives are both unclear and to a degree contradictory as to exactly what happened next, but it would appear that at this point the filibusters went after a large *caballada* reported to be guarded by upward of fifty Mexicans. They initially failed to find it, for "the guard had got wind of us and returned to the city." But "finding the Rancheros in possession of a quantity of fine Horses, and anxious to dispose of them, we purchased about an hundred excellent ones for the most part of which we paid the Cash, and for those we did not, we gave certificates which was perfectly satisfactory to the owners. We then returned to the place where we had left Col Johnson and were re-united."[7]

Despite the urgency of the situation, all this horse buying inevitably took some time, and as a result it was not until sometime between February 18 and February 21 that they got back to Santa Rosa.[8] Pearson's company could now be properly remounted, but the horses also attracted a new and unexpected hazard. The unsettled state of the country was arousing an unhealthy interest on the part of the local Indian tribes and in particular the Comanche. For some time now, their bands had been hanging around Santa Anna's army as it advanced along the Camino Real, scavenging its campsites and picking off stragglers. Others, perhaps driven off by the presidial companies ordered to protect Santa Anna's rear, were now ranging down into northern Tamaulipas in search of easier prey. The caballada Grant and his men unsuccessfully sought was being guarded not against them but against the Comanche, and in the single worst incident on February 20, a wagon train of settlers fleeing from Beales's colony at Dolores was caught and massacred by one band on the Matamoros road. Other bands were already roaming eastward as far as San Patricio, where three men were murdered and all the horses run off by Comanches on February 19. Now it was James Grant's turn at Santa Rosa. "On that night," remembered Brown, "we anticipated an attack from the Indians, our camp being literally surrounded with them, and the wood resounding with their yells until nearly day—when they disappeared." Given their location and the probable date of the Comanches' appearance, this may have been the same band that had wiped out the Dolores colonists, but if so they evidently decided Grant's men, all armed to the teeth, were an altogether tougher prospect.

Nevertheless, there would be another effort to gather horses. "On the following morning while we were making preparations to return to San Patricio, and from thence join Fannin at Goliad with the Horses, a Ranchero came to our Camp and informed us of a large quantity of Horses about sixty miles up the Rio Grande, and said if we would go after them he would act as a guide for us." This, presumably, was the same herd that had eluded them earlier, and Grant immediately proposed doing just that. He must have known that in doing so he was running a considerable risk, both from the Comanches and from the rapidly approaching Centralistas, which raises the question of why he was so eager to go. As Johnson no doubt argued, the immediate crisis had been settled with the remounting of Pearson's men, and there was a useful surplus besides with which to mount Fannin's men if they were indeed coming down through San Patricio. There was therefore no obvious justification for plunging deeper into potentially hostile territory; other horses could have been found closer at hand along the Nueces.

Grant's real motives for going up the river may have been based on nothing more complicated than sheer bloody-minded frustration and a refusal to relinquish his hard-won authority, for he would have no standing in Fannin's army, especially after those parting letters to Cooke. In reality the horses were no more than a convenient excuse for making one last desperate attempt to reestablish contact with Captain Canales and his Federalistas, for it is no coincidence that both they and the elusive caballada had last been reported farther up the Rio Grande at Camargo. At all events Johnson said he disagreed with the proposal, but Morris, who had likewise burned his boats, sided with Grant and Benavides, and so in the end they split up. Johnson went north with Pearson's company and all the horses gathered in so far, while Grant and Benavides, accompanied by Morris, Lewellen, and about twenty Americans and as many of Benavides's Federalistas, went west to the Camargo ranches in search of Canales.[9]

Undisturbed by Comanches or anyone else, Johnson thus returned safely to San Patricio on February 24—the day after Santa Anna's army swept into Bexar and began to besiege the Alamo. Fannin of course had ignored Johnson's February 9 letter urging an immediate advance, and instead Cooke had gone off with the guns, leaving only Pittman's little detachment to greet the returning raiders. In the circumstances Johnson can hardly have been surprised by this, but he still felt obliged to wait for Grant. In the meantime he sent the horses out to Don Julián de la Garza's ranch some three miles below the village, guarded by a detachment of men drawn from Pearson's company and some Tejanos, while according to McMullen the rest of the Americans were quartered "in three different houses, Capt. Thos. K Pearson with Eight men was lodged on the Public Square and at about Eighty yards from him the other five hundred yards from him." Dangerously, although he had heard nothing from Grant since they had parted at Santa Rosa, Johnson was relying on Grant's men being between him and the Centralist forces, who were still assumed to be at Matamoros. He therefore took no real precautions against an attack and, according to McMullen, was encouraged that "several mexicans come in during the day, but all giving the Same information that there was no fear of an enemy Coming. . . . On the morning of the third day 4 A.M. all laid down to Sleep little thinking it would be The last for Some."[10]

Unbeknownst to them, leaving nearly two hundred men behind to ensure the uncertain loyalties of General Fernández and the Matamoros garrison, Urrea had already crossed the Rio Grande as early as February 17 with 205 infantry and 188 cavalry.[11] He must narrowly have missed the filibusters then immobilized at Santa Rosa—which suggests either that his own intelligence was not always as good as he claimed or that he had reasons of his own for not going after Grant immediately. Now that Grant and Johnson had split up, however, he set off in pursuit of the latter on February 25. Following the filibusters was easy enough, for the large herd of horses being driven by Johnson's men left an unmistakable trail, and Urrea's official campaign diary relates what happened next:

> We resumed our march at four in the afternoon and went ahead with 100 infantry and 100 dragoons. At seven o'clock that night a cold and penetrating norther began to blow. At ten I was informed by the scouting party that the enemy was occupying San Patricio. In view of this, I ordered the infantry to continue its march. Six soldiers of the battalion of Yucatán died from exposure to the cold. I moved forward our cavalry until I joined the observation party that awaited in a woods, two leagues on this side of Santa Gertrudis, where I arrived at half past eleven that night. I immediately wrote to Don Salvador Cuéllar, who lived in that town and [from] whom I expected exact information as to the enemy, asking him to come out immediately and meet me on the march.[12]

This added another intriguing wrinkle to the story, for Don Salvador was none other than a brother of Jesús Cuéllar, who had so recently been acting as a go-between for Grant and Fernández. The lieutenant's defection at Bexar was said by Creed Taylor to have been prompted by Santa Anna's execution of another brother at Zacatecas, but there was seemingly no doubting Don Salvador's centralist sympathies, and McMullen for one reckoned that like Fernández, Don Jesús was also now playing a double game.

Be that as it may, the next day "the infantry arrived at the above-mentioned place at dawn, led by the guides which I had sent for the purpose," declared Urrea.

It began to rain at three in the morning and it looked like snow. I immediately gave orders to Lieutenant Colonel Nicolás de la Portilla for the infantry and the mounted cavalry to encamp [in] the woods, with instructions not to break up camp until the following day, provided the rain ceased. Taking advantage of bad weather, I moved forward immediately. Leaving the road to our right we made our way through woods and across creeks until eleven that night when we came upon the Nueces, a league above Lipantitlán. Not being able to cross at this point I had to retrace my steps to the said town where I succeeded crossing with much difficulty. I took a position on its left bank. Cuéllar, with two companions, came to inform me that there were seventy Americans at San Patricio, waiting to be reinforced by Dr. Grant and his sixty men who had gone to the Río Bravo to round up horses. The night was very raw and excessively cold. The rain continued and the dragoons, who were barely able to dismount, were so numbed by the cold that they could hardly speak. Nevertheless, being as brave as they were faithful, they showed no discouragement and we continued our march.

I arrived in San Patricio at three in the morning, and immediately ordered a party of thirty men headed by Capt. Rafael Pretalia to proceed to the ranch of Don Julián de la Garza (a league distant) to attack twelve or fifteen men who were guarding 150 horses there. I ordered forty dragoons of the remaining force to dismount; and, dividing them into three groups under good officers, I gave instructions for them to charge the position of the enemy, protected by the rest of our mounted troops. The enemy was attacked at half past three in the morning in the midst of the rain.

According to tradition, before he attacked, Urrea sent word for the loyalists in San Patricio to place lights in their windows so that those houses occupied by the filibusters could be identified more easily. By sheer chance, although Urrea's attack went in at about 4:00 A.M. on February 27, Johnson and Grant's old business partner, Daniel Toler, were still awake and busy with papers when the attack began. Two other men, James Miller and Reuben Brown's friend John Love, were also in the house, and at first it seemed as if the four of them might be overlooked; but then they made the understandable mistake of dousing the light.

"The house was soon surrounded," said Johnson, writing as usual in the third person, "and an order was given to open the door. There being no light in the house, the Mexican ordered a light to be made. Toler, who spoke the Castilian language, kept the officer in conversation while he pretended to be complying with the order. While thus engaged, fortunately for the inmates of the house, fire was opened on the street in front. This drew those in the rear of the house to the front. Apprised of this, Colonel Johnson gave the order to open the rear door and to pass out and escape if we could."[13]

The shooting came from Captain Tom Pearson, who had those eight men in a house fronting onto the town square. "When asked to give himself up," said McMullen, "he answered 'No' and commenced to fire encouraging his men to do . . . (the same). They killed the Mexican Col. and two men wounded; four men died after." Naturally enough this provoked a general fusillade on both sides, but after three more Mexicans were wounded and a fourth killed, the dragoons gave over the one-sided exchange and instead ostentatiously fetched up a quantity of combustibles. "Some of the Texians seeing from within that they was going to set fire to the house called to Capt Pearson to Surrender to which he answered no," remembered McMullen, "but the men Called Surrender; and in going out to give themselves up the[y] ware Shot or lanced, among them Capt. Thos. K. Pearson, Dr. J. Hart, Benjamin Dale, Liet. [Henry] Cooney of New York, all which ware Intered next day by the Revd. T. J. Malloy in the Church yard of the Same Place."[14]

Elsewhere in the village Sergeant Pittman and seven other members of Lewellen's company had already surrendered promptly enough to avoid a similar fate, and by dawn it was all over. Urrea was never slow to embellish his own achievements, and in the circumstances it is understandable that he should want to represent the squalid little brawl to Santa Anna as a proper military victory. He therefore all but denied having fought in the village at all, instead writing up his official campaign diary to read as if the Americans had been defending the abandoned ruins of Fort Lipantitlán—on the other side of the Nueces: "Although forty men within the fort defended themselves resolutely," he claimed, "the door was forced at dawn, sixteen being killed and twenty-four being taken prisoners. The town and the rest of the inhabitants did not suffer the least damage. I captured a flag and all kinds of arms and ammunitions. . . . In these operations one dragoon was killed and one sergeant [presumably McMullen's "colonel"] and three soldiers wounded."

Out at Julian's rancho, Captain Pretalia was equally successful. The horse guard there was a party from Pearson's company led by Sergeant William Langenheim and consisting of Edward Hufty, Johan Spiess, George Copeland, William Williams, Gustav Bunsen, Phineas Mahan, and "one other whose name is not remembered, besides an equal number of friendly Mexicans to assist us in herding." The two parties were supposed to be taking turns to sleep and stand sentry, but as Mahan all too graphically recorded, that night "the Americans were all asleep, heads covered up, a heavy norther blowing; the Mexicans, I believe, in the same situation." Pretalia's men were therefore able to surround them. "The first intimation we had of their presence," continued Mahan, "was a volley poured into our sleeping quarters in the corral. The first volley wounded Spence [sic] and Hufty; the second volley grazed Baron Von Bunsen on top of the head. The last I saw of him alive was his endeavouring to remove the cover from his rifle, the next dead, and his body horribly mutilated. Williams had succeeded in climbing over the corral, but was assaulted by a large number of cavalry and literally chopped up. He was an Englishman, and had fought at Waterloo. He had frequently said on our march that he would never become a prisoner. . . . Langenheim called out in Spanish "We surrender."[15] All in all, as Urrea reported with some satisfaction, "Captain Pretalia reported at six o'clock that he had surprised the guard in charge of the horses, had captured all of these, killed four men, and taken eight prisoners." Since only three of the latter—Langenheim, Mahan, and Spiess—belonged to Pearson's company, the others were presumably Tejanos.

In the end only about five or six of the Americans escaped from the debacle, and as Johnson told it: "Toler, Love and Miller kept together, and made their way as best they could for Refugio. The night was dark and greatly favored their escape. The next morning Johnson overtook them and they proceeded together, keeping in the brush, and halting and secreting themselves in clumps of bushes as long as they could for the coldness of the weather. In this way they traveled until night . . . struck the road to Refugio. . . . Here they were joined by another companion [John F. Beck] who had made good his escape."[16] And so at last, said McMullen, reached safety "without hat, shoe or coat."

From Refugio an express rider was immediately dispatched to Goliad by a shadowy character called Edward Gritten, and at 6:00 P.M. on February 28 Fannin first heard of the disaster. It could not possibly have come at a worse time.

When he accepted his appointment as the council's agent, Fannin expected to have to do little more than organize the various groups of footloose volunteers and march them down the coast to occupy Matamoros. Exactly what they were all supposed to do once they got there was never really made clear to Fannin, or rather never properly thought through by the council or anyone else in the Texian ranks. James Grant of course had his own very definite plans for the volunteers, but no one at San Felipe or anywhere else seriously anticipated that they might actually have to fight their way into the city, far less face an invasion force coming the other way. What was more, Fannin had become uncomfortably aware that in Sam Houston's absence he was the Texian army's ranking officer, and with that chilling realization, his self-confidence evaporated. As we have seen, gratefully seizing on Robinson's authorization to abandon the expedition, he had ordered the army to concentrate at Goliad in anticipation of a Mexican advance, but somehow he never quite succeeded in achieving even that modest goal. His orders, in short, were ignored, and supplies and reinforcements—including the long-awaited New York battalion (which was now at last in Texas)— simply failed to materialize. Moreover, since falling back to Goliad he had become steadily more unsettled by reports of Mexican troop movements. They were not always accurate in themselves, but there was no doubting that a major offensive from two or even three different directions was imminent.

As a result Fannin grew ever more pessimistic about his increasingly isolated position, and the reorganization of his little army with its obligatory elections only made matters worse. He was duly confirmed without opposition as colonel of what had now become the 1st Texas Volunteers, but the ballot for the field officers of its two battalions took its toll. "Stir up the people, but do not allow them to come into camp unless organized," he pleaded. "I never wish to see an election in a camp where I am responsible in any manner." By February 22 he was reduced to admitting in a self-pitying letter to Robinson that: "I am a better judge of my military abilities than others, and if I am qualified to command an army, I have not found it out. I well know I am a better company officer than most men now in Texas, and might do with regulars &c for a Regiment. But this does not constitute me a commander."[17]

Then just three days later he received a desperate plea for assistance from William Travis and James Bowie, announcing that the Mexican Army was actually in Bexar: "We have removed all our men into the Alamo, where we will make such resistance as is due to our honour, and that of our country until we can get assistance from you, which we expect you will forward immediately. In this extremity, we hope you will send us all the men you can spare promptly. We have one hundred and forty-six men, who are determined never to retreat. We have but little provisions, but enough to serve us till you and your men arrive." The two men closed by pointedly adding: "We deem it unnecessary to repeat to a brave officer, who knows his duty, that we call upon him for assistance."

Fannin, naturally, had no choice but to respond to such an appeal and, having sent an advance guard forward to the Cibolo later on that day, eventually got the greater part of his men moving on February 26. Ira Westover and his little band of regulars were left behind to garrison Goliad, but the 1st Texas Volunteers, some 320 strong with four guns, took up the line of march for Bexar—and got just two hundred yards down the road! At that point a wheel came off one of the supply wagons. Once it had been unloaded, repaired, and loaded again, another problem arose when the party discovered that "it was necessary to double teams in order to draw the artillery across the river, each piece having but one yoke of oxen." By now it was late in the afternoon and with darkness coming on they halted for the night—still within sight of Goliad. It was an inauspicious start, and next day was no better. Unfortunately, as the Texas historian Harbert Davenport remarked, the American volunteers were brave and had the makings of good soldiers, but they were neither frontiersmen nor farmers and lacked practical knowledge and skills.

Consequently much of the morning was wasted in rounding up the draft oxen, which had carelessly been allowed to stray during the night. In the end a thoroughly disgruntled council of war determined that "inasmuch as a proper supply of provisions and means of transportation could not be had; and, as it was impossible, with our present means, to carry the artillery with us, and as by leaving Fort Defiance [as they had recently voted to name the old presidio] without a proper garrison, it might fall into the hands of the enemy . . . it was deemed expedient to return to this post and complete the fortification."[18] And that was the end of the attempt to relieve the Alamo and its gallant little garrison. In truth, Fannin had needed little persuading to turn back, but while it is easy to condemn his lack of determination, the fact remains that the crucial factor was a crippling shortage of horses—which ironically enough had provided the ostensible justification for Grant and Johnson's foray to the Rio Grande.

Now the news that Urrea was just a few miles to the south confirmed, in Fannin's own mind at least, the wisdom of staying put and at the same time completely destroyed what little remained of his confidence. Nor did it help that when a thoroughly shaken Frank Johnson turned up the day after Gritten's messenger, he hung around only long enough to confirm that his command had been destroyed and that Grant was missing before continuing to San Felipe and then to all intents and purposes riding out of the story entirely. Toler and Love went with him, while John Beck, James Miller, and Edward Hufty all chose to stay with Fannin's forces at Goliad and would die with them there.

However, although Fannin was now nervously expecting an imminent attack, Urrea was taking his time about advancing on Goliad. Despite his easy victory over Johnson, he was acutely aware that he presently lacked sufficient men to tackle the Americans head on, so while he waited for reinforcements from Santa Anna, he instead turned south again in search of Grant. It is not at all clear whether the Mexican authorities ever realized that Grant was actually a British agent, but they were certainly particularly keen to see him dead, and Santa Anna responded to Urrea's report of his victory at San Patricio by noting that "Your Excellency is occupied in pursuing the foreigner Dr. Grant, and I do not doubt that he will soon be taught a lesson, as he deserves."[19] There was no mistaking his meaning, for by accounting Grant a "foreigner" rather than the citizen of Mexico he had been for the past five and a half years, Santa

Anna was making it plain that if captured, Grant was to be executed in accordance with a *circular de la secretaría de guerra* of December 30 1835, instructing that any foreigners (*extranjeros*) coming armed into the republic were to be treated as pirates.

Urrea did not have long to wait. "Having been informed that Dr. Grant was about to arrive," he commented, "I sent some Mexicans to watch the roads by which he was expected," and after two days of waiting, the news came.

As Reuben Brown told the story in 1858, when Grant and his men parted from Johnson at Santa Rosa on about February 20, "we . . . made an early start, but when we came in sight of them [the Mexicans guarding the caballado] we found them moving off, and driving their horses before them. We pursued them to the Rio Grande, where we overtook them, and, as they were attempting to cross pel-mel, some of them were drowned." Disappointingly enough he said nothing of this exciting incident in the rather more sober account presented to President Lamar twenty years earlier, which merely recorded: "We proceeded to the place spoken of by the Mexican, with him for our guide, but found the distance to be near an hundred miles." Nevertheless he was telling the truth about crossing the Rio Grande, for they did end up at the Camargo ranches, but if Grant was still hoping in spite of everything to meet up again with Canales there, he was sadly disappointed. Instead, according to Brown, "on our arrival, we were informed by the Rancheros that there had been about thirty Mexican soldiers in that vicinity for the purpose of protecting them against Indians, but had left, on hearing of our approach." It was at last all too obvious that so far as his former federalist friends were concerned, James Grant was now very bad news, and his supposed ally, Antonio Canales, was only too ready to demonstrate why he would be known as the elusive El Zorro.

In the meantime, the Camargo rancheros appeared friendly and were willing to sell their horses at the going rate, and they also told Grant and his men that "the lower division of the Mexican army was concentrating at Matamoros, and would march in the Course of two weeks for Texas." That particular piece of intelligence was at best stale, and if Zorro had anything to do with it, more than likely knowingly false, for by now Urrea had been across the river for over a week. Nevertheless, encouraged by these false assurances of security, Grant remained at Camargo for three more days before recrossing the Rio Grande on February 27 and at last heading back up the trail toward San Patricio. According to Brown the party traveled steadily for four more days before reaching what he called the "Rancho Persaniath"—the Rancho los Presenos—on San Fernando Creek, a little to the east of the present city of Alice. They were still about twenty-five miles away from San Patricio at that point, and so, "the day being far advanced, we concluded to remain there until the following morning. We were there informed that Col Johnson was still at San Patricio in wait for us. We were treated with kindness and hospitality at this Place but after I became a prisoner I understood that it was all feigned for while entertaining us in the most friendly manner they had secretly sent to the Mexican General then at San partricia informing him we were there."

This was confirmed by Urrea himself, who recorded in his campaign diary for March 1 that he "received news that Dr. Grant was returning from the Río Bravo with a party of forty or fifty picked riflemen and I marched that night, with eighty dragoons, to meet him. The north wind was very strong and the cold was extreme for which reason I decided to wait for the enemy ten leagues from San Patricio, at El Puerto de Los Cuates de Agua Dulce where he would have to pass."

Urrea had chosen his ground well. It was an ideal spot for an ambush. As its name suggests, Los Cuates—the forks—was a well-known crossing point where the trail passed over two branches of Agua Dulce Creek, just below a cluster of miserable jacales or huts dignified by the same name.[20] The creek itself was a substantial watercourse described in 1848 as having "all the appearance of a lagoon" and "the width being from forty to fifty yards and very deep." For much of its length in this area it is bordered by steep bluffs, except at the two-hundred-yard-wide *puerto* or crossing point, where the creek banks open out to slope much more gradually. Then as now, the area was fairly heavily timbered, and Urrea divided his force into six groups and concealed them behind two large mottes or thick clumps of oak. While there is no reason to doubt his statement that he took no more than eighty dragoons drawn from his old regiment, the Cuautla Permanente, rather than the five hundred or one thousand troopers that would be variously reported by a thoroughly intimidated Reuben Brown, Urrea's report reveals that in addition he had an unknown number of infantry under Colonel Martín Garay of the Yucatán Battalion. Other accounts also point to his being accompanied by some of Carlos de la Garza's locally recruited scouts and even by a few presidial troopers under the irrepressible Nicolás Rodríguez; hence an estimate by some of the surviving Americans that the whole lot amounted to about 150 is probably fairly accurate.[21]

Similarly, Urrea's assertion in both his diary and his official report that Grant was leading a total of as many as fifty-three riflemen raises an interesting question, for all the American accounts are agreed that there were no more than twenty-six of them—of whom less than twenty can be identified by name, and some of those only tentatively. At first sight it looks as though Urrea may simply have been guilty of inflating the numbers and the scale of his victory, but on closer examination it becomes clear that those twenty-six men did not include any of the Tejano volunteers riding with Plácido Benavides that morning. Indeed the presence of these Federalistas throughout the campaign is all but ignored, yet a month earlier Frank Johnson reported that there were forty-seven of them at that time, and some simple arithmetic suggests that if Urrea was telling the truth, there were still at least twenty-seven at the Agua Dulce, thus accounting for fully half of Grant's party.[22]

Having comfortably sat out the previous night's norther at the Rancho los Presenos, and expecting to be in San Patricio by nightfall, Grant and those fifty-odd men were in good spirits by the time they reached the Agua Dulce shortly before midday on March 2 and, all unsuspecting, had allowed themselves to become badly strung out as they herded the horses. Chester Newell's highly derivative 1838 account claims that they "were suddenly attacked whilst watering their horses and cattle."[23] While none of the known survivors' testimony directly corroborates this, it would certainly explain why Brown reckoned that "Grant, Placedon [*sic*] and myself were two or three hundred yards in advance of our company when all at once we saw the enemy charging upon us from every direction."

Grant's nemesis, Nicolás Rodríguez, wrote three days afterward that the surprise was so complete that the Americans and their allies "did not perceive us until they were in our power." As John McMullen later heard it at San Patricio, Grant's men immediately "all took to run but the enemy in coming up to them Speared or lanced them off their horses, Shewing no quarters stripping them naked before yet dead." But not all of them ran, and picking through the fragmentary stories reveals that there was indeed a fight of some kind, albeit a brutally brief one. When William Scurlock and the other survivors reached Goliad they told how they "were bringing on a large herd of horses, and in the attempt to save them, and at the same time, fight the enemy, who amounted to 150, they were cut to pieces."[24] Amid the milling confusion of loose horses and cattle, frightened men, and red-jacketed lancers, a fair number of men dismounted and ran toward the village, where they could use their deadly rifles. As they did so, James Grant also came roaring back into the fight. "Wheeling around," continued Brown, "we discovered our little company surrounded. In this critical situation we did not hesitate But determined to join our little band and sell our lives as dear as possible."

It was only natural that the Americans, few if any of whom had swords, should try to shoot it out on foot, but Urrea had carefully anticipated this by posting some of Garay's infantry as a backstop, and in his official report to Santa Anna, he told how "five escaped to the villa where they were received by an advance of infantry that followed them through the woods where they went after they were fired upon." Although forced to split up, most of that group got away, but at least two other men, Stillman S. Curtis and Nelson Jones, were captured at this point. In the meantime Reuben Brown had also dismounted, presumably in order to join those men he thought were still fighting, but when he came to revise his story in 1858, the move became an involuntary one. "My horse was quickly killed with a lance," he wrote, "but Grant told me to mount Maj. Morris' horse, as Morris had just been killed. I did so, but without seeing any object to be accomplished by it."

Grant may indeed have grimly resolved, as Brown said, to "go in and die with the boys," but it was already far too late. Benavides's men were scattered and ridden down by the lancers, Morris was dead, Lewellen was dead, and all their men with them, and so he decided to make a run for it after all. Having got Brown up on to Morris's horse, "Grant observed to me to make your escape if you can, and at the same time he made a rush to force himself through the enemy who were all around us, he fired his pistole at an officer & shot him from his horse, he passed through, also Placedon [sic] went through at the same time. I made two attempts and failed, also received several Blows from their swords."[25]

Things were now looking decidedly nasty, but then, as he told the story in 1858, "just at that moment the horses took a stampede, and broke the lines of dragoons, and Grant and myself finding ourselves the only survivors of our party, followed in the wake of the horses, the dragoons shooting after us, and wounding our horses in several places, but not badly." Thus with one bound as it were, he seemed to be free for the moment, although in his earlier and more breathless account, written for Lamar, he told a different story:

I fired my gun & one pistole, two men fell, I charged over them, by that time Grant & Placedon was about two hundred yards off; and appeard if there was about fifty Mexicans close behind them. I had no time to reflect what would be my best course but kept on after Grant, with a great number of Mexicans fireing and yelling close behind me—that attracted the attention of those in pursuit of Grant, as soon as they discovered me approaching pretty near them they wheeled on me but I could not stop for those behind was almost reaching me with their lances, I put my Pistole almost against a man's breast, fired and rushed through I received a blow on the head that came very near putting me on the ground. I soon came up with Grant & Placedon, my wound on the head was bleeding in a stream—they were much surprised to see me.

And well they might be, but the three were not out of danger yet. "I ast them if they had any hopes of escape, they said if we could get to timber we might probably get shut of them—at that time there was about two hundred of them within thirty yards, they would frequently come very close as though they would dismount us with their lances, we would wheel on them with our pistols, they would halt and attempt to surround us, discovering their intentions we would set off again, finally our horses began to fail."

By now they had run hard about six or seven miles away from Agua Dulce, in the direction of Banquette. There are various accounts of what happened next, the most straightforward of which came from McMullen: "Col. Grant ran his horse 7 miles before he was taken. On the Lieutenant who killed coming close to him he Grant fired one of his Pistoles and Pared the leafe of his hat, the Second he fired without effect, when the other came up and lanced him through the back."

Brown, as might be expected, told a different story, or rather a series of quite different stories. The Mexicans, he said in 1858, were still "occasionally coming up with us, and crying out to us to surrender and our lives would be saved. But we knew better, and continued to fly, but the number of those overtaking us became larger and larger." At last, however, as he told Lamar, the fugitives recognized that it was all over: "Placedon being better mounted than Grant or myself, we told him to go on & save himself if he could, the officers seeing us separating forced them [the dragoons] to make a charge, they came up, we wheeled on them as before but they came ahead. I attempted to shoot one of them, that had his lance up to plunge, with a pistol. I had loaded while running, the cap exploded but did not fire. Grant fired at him after he had give me a blow, he shot him in the shoulder, another one raised his sword to strike me. I threw my pistole at him and struck him in the face. I jumped from my horse & got the lance from the man that Grant had wounded & keep them off until an officer came & forbid their killing me, by that time Grant was dead."[26]

However, the story he told to Rueben Marmaduke Potter while he was in prison at Matamoros shortly after the fight was altogether more convincing and in its way far more chilling: "He said that while he was flying in a course parallel with that of Grant, but a few hundred yards from him, he saw Grant, who was hotly pursued by a dragoon while his horse was failing, suddenly make signs of surrender by throwing down his sword and pistols and dismounting. The horseman rode up to him, but as yet showed no disposition to violence; but while Grant was speaking to him, another trooper charged in and ran Grant through with his lance, and then both of the soldiers joined in mangling the body of the fallen man."

Afterward, said an understandably shaken Brown; "I saw some ten or a dozen officers go up and run their sword through his body. He was well known to them, having lived a long time in Mexico. They had a bit of a grudge against him." That at least was obviously something of an understatement, but it plainly emphasizes an intriguing determination to make sure that Grant was well and truly dead.[27] While it is possible that his death after having surrendered may simply have been one more random slaying by overexcited men, the shocking circumstances as relayed to Potter are much more suggestive of a deliberate cold-blooded murder—as would be alleged in Grant's daughter's obituary. Santa Anna for one certainly wanted him dead, but Urrea and his federalist friends may have had reasons of their own for ensuring that James Grant died quickly and above all quietly. As a live prisoner with an intimate knowledge of that general scheme of revolutionizing, he could have been a dangerous embarrassment.

Reuben Brown was far luckier. Having been roped with a lasso and taken captive, "I was then lashed upon a horse and taken to the ground where the fight first commenced, where I saw most of our men lying dead. Among others whom I recognised was one poor fellow named [Joseph] Carpenter, from Tennessee, who was fatally wounded, but not quite dead. When it was discovered that he was alive, one of the dragoons was ordered to finish him. He dismounted, and, while poor Carpenter was asking to have his life spared, he struck him on the head with his escopeta, and thus ended his existence." Even then, Brown himself narrowly missed a similar fate, for as he was being carried along "one of them road up within eight or ten feet, fired at my head with my own pistole, the one that failed to fire and I had thrown it into one of their faces."

Finally, just before they all reached San Patricio, "an officer came up and drew his sword which was perfectly bloody, and ask me how I liked it. I told him he was one of the men I recollected seeing run his sword through the body of Grant, he turned off and said nothing mour."

There was indeed no more to be said. James Grant's body was left, with those of his men, lying where he fell. Any last lingering prospect of a federalist uprising in Tamaulipas—however remote or unrealistic it might have been by this time—was well and truly gone.

8 • *From Sea to Shining Sea*

ON THE SAME DAY Grant was killed, the reconvened Texian Convention issued the long-expected formal Declaration of Independence from Mexico. Few of the signatories, who included Sam Houston, seem to have been in any doubt at all that this declaration was merely a temporary arrangement pending an annexation of Texas by the United States. Just five days afterward Houston asked a fellow delegate's opinion regarding a resolution "that Texas is part of Louisiana, and the U. States by treaty of 1803," as earlier noted.[1] Grant, it seemed, had fought and died in vain to prevent this, but it took more than two months for the news of his death to reach London, and a great deal happened in that time as Mexico first came close to regaining Texas before dramatically losing it forever; and in the process American ambitions were quite unexpectedly thwarted.

Two days after the declaration Houston, in the ascendant once again, was reconfirmed as commander in chief of the Texian army, "regulars, volunteers and militia, while in actual service." He insisted on this reaffirmation ostensibly because his earlier appointment had been made under the authority of the Mexican Constitution of 1824 and now had no legal standing under the new regime. Strictly speaking this might have been so, and given the number of lawyers involved it was only prudent, but no one was in any doubt that his real purpose was to gain undisputed command of both the volunteers and the militia as well as his little handful of regulars. Recognizing the sense of this, the government agreed to the extension of his authority but insisted that his first job was to organize a relief force to go to the aid of the Alamo. Yet this was something he seemed oddly reluctant to do, and he delayed leaving Washington until March 6. Even then it took a clear threat of dismissal to get him going, and all the while he was assuring anyone who would listen that "all those reports from Travis & Fannin were lies, for there were no Mexican forces there."[2] It is inconceivable he actually believed this, but he was shrewd enough to realize the futility of tackling the Mexican Army head on with the slender resources then available, and so he dragged his feet, taking five days to reach the rendezvous at Gonzales. There he was justified in his reluctance with the news that it was all over.

"Upon my arrival here this afternoon," he told Fannin, "the following intelligence was received through a Mexican, supposed to be friendly. . . . I fear a melancholy portion of it will be found too true. He states that he left Fort San Antonio on Sunday, the 6th inst; that the Alamo (citadel) was attacked on that morning at the dawn of day, by about 2,500 men, and was carried a short time before sunrise with a loss of 520 men, Mexicans, killed and as many wounded. Col. Travis had only 150 effective men, out of his whole force of 187. After the fort was carried, seven men surrendered, and called for Gen Santa Anna and quarters. They were murdered by his order. Col. Bowie was sick in his bed, and was also murdered."[3]

Sadly, all the intelligence except the overoptimistic assessment of Mexican casualties was indeed true. On March 3 Santa Anna had heard from Urrea that the rebels had been routed at San Patricio and that he was in pursuit of Grant. There was no longer any danger of a federalist uprising in his rear, and so the assault was fixed for the predawn hours of March 6. It was, as he afterward declared, "a small affair." Two or three men may have escaped during a mass breakout over the east walls, but otherwise the whole garrison was massacred. In both human and political terms the fall of the Alamo was a disaster of the first magnitude for the Texians, and Houston never really lived down his failure to try and save its defenders. For the present, however, he immediately sent Fannin instructions to evacuate Goliad and retreat to the line of the Guadalupe.

Unfortunately, only a day or two earlier, nearly half of Fannin's men, under Lieutenant Colonel Ward, had gone down to Refugio to evacuate the Ayers family and other American colonists, only to be caught by Urrea before they could get away. After a day-long battle on March 14, all of them were killed, captured, or scattered when they tried escape under cover of darkness. At first unaware of this disaster, Fannin wasted three precious days waiting for their return before commencing his retreat on the morning of March 19. By then it was too late; Urrea caught up with him in the afternoon on the open prairie just short of Coleto Creek.

Despite their never having reached the creek, American accounts refer to the engagement by that name, but their Mexican adversaries knew the place as the Encinal del Perdido—the "wood of the lost ones"—for Fannin and his men were not the first adventurers to stand and die there. Fringing the prairie were belts of woodland, and on June 19, 1817, a now forgotten little battle had been fought in the woods just a mile to the north of Fannin's present position, between the forces of Colonel Antonio Martínez, the last Spanish governor of Texas, and a Mexican Republican "army" on its way to capture Goliad. The Republicans had forty-two men under Colonel Henry Perry and Major James H. Gordon, both former U.S. officers and veterans of the 1815 Battle of New Orleans. Despite being outnumbered by three to one, Perry and Gordon refused to surrender tamely and in the fight that followed were killed along with more than half their men. Now Urrea's men used those same woods for cover and to conceal their movements as they prepared to destroy another army of filibusters.

Formed in a square, Fannin and his men successfully fought off attacks all through the afternoon and into the night. But short of ammunition and above all of water, and with all their draft animals killed and a lengthening toll of wounded, they eventually recognized that there was no way out; they surrendered the next morning. The capitulation that followed was a controversial one. Encouraged by a Mexican colonel named Holzinger, Fannin understood that after surrendering, his men would be marched either to Copano or perhaps Matamoros, and then repatriated to New Orleans; but afterward Urrea flatly denied ever offering anything better than an unconditional surrender. Indeed, as Santa Anna himself firmly reminded Urrea, he had no authority to do so, since the *circular de la secretaría de guerra* of December 30, 1835, expressly instructed that all such prisoners were to be executed.

After the battle they returned to Goliad and were imprisoned there for a week before pulling on their knapsacks and marching in three groups on the morning of March 27. It was Palm Sunday, and they were told they were marching to Copano and the ships that would carry them home to New Orleans. Instead, a short distance down the road they were halted and "ordered to sit down with their backs to the Guard. Young [Robert] Fenner . . . rose on his feet, and exclaimed "Boys, they are going to kill us—die with your faces to them, like men!" At the same moment two other young men, flourishing their caps over their heads, shouted at the top of their voices: "Hurrah for Texas!" Then the firing began. In the confusion a number of men managed to escape, including Herman Ehrenberg and John Duval, but at the end of the day the best estimate is that 342 were murdered in cold blood, including Fannin himself and all the other wounded.

From the Mexicans' point of view and in strict legalistic terms, there was justification enough for this harsh measure. No matter how they might be dressed up at the time and afterward, "the soldiers of Travis at the Alamo, those of Fannin at Perdido, the riflemen of Dr. Grant . . . with but few exceptions, were publicly known to have come from New Orleans and other points of the neighboring republic."[4] As General Filisola put it, they were "men who were fighting without a banner, murdering Mexican detachments, burning houses, attacking the property of legitimate owners and peaceful citizens, and were trying in addition to steal a great part of the national territory."[5] In short they were indeed filibusters, fighting under no recognized flag and hence considered under international law to be pirates. There was, however, a difference between executing a few ringleaders for the sake of example and indiscriminate slaughter on such a scale, which led to a chorus of condemnation from both the British and French governments as well as from the United States.[6]

In the meantime, there was never going to be any realistic prospect of Sam Houston managing to hold the line of the Guadalupe, and the retreat began on the night of March 13—even before his messenger reached Fannin. By March 17 Houston was safely over the Colorado at Burman's Ferry, but with only 374 men he was obviously in no condition to fight Santa Anna. On March 26, hearing of Fannin's defeat, he fell back first to San Felipe and then farther up the Brazos to Groce's Plantation. Joined during the retreat by more Texian militia and a handful of American volunteers, Houston's army was some eight hundred strong when he broke camp on April 12 and headed east toward the Redlands of East Texas and the Sabine River—where a United States army was waiting under the command of General Edward Pendleton Gaines. The general, as it turned out, had some very odd orders indeed.

On December 28, 1835, a detachment of U.S. regulars led by Major Francis Dade had been ambushed and massacred by Seminole Indians near Tampa in Florida. Within the week the news reached New Orleans, where Gaines promptly gathered a force of some three hundred regulars and seven hundred Louisiana militia. They headed east and were at Fort Brooke, Florida, by February 9 when instructions to do something quite different caught up with them. On January 23, U.S. Secretary of War Lewis Cass had ordered Gaines to proceed to the western frontier with Texas. There he was to prevent any incursions by "parties" into Mexico, which might appear to suggest that he was to intercept the various volunteer companies proceeding to Texas, were it not for Cass's pointed emphasis on U.S. treaty obligations to prevent incursions into Mexican territory by Indians![7]

Understandably Gaines was reluctant to ignore an actual emergency in order to deal with a hypothetical one and so did not return to New Orleans until March 28, but by then he was in no doubt as to what was really required of him. His instructions were ostensibly framed to prevent the conflict spilling over onto American soil—but there lay the opportunity, for back in February 1819, when John Quincy Adams had formally conceded that Texas was indeed Mexican territory, article three of the treaty he signed with Don Luis de Onis de Gonzáles defined the international border as running along the Sabine River. However there was a delay in ratifying the treaty, and the Jackson administration began arguing that the border should lie farther west, along the Neches River. Consequently the boundary question had never been properly settled— in the 1820s Henry Ward was particularly exasperated by Mexican reluctance to force the issue—and the twenty leagues separating the two rivers came to be regarded as neutral ground. Notwithstanding some sensationalist newspaper reporting, no one in Washington or anywhere else really expected the Mexican Army to come storming across the Sabine, but it was hopefully anticipated that Santa Anna's supposed Indian allies might be a different matter entirely.

"Should I find any disposition on the part of the Mexicans or their red allies to menace our frontier," wrote Gaines, "I cannot but deem it to be my duty not only to hold the troops of my command in readiness for action in defence of our frontier, but to anticipate their lawless movements, by crossing our supposed or imaginary national boundary."[8] His superiors in Washington understood him perfectly, and Cass quickly responded that "the President approves the suggestion you make, and you are authorised to take such position, on either side of the imaginary boundary line, as may be best for your defensive operations."

What had been serving as the border for the last seventeen years was now just an "imaginary boundary," and the only constraint placed upon Gaines was a prohibition on moving farther west than Nacogdoches. Disappointingly, the local Indian tribes proved uncooperative. Instead of going on the rampage, they seemed just as anxious as the settlers to move out of the battle area. Nevertheless, by the time Gaines had his men fully in place in early April it was obvious that the Texians were taking a beating, and so he requested the governors of Louisiana, Mississippi, Alabama, and Tennessee to call out their militia. He had no authority to do so, and all of them more or less politely declined his invitation, but on April 14, two days after Houston abandoned the camp at Groce's and headed east, Gaines suddenly received warning of a concentration of 1,500–2,000 Indians; "and a conjunction of their forces with about one thousand *Mounted* Mexicans. This is the detachment no doubt, which Jo. (Colo. Travis servant) spoke of as having left San Antonio and which took the Bastrop road."[9] Breathless reports also came in that Nacogdoches had been attacked and burned. Nothing of this curious flurry of alarm was true, but it was just the excuse Gaines had been waiting for. He immediately ordered thirteen companies of regulars belonging to the 3rd and 6th Infantry to march westward that evening, with thirty-five rounds a man, two cannon, and twelve days' provisions, in the full knowledge that any contact with Mexican troops would inevitably bring on a war. Instead, something quite unexpected happened.

Had Sam Houston's army been built around a solid core of those American volunteers whom he had himself invited from "the old states," there would probably have been little to prevent him from retreating all the way to the Redlands and a rendezvous with Gaines. Instead, thanks to Grant and his "wild scheme," most of those volunteers lay dead at the Alamo or along the Atascosita Road. In their place Houston's army now consisted almost entirely of Texian militia; all of them bitterly angry at the abandonment and destruction of their homes and plantations and angrier still that no attempt was being made to slow down or stop the Mexican advance. They also had some definite views about the limits of their commander's authority, and instead of obeying him as the U.S. volunteers might have done, they forced an unwilling Houston to turn and fight at San Jacinto on April 21.[10] There another factor came into play, for with the original filibusters all dead or scattered, Santa Anna understandably enough assumed that the real military campaign was effectively over and that now it was simply a matter of scouring the remaining rebels over the Sabine. The better to accomplish that task, his army was spread right across Texas to hunt them down, and he himself had just twelve hundred men under his personal command when the battle began. His force still outnumbered Houston's, but not by nearly enough; sheer ferocity won the day for Texas in just eighteen bloody minutes.

The unexpected victory at San Jacinto and Santa Anna's even more fortuitous capture the next day meant that Texan independence was for the moment assured—not just from Mexico but from the United States as well, for failing that rendezvous in the Redlands, Houston, Jackson, and Gaines could not bounce America into a war with Mexico, and without that war, annexation was to be set back by ten years. In the meantime, however, disregarding enthusiastic proposals to lynch Santa Anna on the spot, Houston had secured from his illustrious captive a promise to order all remaining Mexican troops to evacuate Texas—and to recognize Texian independence. The first was easily accomplished, but in choosing to send Santa Anna home by way of Washington, the Texian government made a bad mistake, for although it ensured the general could not renege on his promises by rallying his troops, it underlined to the world that San Jacinto had indeed been an *American* victory. This impression was only strengthened when in September 1836, following Sam Houston's election as president of the new republic, a resolution by his government to seek annexation was approved almost unanimously. The reaction was not what the Texians expected. Santa Anna, not unreasonably, declared that he had consented to recognize the independence of Texas, but not its annexation, while in the United States the response was equally frosty.

Although there was obviously enthusiastic support in the southern states for the acquisition of Texas, northern abolitionists, led by John Quincy Adams in particular, were fervently opposed to the prospect of adding another slave-holding state to the Union. So great was their hostility that neither Andrew Jackson nor his designated successor, Martin Van Buren, dared formally introduce the question of annexation on Capitol Hill. Even diplomatic recognition of an independent Texas was pushed through by just the very narrowest of margins, and the bill was signed only on March 3, 1837, barely twenty-four hours before Jackson left office.

Indeed for a time it seemed that no one wanted Texas, for on July 1, 1836, Richard Pakenham, the British minister at Mexico City, had penned a remarkable report to Lord Palmerston at the Foreign Office, advising him:

Whatever may be the expectation of the [Mexican] Government with regard to the temporary subjection of Texas I believe that they are impressed with the conviction that after what has happened to retain permanent possession of the Territory would be beyond the power of the Country, and I am assured that in order to get rid of so onerous a possession and at the same time to establish a barrier against further encroachments from the United States, they had some time ago conceived the singular project of offering the Sovereignty of Texas to England. Certain observations lately made to me by the Minister of war [José María Tornel] whom I consider at present the leading Member of the Administration, convinced me that they really did entertain such a design.[11]

That design was of course not too far removed from what Henry Ward and his agents had aimed at in holding out the prospect of British protection to the Fredonian rebels all those years ago—as Tornel may have been aware. The difference was that now Mexico was in no position to transfer the sovereignty of its wayward province, and moreover Palmerston had no desire for Britain to be thrust quite so provocatively into what even he recognized as America's back yard. Therefore when an alarmed American consul reported from Mexico City in May 1837, that a proposition was before the Mexican Congress to sell Texas to Britain in order to pay off its debts to that country, then amounting to some $68 million, Palmerston sidestepped the inevitable questions by blandly assuring Andrew Stevenson, the U.S. minister in London, that while Mexico had indeed applied for aid against the Texians, he had declined to provide it.[12]

There the matter rested, but in the meantime in April 1837, Pakenham had sent Crawford, the British consul at Tampico, across to have a look at what was going on beyond the Rio Grande. As the *Telegraph and Texas Register* of May 2, 1837, confidently asserted: "The object of this gentleman's visit to Texas, is we understand to investigate the civil and political condition of the country and report to the British government."

This he did with some thoroughness, concluding that the Texians were now confident they could stand by themselves and that instead of seeking annexation, they were "very anxious to have a Separate, free and recognised Independent Government, to trade directly with other Nations, giving the Raw produce for the Manufactures they require, for it must be long ere there are Manufactories in Texas. I am not aware whether other Instructions are sent to the Minister in Washington but I know that annexation to that Government is not wished by the people or the Government of Texas, nor will it now be sought for."[13]

Crawford may simply have been told what he wanted to hear, but the hint could not have been plainer, nor unconnected with Houston's appointment of General J. Pinckney Henderson to serve as the diplomatic agent of Texas in securing British and French recognition of the new republic. Nevertheless, despite the optimistic tone of Crawford's report, Palmerston at first prevaricated when Henderson presented his credentials on October 13 and then declined to enter into any negotiations. As he commented to the chancellor of the exchequer, Thomas Spring Rice, "it would not do for us to make a Treaty with a self-denominated State, till events had proved such a state could permanently maintain its independence."[14] At that point Palmerston still regarded the annexation of Texas by the United States as both inevitable and imminent, and he consequently saw no point whatsoever in unnecessarily antagonizing Mexico by prematurely recognizing it in the meantime.

Furthermore, just as the slavery question impeded annexation by the United States, it also discouraged British interest. As we have already seen, the crucial parliamentary debate of August 5, 1836—(before Pakenham's report of Tornel's proposal reached London)—not only articulated widespread unease among British politicians over the prospect of American expansion into Texas but also revealed an even greater anxiety over the continued presence of slavery there. The institution was supposedly illegal in Mexico but had been quietly tolerated in Texas until the revolution. The new republic's constitution proclaimed slavery to be lawful and actually required the enslavement of any free Negroes who might enter its borders! This was hardly calculated to engage British sympathies, and so on January 27, 1838, Henderson was formally advised that Texas could not be recognized.

Palmerston, for the moment, enjoyed the best of all possible worlds. The expansionist tendencies of the United States had been blocked, at least temporarily. Mexico, although disappointed at Britain's failure to challenge the Texan blockade of her northern ports, remained an ally and important trading partner; while at home the abolitionists were satisfied that no encouragement was being extended to the slave holders. Nevertheless, with the passage of time it gradually became clear that there was no immediate prospect of the republic becoming extinguished after all, either by a resurgent Mexico or by the long anticipated annexation, and so in due course Henderson was followed in turn by another envoy, General James Hamilton. A former governor of South Carolina, slave owner, and prominent advocate of states' rights, Hamilton arrived in England in December of 1839 with instructions to seek that elusive recognition and to negotiate a variety of treaties with the British government. In a curious echo of Wavell's embassy on behalf of Iturbide all those years ago, he was also engaged as a loan commissioner in trying to raise capital for the republic through the sale of bonds both there and elsewhere in Europe, and at first this seems to have assumed a higher priority, for it was not until the following November that he reported any progress on the treaties.

That progress could be made at all was a simple reflection of the fact that on December 10, 1838, Sam Houston had been succeeded as president by Mirabeau Buonaparte Lamar. A flamboyant politician from Georgia who had distinguished himself at San Jacinto, Lamar believed that Texas could survive as an independent nation. Annexation was no longer on the political agenda. Therefore, on November 13, 1840, Palmerston effectively recognized the republic by putting his hand to a treaty of amity and commerce. This he followed by signing another treaty committing Britain to using its good offices as a mediator between Texas and Mexico, in return for which Texas was to assume responsibility for £1 million of the Mexican debt. So far so good, but then came a third treaty, which he also insisted upon, giving mutual right of search of vessels suspected of being engaged in the African slave trade, and thereby the whole thing collapsed. Hamilton was deeply unhappy with Palmerston's insistence on this particular treaty, but he could hardly refuse to accept it. Britain already had a similar treaty with Mexico; until now the only concession that had been allowed to vessels sailing under the flag of Texas was that they should be regarded for customs purposes as Mexican vessels—and therefore, although it was not spelled out, subject to the same stop and search rights. Politically it was impossible for Palmerston to relinquish these rights, for the root of the problem lay not with the continued existence of slavery on Texan soil but with the importation of slaves and, it was widely supposed, their subsequent transfer to the United States.

The first and second treaties were sent to Texas for ratification on December 3, 1840, but the third was held back for a month due to Hamilton's insistence that it should be carried home by a friend, Albert Burnley, who could explain to his government just why Hamilton had signed a treaty he had had no authority to negotiate in the first place. Naturally enough it was suspected that the real reason for the delay was a hope that if Texan approval of the first and second treaties were received swiftly enough, Britain would proceed to ratify them without waiting for the third, which could then be allowed to lapse. The result was predictable. Texan sanction of the first and second treaties was indeed duly transmitted to Hamilton on February 12, 1841, but Burnley did not even submit the slave trade treaty until February 21, far too late for approval by Congress, which had adjourned more than two weeks earlier. Unimpressed by this all too transparent maneuvering, Palmerston rightly insisted on exchanging ratifications of all three treaties at the same time, and thus all were delayed until June 28, 1842.[15]

By that time there had been a change of government in Britain as well and another shift in attitudes toward American ambitions, which did not entirely spring from the substitution of Lord Aberdeen for Lord Palmerston at the Foreign Office. In part it also arose from the tragic-comic "Battle of the Windmill" in November 1838. Inspired by the recent success of the Texas Revolution, an extremist Jacksonian group called the Hunters launched a filibustering invasion of Canada that ended in a five-day-long siege near Prescott, Ontario. To the Hunters' dismay not only did the supposedly oppressed Canadians decline to rally to liberty's banner, but the U.S. Army intervened—and not to assist them, as Gaines had just done in Texas and Andrew Jackson himself had done in West Florida all those years ago, but to intercept and disarm any reinforcements and even arrest some of the fugitives afterward.[16] From the Foreign Office point of view this cooperation was a welcome vindication of Palmerston's policy of engagement and accommodation with the United States, but the Colonial Office—or rather its officials on the ground, for Glenelg was as incompetent as ever—saw it rather differently. Having just been invaded after facing down a domestic revolt in Canada the year before, they took the possible threat of further filibustering attempts very seriously.

One of those most closely involved in the counterinsurgency work was a man named William Kennedy—another Scot—who was employed by the then Canadian governor general, Lord Durham, in the outwardly innocuous role of "municipal commissioner," in which he was actually charged with investigating the penetration of local government in the colony by the Hunters or their sympathizers. After Durham's recall, however, Kennedy proceeded to the United States in 1839, on what was ostensibly a private visit; "first to examine the working of the State Legislatures, and secondly to visit Texas." In the curious way of confidential agents in those days, a book followed in due course, mildly titled *The Rise, Progress and Prospects of Texas,* which described the country and its history at some length but said remarkably little about why Kennedy was given a letter of introduction to the British minister in Washington, Henry Fox, or about the nature of his subsequent talks with President Lamar of Texas.

What the Colonial Office may have learned from his findings does not appear, but in October 1841, with a change of government in August and diplomatic recognition suddenly back on the agenda, Palmerston's successor, Lord Aberdeen, instantly accepted an offer by Kennedy to go back to Texas in a quasidiplomatic role—and at the same time to establish a proper espionage network in the republic.

Kennedy made no bones about the necessity for his doing so, for as he told Aberdeen, he was "thoroughly convinced that, unless English influence be employed in raising up a stable independent power on the South-Western and North Western frontiers of the Union, a very few years will suffice to place the whole of the territory they covet under the Sovereignty of the United States. *There* lies the danger to the Maritime and Commercial supremacy of Great Britain."[17]

There too in a nutshell was the old worry successively articulated by Canning, Huskisson, Ward, and their various agents, including of course James Grant. Aberdeen therefore had no hesitation in accepting Kennedy's offer to go out "in the capacity of an unaccredited Agent . . . for the purpose of Watching events, and exercising whatever influence I might possess for the benefit of my Country." His immediate problem was that just before Palmerston departed from the Foreign Office, a commission was drawn up appointing a Scottish naval officer, Captain Charles Elliot, as consul general for Texas. However, at the time Elliot was still making his way back from another diplomatic posting to China and would not even learn of his appointment until December 6. Even then, understandably enough, he first requested a further month's grace in order to set his affairs in order and then was detained to await the outcome of Kennedy's mission. In the meantime doubts were suddenly appearing over the supposedly dormant question of American annexation. President Lamar had overreached himself in establishing a ruinously expensive regular army and navy that Texas quite literally could not afford, and on February 5, 1841, Congress adjourned without appropriating any funds to extend the soldiers' three-year enlistments, which were due to expire that August. Not only was Texas about to lose the means of defending itself, but fresh elections were also due, with every prospect of seeing Sam Houston returning as president. News of his reelection arrived in London on November 6, and three days later Kennedy breathlessly seconded this unwelcome news with a brief private note: "I have just been assured," he said, "that the United States are actively intriguing to effect the Annexation of Texas, and that the newly elected President, General Houston (the friend and protégé of General Jackson) is not unfavorable to their object."[18]

Kennedy's immediate task was to assess what was going on, by whatever means at his disposal, and to endeavor to secure Texan ratification of the antislavery treaty before all three treaties lapsed on August 1, 1842. He was certainly in no doubt as to the importance of this issue. One of his earlier letters alluded to

the subject of domestic Slavery, which the Slave holding people of the South will not even *discuss* except with those in whose fair dealing and friendly intentions they repose full confidence. The trust of the Texans in me, as the disinterested chronicler of their social rise and progress, is admitted to be considerable and, were I in a suitable position to give strength to my opinions, I indulge the hope that I might succeed in effecting some mitigation of the system, as inducing them to assent to its early abandonment. A leading member of the Anti-Slavery Society—(a body whose mode of operating upon Foreign States is perhaps more zealous than judicious) admitted, when discussing the matter with me, that any representations I might make were likely to have peculiar weight with the planters of Texas.[19]

Just how much influence Kennedy actually possessed may be open to question, but there was no doubting the urgency with which he undertook his mission. He was in Galveston by January 10 and reached the city of Austin a week later, where he "fortunately found Congress still in Session, and both the Government and the people well disposed to listen to my representations." It can hardly have been coincidental that Houston had introduced the matter of the antislavery treaty on January 12, two days after Kennedy reached Texas, and that it was read for the first time on January 14. Consequently Kennedy's arrival in Austin on January 17 was rather more than timely, and "in consideration of my work in Texas, I received a vote of thanks from both Houses of Congress, and was invited to a Seat within the bar of the Senate and Chamber of Representatives."

No one there could therefore have been under any illusions as to his real status, and "on inquiring respecting the Slave Trade Treaty, I was informed that, at the Special request of General Hamilton its presentation to the Senate had been delayed until his arrival in Texas, where he has not yet appeared. Apprehending nothing but Mischief from another twelve Month's delay, I urged the immediate ratification of the Treaty upon the President and Senators, and am happy to say that on the 22d Inst. it passed the Senate by *a unanimous vote.*"[20]

Although Kennedy's exertions certainly merited a degree of self-satisfaction at the outcome, he was pushing at an open door, for the plain fact of the matter was that Houston wanted that promise of British mediation with Mexico and was also keen, for reasons of his own, to see the matter settled before Hamilton returned from Europe. Consequently the South Carolinian addressed a furious letter of denunciation to Aberdeen, alleging:

He [Kennedy] reached Texas before me, and finding from the Jealousy of the present President of Texas, Gen. Houston to myself (lest I should supplant him in influence with the people of Texas) that he would obtain favour by joining in the current of prejudice which thro' the instrumentality of the President was running against me, and strange to say (he an Englishman and I a Slave Holder) one of the grounds of his assault was, that I was confederating with an association at Exeter Hall to abolish slavery in Texas.

His flattery of President Houston (who to say the best of him, is one of the least respectable persons in Texas) has secured to him a large Empesari or Grant of Land, and the understanding that Mr. Kennedy is to write Gen. Houston's Life, has perhaps been equally influential in procuring for him the Consul Generalship to Great Britain. . . . Lord Palmerston will give you some items of intelligence respecting Kennedy, which will let you not the less understandingly into his character. If you were to refuse to recognise him as Consul Genl. you would gratify a great many of the most influential and respectable of the people of Texas, who have regarded his ingratitude to me and sycophancy to Houston with unspeakable disgust.[21]

To underline the point Hamilton also challenged Kennedy to a duel, informing him that "you will find me on your way through the States to Charleston until the 1st. July—In this as in all other Cases responsible for my own acts and seeking neither shelter or concealment." Kennedy sensibly ignored the bellicose general and returned home to assume temporarily the post of *Texan* consul general in London!

By then, as he assured Aberdeen, who was similarly indifferent to Hamilton's chagrin, matters had again assumed a critical turn. The reason for Houston's eagerness to embrace a British alliance was now clear. Santa Anna was back in power in Mexico, minus a leg lost in repelling a French invasion but with his power and prestige enhanced thereby. Nevertheless, his position, as always, was sufficiently precarious that he could not entertain any proposals to give up Mexico's claim to Texas, and on March 5, 1842, a small Mexican army led by General Rafael Vásquez made this clear by occupying San Antonio, and causing panic among the border settlements, before pulling out again two days later. Lacking an army, Texas more than ever needed the protection of either Great Britain or the United States. Kennedy reported:

I do not think I arrogate too much to myself in saying that the Confidence reposed in me by the Government and people of Texas materially contributed to allay the excitement in favour of immediate annexation to the United States, which prevailed at the period of my arrival in the Country. I obtained, at all events, a suspension of the question until the dispositions of Great Britain could be known. The position of that question is now materially altered by the Mexican invasion. Unacquainted, as I am, with the views of Her Majesty's Government, and the information in their possession, I am reluctant to hazard an opinion as to the probable result of the invasion, but I greatly fear that it will eventually prove as injurious to English interests, as it will be *temporarily* detrimental to Texas, and *permanently* injurious to Mexico. A few Months will determine every thing.[22]

With all three treaties now approved by the Texian Congress and ready for ratification, Elliot was at last instructed to proceed to Texas on May 26. With the ratification of the treaties taking place on June 28, he actually went out as *chargé d'affairs* rather than as consul general, and Aberdeen, mistakenly concluding that annexation had thus been decisively blocked, specifically forbade him from undertaking any clandestine activities once he got out there: "With reference to our political relations," Elliott was firmly instructed, "I shall wish that you should, at first, assume the attitude, rather of an observer than of an actor, of a passive, but not inattentive spectator rather than of an energetic agent or counseller. You will watch closely all the proceedings of the Texian Govt., not with any hostile view, but simply with the object of putting Your own Govt. in possession of such facts and circumstances as may enable them to form a just estimate of the power and character of the Texian Govt. and Nation, and to judge thereby of the value of the new relations which H.M. has formed with that Republick."[23]

Kennedy was similarly instructed. Agreeably combining his dual roles as Texan consul general in London and British spymaster, he had continued to forward intelligence reports to Aberdeen throughout that summer, and when Elliot's promotion created a vacancy for a consul at Galveston, Kennedy was the obvious choice and was duly appointed to the post on September 29. However, although Aberdeen personally drafted a short note to accompany his official instructions, warning Kennedy against "involving yourself in difficulties with the Ruling Authorities of Texas" and reminding him that his official duties "are confined to the care of British Interests at the Port of Galveston and its immediate neighbourhood," Kennedy nevertheless continued his intelligence-gathering role after his arrival there in February 1843.[24]

This was perhaps all the more necessary because throughout this period a rather desultory war had been spluttering along the western frontier, and in August Mexican forces, led this time by General Adrian Woll, captured Bexar—or rather San Antonio, as it was now becoming more commonly known—and then got the better of the Texian militia in a fight on the Salado on September 17. Afterward Woll withdrew, unmolested, and pressure grew for a retaliatory strike across the Rio Grande. This was precisely what Sam Houston had hoped to avoid, and his reluctance was justified when the mismanaged expedition quickly fell apart. Most of the men, thoroughly soaked by near continuous rain, simply went home; but a significant number barged into the Mexican town of Mier and were promptly attacked, surrounded, and captured by a mixed force of Mexican regulars and militia.

It was now obvious to everyone concerned that while the Mexican Army was incapable of recovering Texas, what passed for a Texan army was equally incapable of holding the frontier against cross-border incursions. However, mediating between the two turned out to be difficult. A proposed joint endeavor with France and the United States was declined by Britain for the perfectly understandable reason that Mexico's relations with both countries were far from cordial, and their interference was more likely to inflame than to calm the situation. Britain's own efforts also seemed to get nowhere, and by June 10, 1843, Texas was driven to announcing that unless there was a cessation of hostilities by December, the republic would assume an "offensive war" against Mexico. Coming as it did in the wake of the Mier fiasco, this threat was decidedly hollow, but quite coincidentally just the previous day Elliot heard from Percy Doyle, the new *chargé d'affairs* in Mexico City, that Santa Anna had agreed to suspend hostilities if Texas would do the same.

This sounded promising, but it soon turned out that Santa Anna was still not prepared to compromise on the issue of sovereignty—his own political survival depended on it. Elliot nevertheless encouraged the Texians to negotiate, arguing that in return for a purely nominal acknowledgment of Mexican sovereignty, they would obtain a permanent cessation of hostilities and de facto independence. Unstated of course was the thought that once acknowledged, that Mexican sovereignty might be transferred to Britain at a later date, if it ever became expedient or desirable to do so. Aberdeen, however, was less sanguine about the prospect and declined to get involved, since he was already embroiled in some less than cordial exchanges with his American counterparts over the issue of slavery.

In July of 1842 some informal proposals had been floated, almost certainly by Glenelg's abolitionist colleague Lord Brougham, that Texas might be reimbursed by Britain for the financial costs arising out of the total abolition of slavery within its borders. These proposals did not actually emanate from the Foreign Office, but it was hinted that Aberdeen knew about and approved of them. At the time nothing came of them, but they resurfaced during an antislavery conference held in London in the summer of 1843 and were subsequently alluded to by Brougham in a debate in the House of Lords on August 18. Rather to everyone's surprise Aberdeen responded to him by hinting that he was already engaged in negotiations on the subject. In a later interview with a startled Edward Everett, the American minister in London, Aberdeen denied that this was so and assured Everett that the negotiations alluded to were being undertaken with the Mexican government rather than the Texan one.

This verbal denial notwithstanding, Aberdeen was soon constrained to send a letter to Pakenham, now promoted to the Washington embassy, stating unequivocally that Britain had no desire to acquire any undue influence in Texas, and that while firmly committed to the universal abolition of slavery, Britain had no intention of influencing the United States through Texas. Pakenham was instructed to show the letter to Abel P. Upshur, the American secretary of state, but the initiative failed, for he was unable to do so until February 26, 1844, just a few days before the latter's untimely death—killed by the explosion of an experimental cannon. Of itself this was a wholly unanticipated setback, and one that quite "disarranged" the State Department, but it was rendered all the more fatal by the appointment of John C. Calhoun as secretary of state in Upsher's place.

Calhoun was at once the most vocal and formidable proponent of slavery in North America and no doubt took considerable satisfaction in advising Pakenham on April 18 that since the abolition of slavery in Texas would be injurious to the interests of the United States, it would be necessary for his country to adopt the most effectual measures to prevent any interference by Britain in bringing it about. Calhoun then underscored the point by adding almost as an afterthought that he had just negotiated a treaty of annexation with Texas.

The announcement should not have come as a surprise, for in March the then Texan secretary of state, Anson Jones, had admitted to Elliot that since Texas had given up hope of a peaceful settlement with Mexico, General Henderson had been sent to Washington with a view to reopening the question of annexation with the altogether more welcoming Calhoun. As it happened, although the treaty was duly signed on April 22, ratification was refused by the U.S. Senate on June 8. Nevertheless, as Kennedy reported in September, this was seen as merely a temporary setback, and the matter was becoming critical: "Had the project of Annexation been favourable to the interests of the traders resident at Corpus Christi, I have good grounds for apprehending that United States' troops would, before this time, have been camped on the Texan territory. If I have not been misinformed, it was suggested to the traders that, if they would manage to 'get up' a pretext for their presence, they would soon be forthcoming."

He had been told, he continued, that "after the failure of the Treaty of Annexation in the Senate of the United States' Congress, General Henderson, the Special Minister of this Republic at Washington, recommended President Tyler to take Military possession of Texas. This has been conveyed to me from a usually well-informed source."[25]

Galvanized into action by the rapidly deteriorating situation, Aberdeen had already informed Ashbel Smith, the new Texan secretary of state, that if the present annexation treaty failed to be ratified, England and France would act jointly to impose a settlement on Mexico and guarantee Texan independence in return for a veto on any future annexation. What was more, from the other side an equally alarmed Santa Anna expressed a willingness to concede recognition of an independent Texas with a frontier on the Colorado—in other words, if the old Hispanic department of Bexar were returned to Mexico, he was prepared to relinquish sovereignty of the rest.[26] As a bargaining position this was at least a start, and even more encouragingly, the proposal survived both his removal in a coup in early December, 1844, and a less dramatic change of government in Texas. But in the meantime, Kennedy's reports were becoming steadily more pessimistic:

I have learned, from competent sources that it will not be owing to General Green's endeavours as a peace-maker if events do not justify the alleged apprehensions of Mexico.—He has urged more than one

Member of the Texan Congress, during his sojourn at Galveston, to declare for the invasion of Mexico—with the view that further territorial aggrandizement,—(even it is said, Southward and Westward of the Rio Grande),—should accompany the Annexation of Texas to the Confederacy of the North.—Before the "espousals" are perfected, it is desired that the bride should bring a still more ample dowry. Nor does it seem likely that the affianced will be backward in supplying needful aid for the accomplishment of this provident object. A Correspondent on whom I can rely thus addresses me from a locality in the United States favourable to apposite observation.

—"Be assured that no child's play operations are at hand. The present moment demands all the devotion and energy of British Servants in this quarter. The accumulation of Military Stores on your frontier still goes on. And Arms, Ammunition, Camp equipage and Ordnance Stores for ten thousand men have already reached Fort Jessup. Mr Calhoun and his party, or section of a party, would prefer war with England to the non-acquisition of Texas, and, to precipitate that calamity upon the United States, or to commit some iniquitous overt act, from which the pride of the people would be unwilling to recede, is, in my opinion the end and aim of the present Administration."

The same Correspondent further remarks—"Texas, it is now sufficiently apparent, is the Key to Mexico, and the fall of the latter and its subjugation by these States are talked of here in a way not to be misunderstood by any but those who are too wise in their own conceit to derive instruction from what is passing around them."[27]

The momentum for annexation, with or without any military intervention, was in fact becoming inexorable on both sides of the Sabine. A joint resolution of the U.S. Congress had finally approved annexation and had been signed on March 1. Thus although at the end of the month Texan Secretary of State Ashbel Smith signed preliminary proposals for a treaty whereby Mexico was to recognize Texan independence providing the republic agreed not to seek annexation by another country, it was too late. The door was now open if Texas wished to enter the Union as a fully fledged state; encouraged by the arrival of a "Corps of Observation" commanded by General Zachary Taylor (just as predicted by Kennedy and his informants), a special convention at Austin duly approved the terms of annexation on July 4, 1845.

9 • *Postscript*

FOR THE UNITED STATES the annexation of Texas paved the way for the final stages of the march to the Pacific Ocean. As William Kennedy noted: "In a letter written by General Andrew Jackson, and published some months before his death, he observed—(on behalf of the American people)—'We want Texas because we want California.'—The Ex-President might have added,—'And we want California because we desire to obtain Maritime ascendancy in the Pacific, with the advantages consequent on an easy and comparatively speedy communication with India and China.'"[1] Just three months after the annexation Zachary Taylor's men were at war with Mexico, and by the end of the hard-fought but ultimately one-sided conflict, Washington had gained the greatest prize of them all: California. In the meantime, on June 15, 1846, a separate but not entirely coincidental treaty was signed between Britain and the United States, settling the last remaining point of contention between the two countries—the Oregon question. Sold to the United States by France as part of the Louisiana Purchase, the Oregon country was claimed by Britain for more than thirty years through right of occupation by its Hudson's Bay Company. But now the issue was pragmatically settled by the concession of an international boundary running along the forty-ninth parallel and by withdrawal of American demands for a foothold on the southern tip of Vancouver Island.

At last the boundaries of the United States extended from sea to shining sea. In retrospect at least, this may seem to have been an inevitable process, but for twenty years and more it was an outcome that Britain and its agents, both authorized and unauthorized, had fought hard to prevent.

The seeming inevitability of the process by which the United States first acquired Texas and then the other North American states of Mexico to gain that permanent foothold on the Pacific Coast, and that "American Road to India" so feared by Henry Ward and the East India Company people, casts a long shadow over James Grant's "visionary" attempt to block the extension of power by forging a republic of northern Mexico.[2] Yet had Fannin been able to move with Grant in late January or early February 1836, it is unlikely that Urrea could have stopped the filibusters and their federalist allies with just one regiment of regular cavalry and a single battalion of untrained conscripts—or even wanted to do so. Grant might well have united with Fernández at Matamoros and so sparked that federalist uprising after all. In September 1839, Antonio Canales—El Zorro—and Grant's old friend Colonel José María Gonzáles did in fact lead another federalist rebellion in the area and proclaimed the independent but short-lived Republic of Rio Grande. This was boldly intended to comprise those self-same states of Tamaulipas, Nuevo León, and Coahuila that were to have been the core of Grant's proposed republic of northern Mexico. To help them win it, Canales and Gonzáles enlisted a whole regiment and more of Texan filibusters, with the tacit approval of the Texan government. They even fought under the Lone Star flag of Texas. But Canales was unable to capture Matamoros and eventually switched sides yet again, betraying his Texan allies in the process and ultimately becoming a brigadier general in the Mexican Army.

Whether Grant could have done any better in 1836 is a moot point, but the prospect itself was clearly far from visionary. It is easy to overlook just how unstable the region was in the early part of the nineteenth century. The United States was itself not much more than half a century old when Grant rode south from San Patricio for the last time, and Mexico had been an independent country for just over a single turbulent decade. It was still an uncertain federation of disparate provinces, and there was no reason why some of them should not make common cause and form a breakaway new republic—or, perhaps, why a Scottish adventurer could not aspire to become its president.

Even the level-headed Charles Elliot thought that such a buffer state might have been a feasible proposition. In a carefully considered memorandum on the possible future of Texas, written in November of 1842, he mused:

Meditating on the situation and prospect of this Country [Texas], and other interests connected with it, I cannot help lamenting more and more that free labor has not been its foundation Stone. The advantages to the Country itself would have been vast indeed, not merely on the results springing from Men's sense that they were laboring for their own and their Children's advantage, not merely in beginning upon sound, instead of rotten principles, not merely in drawing to the land much larger proportions of the orderly and enterprising settlers from the free States of the American Union rather than the reckless people of the South, but because immediately considered it would have left Texas clear of a very dangerous state of circumstances, if the Mexicans do invade the Country, and indeed I cannot but think that to have made Texas a fine State, would have been at once to disarm the hostility of Mexico against its consolidation, and advancement.

Texas, with a free population would of course have been an object of great dislike and suspicion to the South Western States of America, and therefore an effectual barrier between them and Mexico. And it is manifestly the permanent interest of this Country to cultivate more intimate and friendly relations with the people and things Westward of the Rio Grande, than with those East of the Sabine. If wise Councils could be heard here, I think they point to a course which it may not yet be too late to pursue, and which I do fairly believe would be attended with vast advantages to this Country, to our own substantial concernment, and to the great interests of humanity. My scheme supposes another Convention in this Country. Slavery to be abolished, the entire abolition of political disabilities upon people of Colour, *perfectly free trade* to be declared to be a fundamental principle; the right of voting to depend upon a knowledge of reading and writing, and a pretty high money contribution to the State, with the payment charge to be made in advance, Congress to have power to *lower* the rate from time to time according to the state of the public necessities; stringent legislation against squatting, in the form of a land tax and otherwise, improvements upon the well established failure and folly of a yearly elected Legislature and other liberality of the rodomontade [braggart] school.

It seems to be scarcely doubtful that the Northern and North Eastern part of Mexico, from Tampico on the East Coast, to San Blas on the West (involving the most important parts of the Country), would soon find it their interest to join a State founded upon such principles, or at all events constrain their own Government with the adoption of an equally liberal scheme of Commercial policy.

Foreign Merchants, foreign Capital, and foreign enterprise and principles would soon find their way into those great and rich regions by peaceful means, and the power of the United States on this Continent would be gradually balanced, and yet without motive for collision; Indeed it seems possible enough that the North Eastern States would not be disturbed to see the power of the South and West effectually limited, and a bound marked, beyond which Slavery could not advance. In all such speculation the question immediately presents itself how it is reasonable to expect that a Legislature of Slave Holders will ever consent to make a present sacrifice for a prospective and remote advantage. I have had much experience of such bodies and I know that they talk violently of holding on to their property to the last gasp, of the lawfulness of the System, of the sanction of it in the Bible, Abraham's Slaves. . . . And then there are always many hard words about Irish Slaves and press gangs and the like. But in the main, their circumstances make them a timid and needy people, and ready enough to compound reasonably for a monied consideration.

Neither do I doubt that a sufficient loan could be readily raised in England to enable this Government to compensate the present Slave Holders, upon the frank and full adoption of such a system as I have spoken of. I attach great importance to the entire abolition of disability upon people of Colour. Such a Stipulation would at once bring into this Republic tens of thousands of most abused and intelligent people from the United States, and would be exceedingly agreeable to a very influential and wealthy party.[3]

There was nothing new in this assessment, of course, other than the considerable depth and clarity with which Elliot set out British thinking on the subject—including the proposition of a compensation scheme for Texas slave holders. Not the least intriguing aspect of the memorandum is perhaps that startling reference to the likelihood of Texas being joined by those other Mexican states north of a line "from Tampico on the East Coast, to San Blas on the West." There Elliot repeats almost word for word Jorge Fisher's account to Stephen Austin of the federalists' plans and James Grant's own assertion, as reported by Creed Taylor, that "it would only be a question of time when Tamaulipas, Nuevo Leon, Chihuahua, Coahuila, and New Mexico, would unite with Texas and form a new republic." Clearly, the Foreign Office knew a lot more about Grant's activities in 1835 and 1836 than it was ever willing to admit publicly.

Given better luck and better management, he might have succeeded in creating the Greater Texas that he and Elliot imagined. In the end he was defeated not by destiny, manifest or otherwise, but by Santa Anna and Sam Houston—with more than just a little help from Juan José de Urrea. In defeat, the man who would be king was condemned to obscurity and unjustly remembered merely as an unscrupulous land speculator. But at the time, most of those who knew him regarded him very highly indeed—although we may allow for some humbugging in the words of Abner Lipscombe, President Lamar's secretary of state. "Dr. Grant was an officer, in the service of the Texas Government when he was slain, and no man's memory is held in more respect by the people of this country than his," declared Lipscombe in 1840 in response to Pakenham's representations on behalf of Grant's "numerous children."[4] The story of Grant's will and the search for his money turned out to be as convoluted and mysterious as his life.

Grant wrote his will at Bexar on December 29, 1835, "on the eve of marching on an Expedition and without the possibility of making a Will & Testament in due form." Although it was drafted in some haste and to all appearances cut off short at the end, the outline was clear enough. There was a personal bequest to his younger brother Hugh Grant, who had gone out to Mexico with him, but ultimately his estate was to be divided equally between his nine children, and he named two principal executors; one was his brother, and the other was his business partner, Daniel J. Toler. Both men were to act jointly until his eldest son, Stewart, came of age and could be joined with one or other of them. In the circumstances it was only prudent that he also named two additional executors, Frank Johnson and an attorney named John Alexander Newlands, to act in place of either or both of the others if necessary. That the will survived at all was down to sheer chance, for as Daniel Toler afterward told it: "Mosely Baker going into his Office at San Felipe to rescue all he could previous to the destruction of that place in 1836—Shoved his hand into one of the pigeon holes of a desk & out came the said Will along with some other papers, and he, Toler got it from a friend on the Trinity at the time of the Run-away-scrape."[5]

Having so fortuitously come into possession of the will, Toler then proceeded to have it proven, without reference to Hugh Grant, and succeeded in obtaining Letters Testamentary on May 22, 1838, after Newlands obligingly swore on his behalf that Hugh was "not a citizen of this Republic and is not within the limits of Texas but is a resident of Louisiana in the United States of America." Then on November 1 Toler, together with Newlands, Thomas McKinney, and Augustus Allen, posted a sixty-thousand-dollar bond with the Texas courts in order to have himself officially recognized as the sole execu-tor.[6] As will become apparent, all four of those posting the bond had a strong vested interest in the contents of the will, but Hugh Grant somehow gained word of what was afoot and moved fast to thwart them. When James was arrested by General Cos in the summer of 1835, Hugh had fled to New Orleans and thereafter seemed curiously reluctant to leave the place. Understandably enough, like Toler, he probably "could not go to Mexico again, for fear of his life," but it is less easy to account for his equally firm refusal to show his face in Texas—particularly in view of what was at stake. He knew that Toler was fraudulently trying to gain complete control of the estate, but he may have been intimidated by the involvement of the infamous "Nacogdoches land men" and so feared that his existence might be equally precarious in Texas. At any rate, before the month was out his own agent, another Scot named James Ogilvie, turned up in Texas armed with a power of attorney.[7]

Unsurprisingly, Toler was far from pleased to see him. Immediately upon arriving in the recently founded city of Houston on December 6, Ogilvie called first upon Newlands, who had of course once been James Grant's attorney, and he in turn introduced Ogilvie to Toler the next day. An appointment was thereupon made "for the purpose of convers-ing upon the affairs of Dr. Grant," but Toler failed to show up for the meeting, and it was not until the following week that Ogilvie actually managed to back him into a corner. Even then Toler proved defensive and uncooperative, turning up with Newlands and another associate at his elbow and betraying what was all too obviously a guilty conscience: "Mr. Toler asked if I had any letters from Mr. Hugh Grant for him— none—a power of Attorney was all which he wished to see—on perusal was offended at the words 'fraudulent &c' said he had no objection to let Mr. Hugh Grant be joined with him in the Executorship, but he must come here in person—that an Agent could not execute the duties of the will." Therein of course lay the problem, for that was exactly what Hugh was not prepared to do—and Toler undoubtedly knew it. Nevertheless, nothing daunted, Ogilvie set about petitioning the probate court to be admitted as coadministrator and in the meantime managed to obtain his own office copy of the will.

Notwithstanding some obstruction from Toler's attorney—a rather shady character named John Charles Watrous, who turned out to be none other than the attorney general of Texas—Ogilvie duly obtained from the court on December 31 the necessary authority to act as an administrator. But Watrous sulkily continued to insist "that an agent cannot execute the will of a deceased person in place of a proper Executor—the testator never intended such a transfer & that although the Court had acted upon this belief, it was not according to law. He admitted this practice was, even, common in Louisiana, but that it was proper he was convinced it was not so."[8] Watrous's bluster was unavailing, and Toler, now forced to cooperate rather than simply bow and pass on in the street as usual, rather grudgingly filled out the rather cryptic inventory left by Grant:

Of my Parras property I have nothing to say to men acquainted with my affairs. Newlands will account for a large amount & Dr. Cameron in case of any accident to Newland[s] can give every information on the same head. Samuel M. Williams of the House of McKinney & Williams of Quintana near Brazoria has also to account for the one-half of the proceeds of a joint speculation of considerable magnitude on acct. of which I have received some advances. Williams is also bound to give 50,000 stock to me & my friend in the Texas Bank which is to be divided out in the terms mentioned to my brother Hugh, to Mr. Toler & others. Some government claims in the hands of Hebenstreit, particulars known to St Cruz. And a speculation set on foot between myself, Cameron & F. W. Johnson, but whether it will take effect or not is as yet uncertain. A few soldiers claims who were at the taking of Bexar 640 acres ea. & my own for the same or a larger amount, are worthy of notice & are left with Mr. Alfred Guild to be forwarded to Mr. Newlands or Mr. Cameron: There [sic] merits must serve as I have no time to add more."[9]

As Toler now told it, much of this was worthless. There was nothing of course to be done about the Parras property, which he had recently heard had been valued at $105,000. The Texas bank, as Toler remarked, "turned out to be a Bubble," so there had been no stock issue. Similarly, the proposed "speculation" (whatever its nature) with Dr. John Cameron and Frank Johnson never took effect, and the claims left in the hands of Maurice Hebenstreit were against the now defunct government of Coahuila y Texas and so equally valueless. In response to one of the points in a memorandum Hugh Grant had furnished to Ogilvie, Toler added that "James Bowie was greatly indebted to Dr Grant for money advanced, and that the agreement about the 100 Leagues of Land never was perfected." Finally, the soldiers' claims, it transpired, had indeed been recovered from Guild and related to five Tejano soldiers: Mathias Curbier, Anselm Arredendo, Manuel Flores, Agapita Gartan, and Lucio Emegoy. But like Grant's own headright claim for the same service, they had yet to be confirmed.

All of that, however, was small fry when it came to land matters. The "large amount" to be accounted for by Newlands and the "joint speculation of considerable magnitude" with Samuel M. Williams of McKinney and Williams were both tied up in that purchase of three hundred leagues of land from the state of Coahuila y Texas on April 16, 1835. One third of them, as we have seen earlier, were reserved for Grant himself, who passed them on to Newlands, while another hundred went to John M. Durst, and the remainder were passed to Sam Williams, who was to retain half for himself and sell the rest for Grant, less an advance already made to him of fifteen thousand dollars' worth of supplies for Hacienda los Hornos. Exactly what happened to the certificates relating to all this land was at first unclear, although at one point Toler produced a letter addressed to Grant from an associate in New York, stating that "after much dunning" he had obtained $250 from Sam Williams but had heard that Williams had realized something like $75,000 "for certain Certificates." The implication of course was that these were the certificates given to him by Grant, rather than Grant's own. Williams himself, when later questioned, claimed that those belonging to Grant had all been taken to New Orleans for safekeeping, which may be why Hugh Grant had been able to obtain notarized copies of some of them. The full truth of the matter never came to light, but if Williams did sell some or all of the certificates, he did so doubly fraudulently, for at Sam Houston's instigation the provisional government had suspended the Coahuila land sales and closed down the land offices in November 1835. The Williams certificates were therefore worthless.

On the other hand, however, as Ogilvie had already been briefed by Hugh Grant, the one hundred certificates belonging to Grant himself, which he had given to Newlands when he was arrested by Cos at Gigedo in June of 1835, were subsequently passed on for an agreed price of four hundred dollars apiece to John and Augustus Allen. The Allens were Nacogdoches-based land speculators and businessmen who at the time provided much of the funding for the Texian army and later founded the city of Houston. Once again there was a problem in getting these certificates properly registered, but in this case there was every chance their validity would be accepted for, as was no doubt urged by Grant and Newlands, although they had not yet paid for the certificates, the Allens had had the location surveys carried out "before the Declaration of Independence."[10]

The significance of this was twofold: not only did it mean that the necessary validation procedures for the certificates had been carried out before the provisional government's moratorium, but the very fact that they had been thus processed obviously knocks out a very considerable plank from the lingering accusations that James Grant instigated the Matamoros expedition merely in order to validate the land grants. Furthermore, although the land offices had officially been closed in November 1835, and the Texas constitution had subsequently included a clause annulling all Coahuila land sales after 1833, the admissibility of such retrospective legislation was at best questionable.

This no doubt explained why the attorney, in a chance meeting, congratulated Ogilvie on his progress and commented that "he was also glad on his own Account as he had *considerable depending on it!!!*"[11] Just how considerable may be gauged from the fact that according to the agreement in Hugh's possession, although the Allens were still bound to pay four hundred dollars for each certificate, they were then to divide the profits when the certificates were subsequently sold on for not less than one thousand dollars a time.

In the meantime the matter was before the courts, ostensibly because President Houston's government, relying on the 1836 constitution, had refused to recognize them: "I asked the reason why the Executors had to sue the Government of Texas for the 100 Leagues of Land," wrote Ogilvie, "and not the Allens? and his [Toler's] reply was that as the claim was in Grant's name, it was requisite also to use, his, Dr Grant's name,—Get possession of the lands and then settle with the Allens." It is a measure of just how muddy the business was that Watrous, who had "undertaken the management of the suit against the Government" on behalf of Toler, openly admitted that he had taken the post of attorney general only in order to try the case! Newlands, on the other hand, rather more sensibly agreed with Ogilvie that "the intended suit against the Govt is all folly, we are, or rather the Allens are in possession of the Lands and no one disputes their claim." In fact John Allen was now dead, but the surviving brother Augustus, who had earlier helped post Toler's bond, was sufficiently sure of himself to propose that in settlement of the brothers' claim for over nine thousand dollars, including interest, spent on locating and surveying the lands, he would return forty certificates to Hugh Grant and retain sixty for himself. This was contrary to what Newlands claimed was the original agreement—that they would bear their own costs in locating the lands—but Ogilvie, taking a realistic view, nevertheless forwarded the proposal to both Hugh Grant and his fellow executor, Daniel Toler.

How they responded to it is unclear, but Ogilvie continued his dogged pursuit of the various certificates and, after returning to New Orleans, wrote to Richard Pakenham on August 20, explaining: "Doctor Grant was interested, directly, in contracts with the Government of the State of Coahuila and Texas for the purchase of 350 Certificates, calling for a *Sitio* of land each, in the vacant tracts of the State, and indirectly, in 150 similar Certificates."[12] This total appears to have been arrived at by including all three hundred certificates purchased by Grant in April 1835, even although half of them actually belonged to Durst and Williams, while the other fifty had been privately acquired from another speculator, John T. Mason, only to be lost when the messenger entrusted with them was allegedly killed by Indians. As to those certificates in which Ogilvie claimed Grant had an indirect interest: one hundred were presumably those promised him by James Bowie—which throws an interesting light on the sudden enmity displayed toward Grant by Bowie during the revolution.

At this point the validity of any of the certificates had yet to be recognized, and so Ogilvie asked for Pakenham's interposition, since "unless we succeed in making good these contracts, there will not be sufficient to satisfy the just claims on the Estate, far less to relieve the pressing necessities of his numerous children."

Pakenham duly brought the matter up with the Texian government, only to receive the discouraging response:

> His heirs have large and well founded claims for land in this Republic, there is no doubt, and there can be none, as to there being sustained, without the Agency of Mr Ogilvy. Dr Grant on entering in the war, made a will appointing a Mr Toler a respectable Citizen of this Republic, and Mr Grant his brother in Scotland, his Executors. The former has had the will duly proven, and is qualified, as Executor, and is now making progress in the Settlement of the Estate, Mr Grant has never come to this country. Should he do so, the law will allow him, to join Mr Toler in the Administration, but until he gives and takes the Oath for the faithful discharge of his duty as Executor, Mr Toler will have sole management of the affairs of the estate. He has given bond and Security as required by law, and there can be no doubt, that the interest of the heirs of Dr Grant will be faithfully guarded by him.[13]

Just how "respectable" Toler was may be open to question, but there was good reason for referring to Ogilvie in the past tense and noting that Toler had sole management of the estate, for it appears that Ogilvie was dead by the time Lipscombe wrote this letter. At any rate Adolphus Sterne noted on September 28 that Ogilvie had died at his house in Nacogdoches "some time ago." Just what he was doing in Nacogdoches and whether there were any suspicious circumstances surrounding his death are not clear, but with Hugh Grant still reluctant as ever to accept Lipscombe's invitation to come to Texas, and Stewart Grant still in Scotland, Daniel Toler was indeed the sole executor.

Over the next few years Toler eventually succeeded in securing all of Grant's various bounty, headright, and donation claims in November 1845—although it took the personal intervention of the republic's secretary of war, the same William Gordon Cooke who had once marched with Grant as commander of the San Antonio Greys—and then Toler promptly sold them for a derisory $236.[14] Finally on May 1, 1852, having somehow recovered all of the certificates from Augustus Allen, he also obtained a court order empowering him to sell the one hundred leagues of land purchased by Grant in April 1835; Toler sold them on August 4. At one stage, while the Allens had them, the certificates had been estimated to be worth more than $100,000, but now the only bidder was a certain Henry K. Toler, who paid just $2,000 for them, which sum was immediately applied to the "debts" accrued on the estate.[15] Whether Guadalupe Reyes ever recovered the Hacienda los Hornos is not known, but Grant's Scottish children certainly got nothing.

As for some of the others who, wittingly or unwittingly, found themselves caught up in the story: Hugh Grant died of cholera in New Orleans on May 24, 1855; Grant's cousin Lord Glenelg was eventually forced to resign as colonial secretary in February 1838, since his utter incapacity had by then become all too obvious, even to his friends. As a peer, he continued to sit in the House of Lords, but plagued by increasing financial difficulties, he took no active part in public life and died in comparative poverty at Cannes in 1866. After his return to England, Henry Ward published the inevitable book, *Mexico in 1827*. Its two volumes provided an invaluable description of the country and in particular its mines and industries, but so far as his own activities there were concerned, it was very much a work of fiction. It may temporarily have alleviated the financial difficulties that provided the ostensible cause of his recall, and in 1833 he entered Parliament as the member first for St. Albans and then for Sheffield, gaining a considerable reputation as a radical—and an opponent of Palmerston's stance on the Texas question. He joined the government as secretary to the Admiralty in 1846 but then entered the colonial service as lord high commissioner in the Ionian Islands three years later. Subsequently, he became governor of Ceylon in 1855 and then Madras in 1860—before dying there of cholera in August of that year. His work done, William Kennedy left Texas on sick leave on September 18, 1846, and was not replaced as consul at Galveston until May 1850. His health does in fact seem to have been poor; by that time he had retired on a government pension, and he eventually died in Paris in 1871. Sir Charles Elliot also left Texas in 1846 and afterward successively served as governor of Bermuda, Trinidad, and St. Helena; he died in 1875. Arthur Wavell, on the other hand, never seemed to prosper. After the Fredonian debacle his colonization efforts came to nothing, and his attempts to realize the value of his empresario grants got nowhere. He died in London in July 1860, and is now perhaps best known as the grandfather of Field Marshal Sir Archibald Wavell.

In Texas, James Grant's "bitter enemy" Sam Houston did rather better than all of them, serving two terms as president of the republic. Following its annexation he was elected to represent the new state in the U.S. Senate before becoming governor of Texas in 1859—a post he held until removed from office two years later for refusing to take the oath of allegiance to the Confederacy. The hapless Frank Johnson drifted into obscurity after his escape from San Patricio, but in 1873 he became the founding president of the Texas Veterans Association and then spent the remainder of his long life researching and writing on the history of Texas—an agreeable task that allowed him to claim a far more important role in the proceedings than was probably the case. Another survivor was of course Reuben Brown. After his capture at Agua Dulce he was imprisoned for some ten months in Matamoros before eventually making his escape with Samuel McKneely. Settling in Texas, he became a prosperous planter and then during the Civil War a colonel in the Confederate Army. He died on March 2, 1894—fifty-eight years to the day after he had seen James Grant run down and killed by a Mexican lancer.

Appendix: Grant's Men

A BIOGRAPHICAL DICTIONARY

This is a listing of all the men so far identified as belonging to the two companies that went forward with James Grant to San Patricio at the end of January 1836, and afterward followed him to the Rio Grande. One company was commanded by Captain Thomas Lewellen and the other by Captain Thomas Pearson. Fortunately the transcript of a final roster for Lewellen's company survives in the Land Office Muster Rolls, but none has been found for Pearson's company or Captain Plácido Benavides's Federalistas, and consequently the listing remains incomplete.

The compilation presented here is therefore largely based on the work of the late Harbert Davenport, who included some of Grant's men in an unfinished study of Fannin's command intended to complement Amelia Williams's work on Alamo defenders.[1] A thorough revision and expansion has however been undertaken, and while a number of soldiers have here been added to Davenport's lists, others have been removed or his identifications have been questioned.

STAFF

Colonel Francis (Frank) White Johnson
Born near Leesburg, Virginia, on October 3, 1799, and originally trained as a surveyor, he came to Texas in 1826, laid out Harrisburg in that year, and was afterward the surveyor in the Ayish district and then surveyor-general of Austin's colony in 1832. An able but frequently intemperate Austin supporter, he became alcalde of San Felipe de Austin in 1831, led a militia company during the Anahuac disturbances of 1832, and was a delegate to the constitutional convention in that year. In 1835 he went to

Monclova, ostensibly as an observer at the proceedings of the state legis-lature, met James Grant for the first time, and was associated with Samuel Williams in obtaining some of the controversial land certificates. During the siege of Bexar he was appointed adjutant and inspector general of the army, and during the assault on the town he initially commanded one of the two columns before succeeding to operational control of all the forces in the town after the death of Ben Milam. Subsequently left in command of the forces at Bexar, he and Grant immediately proceeded to reorganize them in preparation for the projected Matamoros expe-dition. However, while Johnson was absent at San Felipe, Grant took command and marched the army down to Goliad. Johnson eventually caught up at Refugio but never succeeded in reestablishing his authority. Surprised by Urrea at San Patricio on February 27, he managed to escape but took no further part in the revolution. Traveling widely and unsuc-cessfully, he was something of a recluse when he died at Aguascalientes, Mexico, on or about April 8, 1884.

Major Robert C. Morris

Seemingly a native of New Orleans and an apothecary by trade, Morris was introduced to Stephen Austin in October 1835, as having served five or six years in a local volunteer unit called the Louisiana Guards; he was recommended to Stephen Austin by J. W. Collins of New Orleans as a "soldier and tactician."[2] He was also, as it turned out, something of an alarmist, but this did not prevent him from successively being elected captain of one of the two companies of New Orleans Greys and then major of the provisional regiment. At the storming of Bexar he was originally second in command of Ben Milam's column, but when all the Texian forces in the town were consolidated after the death of Milam and wounding of Grant, he became Frank Johnson's second in com-mand. Afterward he declined a commission in the regular army of Texas to march south with Grant and stuck by him after Houston's interven-tion at Refugio. In command for a time at San Patricio, he informed William Cooke on February 10 that he was no longer in the service of Texas but had accepted the command of a regiment in the federal service of Mexico and then rode with Grant to the Rio Grande. He was killed in action at Agua Dulce on March 2, 1836, and in 1858 Reuben Brown recalled that after his own horse went down, "Grant told me to mount Maj. Morris' horse, as Morris had just been killed."

Captain Nathaniel R. Brister

A Virginian, he was originally first sergeant of the New Orleans Greys, before being appointed adjutant of Ben Milam's column for the storming of Bexar. Subsequently he stayed on as Frank Johnson's adjutant when the Federal Volunteer Army was organized. At the end of December he accompanied Johnson to San Felipe and rejoined the army with him at Refugio, from where the two followed Grant to San Patricio. When Cooke was recalled to Goliad in mid-February, Brister went with him and was appointed adjutant of Fannin's 1st Texas Volunteers. He was killed in the massacre at Goliad on March 27.

Don Plácido Benavides

Originally a native of Reynosa, Benavides was alcalde of Guadalupe Victoria at the outbreak of the Texan revolt. A committed federalist, he took part in the capture of Goliad and later led a company at the siege of Bexar. Afterward he and his men went south with Colonel José María Gonzáles to raise the Tamaulipas Federalistas and, based at Camargo, acted as a go-between for Grant and the authorities in Matamoros. Escaping from the ambush at Agua Dulce, he returned home to Victoria and was left undisturbed there by Urrea's forces. Unfortunately, after the revolution anti-Mexican feeling eventually forced him to flee to New Orleans, and he died at Opelousas, Louisiana, in 1837. Identifying his men has largely been impossible, beyond the fact that they certainly included four named Arreola, Cayetano, Plaude, and Zambrano, who were taken prisoner at either San Patricio or Agua Dulce. Another may have been a Vicente Aldrete, who witnessed Grant's will at Bexar in December 1835, and they may also have included the five Tejano soldiers whose claims were held by Grant—Mathias Curbier, Anselm Arredendo, Manuel Flores, Agapita Gartan, and Lucio Emegoy—since neither they nor Aldrete appear to have survived the revolution.[3]

Daniel J. Toler

Strictly speaking Daniel Toler was not a soldier but Grant's business partner in Coahuila, but he may have acted as quartermaster after joining Grant at San Patricio at the beginning of February. At any rate he claimed in December 1836, to have supplied Grant and his men with money, mules, horses, and arms to a total value in excess of seven hundred dollars, although he was never able to substantiate it. He was in San

Patricio when Urrea struck on February 27, and according to Johnson it was Toler's knowledge of the "Castilian tongue" that won him and the other survivors precious time to escape. Settling in Washington County after the revolution, he effectively exploited the fact of being one of the executors to gain control of Grant's estate, as described in Chapter 9.

LEWELLEN'S COMPANY

Captain Thomas Lewellen

Lewellen (as he invariably signed himself) originally joined Captain Henry Augustine's company, recruited from around San Augustine, Texas, and became its commander during the fighting at Bexar. In the reorganization of the army that followed the end of the siege he was named as commander of a new infantry company seemingly formed by combining the remains of the various Texas companies with the surviving members of Captain John Peacock's United States Invincibles, an American volunteer company from Mississippi. In January he marched with Grant to Goliad and at Refugio elected to follow him to San Patricio and down to the Rio Grande. The captain and his company were closely associated with Grant in the operations that followed, and Lewellen died with most of them at Agua Dulce.

First Sergeant Hutchins M. Pittman

Captured at San Patricio, Pittman is on a list of prisoners held at Matamoros that appeared in the *New Orleans Commercial Bulletin* for May 27, 1836. There he was described as "Hutchings M. Pittman, aged 26, born in Wilson, Ten. son of William Pittman"; he had actually enlisted at Clinton, Mississippi, as a member of Peacock's United States Invincibles. Released on January 29, 1837, Pittman settled in Bexar County, Texas, and on April 17, 1850, supplied the adjutant general's office with a copy of the company's roster, certified by him as having been correctly transcribed from a pencil original in his possession, which presumably he had retained throughout his captivity.[4]

Sergeant McJohnson

The transcript of Pittman's roster that survives in the Land Office Muster Rolls reads as if McJohnson's given name was "Sargeant," but since Pittman described himself as the company's first sergeant, it is more likely that he was identifying McJohnson by rank rather than by name. The roll has a notation indicating that he was killed, probably at Agua Dulce.

William B. Benson

Benson appears both on Pittman's roll and in the *New Orleans Commercial Bulletin* list of Matamoros prisoners as William B. Benson. Described there as "Aged 20 years, born in Cincinnati, Ohio," he was captured with Pittman at San Patricio. On the Convention roll signed at Refugio on or about February 5, 1836, there appears to be a James B. Benson, who may be the same man.

Reuben R. Brown

According to the 1836 *New Orleans Commercial Bulletin* list, Brown was then aged twenty-two and had been born in Green County, Georgia, but his gravestone gives his date of birth as 1812, not 1814. At any rate he arrived in Texas in November 1835, with Hugh and John H. Love, also of Georgia. They traveled overland from Nacogdoches to Bexar, arriving there the day following the capitulation of Cos, and joined Captain B. L. Lawrence's United States Independent Cavalry Company. At Refugio, however, Brown transferred to Lewellen's company, went south with Grant, and was with him when he was killed. Captured at Agua Dulce, Brown was imprisoned at Matamoros until making his escape with Samuel McKneely in December 1836. Subsequently he wrote at least two important narratives of the campaign (Lamar Papers, no. 1645, and in the *Texas Almanac*, 1858). Settling in Texas, he had a small plantation at Jones Creek and in 1861 became lieutenant colonel of the 13th Texas Infantry. In January 1863, he transferred with the mounted element of the regiment to the 12th Texas Cavalry Battalion, serving in Louisiana until October, after which the battalion was expanded to become the 35th (Brown's) Texas Cavalry, serving in the Galveston area. He died on March 2, 1894, and is buried in the Gulf Coast Cemetery at Jones Creek, Texas.[5]

John W. Bryan

Carried on Pittman's roll, Bryan enlisted at San Augustine, Texas, on October 10, 1835, served at the storming of Bexar, and afterward stayed on under Lewellen. He was taken prisoner at San Patricio and described as "John W. Bryan, aged 26, born in Georgia."

James M. Cass

Cass arrived in Texas as a member of the New Orleans Greys, According to an early printed roster he came from Connecticut, although Reuben Brown thought he was from Philadelphia. Cass was wounded during the siege of Bexar and on some lists, including the *Telegraph and Texas Register* roll, he is included among those killed at Goliad; but Brown specifically recalled that Cass was one of those who went to the Rio Grande, and so presumably he died at either San Patricio or Agua Dulce.[6]

Stillman S. Curtis

A one-time member of Captain John Chenoweth's company, Curtis appears both on Pittman's roll and in the *New Orleans Commercial Bulletin* list of Matamoros prisoners, where he is identified as "S. S. Curtis, aged 23, born in Madison County, New York." Together with Brown and Jones he had been captured at Agua Dulce. Oddly enough Chenoweth has Curtis marked down in his own roll as "killed," presumably knowing only that he had ridden off with Grant and did not come back. This is not the only instance of Chenoweth still claiming one of Grant's men as his own—probably in order to establish himself as administrator of Curtis's estate.

Stephen Dennison

A British-born painter and glazier, Dennison was twenty-four years old when he came to Texas as a member of the New Orleans Greys and was one of those who transferred to Burke's company at Bexar and signed the Convention Memorial at Refugio with them on or about February 5, 1836. He must subsequently have transferred again, this time to Lewellen's company when Cooke took the reinforcement down to the Irish village on February 9, for he appears on Pittman's roll with the annotation "killed"—presumably at Agua Dulce. Dennison is also claimed as an Alamo defender on the strength of a headright claim presented by an H. F. Smith of Louisville, Kentucky, who stated that he died there, but as Dennison must have ridden south with Grant on February 10, this is clearly an error.[7]

Sebastian Francois

Originally a member of Captain Augustine's company, Francois appears on Pittman's roll, showing that after the siege of Bexar he joined

Lewellen's company and was subsequently taken prisoner at San Patricio; he is referred to as a "young Creole from Missouri who spoke Spanish."[8] The *New Orleans Commercial Bulletin* list of Matamoros prisoners identifies him as "Sebastian Francis, aged 20, a native of France, friends in Ohio." Like most of the other Matamoros prisoners he was released on January 29, 1837.

William James Gatlin

Gatlin came to Texas as a member of Captain Thomas H. Breece's company of New Orleans Greys. He signed the Convention Memorial at Refugio early in February 1836, but his name also appears on Pittman's roll of Lewellen's company as well as on the *Telegraph and Texas Register* roster as a member of Burke's company. This indicates that, like Dennison, he transferred to Burke's company at Bexar and subsequently joined Lewellen's company at San Patricio on February 9. Luckier at first than Dennison, Gatlin was one of five (or possibly six) men who escaped from the debacle at Agua Dulce and so rejoined Burke's company, only to die with them at Goliad. Thomas H. Gatlin collected his pay as attorney for and heir to William Gatlin, Sr., his father.

William Hall

Little is known of this man other than that he appears on Pittman's roll and is presumably one of two men of this name who signed the Convention Memorial at Refugio. One of them, William L. Hall, signed his name next to Stephen Dennison on the list and is probably the man in question. At any rate, having been captured at San Patricio, he also appears in the *New Orleans Commercial Bulletin* list of Matamoros prisoners, where he is identified as "W. Hall, aged 24, born in England."

Dr. Charles P. Heartt

Recorded on Pittman's roll is "Doct. Hart"; identification of this man is not entirely certain. Heartt originally came from Mississippi as part of Captain John W. Peacock's company, and it was believed there that he and Horace Ovid Marshall from Grand Gulf died with Grant. However, the subsequent donation grant to Heartt's heirs was for service with Fannin, and he was stated to have died at Goliad. On the other hand, William Brenan of Pettus's Mobile Greys afterward certified his belief that Heartt actually died at San Patricio. A Doctor "Hart" was certainly among those reported killed there, but it is likely that this man's name was really Hort or Hoyt—(see the entry for him under Pearson's company)—and that Heartt may actually have died at Agua Dulce.

Thomas Hicks

Hick's name appears on Pittman's roll with the notation that he was killed, but Harbert Davenport identified him as Joseph W. Hicks and wrote that "Hicks was a Kentuckian, who enlisted at San Felipe Dec. 10, 1835, along with M. Hawkins, A. Swords and A. D. Larison, as volunteers for the reduction of Bexar. At Bexar, Dec. 12th, he joined Llewellyn's Company, and was paid, as a member of that organization for the period Dec. 12, 1835 to March 12, 1836, and his name, somewhat disguised, appears on Pittman's muster roll for that Company. He was not killed, however, at San Patricio or Agua Dulce, but continued in the service of Texas until 1838, when he was either killed or died in the service." Bounty and donation certificates were also issued for Joseph W. Hicks, which would strengthen this identification, although they do not rule out the strong possibility that he and Pittman's "Thomas" Hicks were two different individuals.

J. T. Howard

All that is known of this soldier is that he appears on Pittman's roll with the annotation "killed."

Joseph Smith Johnson

Johnson's name appears without annotation on Pittman's roll, but on January 25, 1841, Branch T. Archer, secretary of war, certified that "Joseph Smith Johnson, deceased, was entitled to pay as private in Captain _____ _____'s Company of Fannin's Command to March 27, 1836; that he entered the service of Texas October 20, 1836, and that W. G. Anderson, as attorney for James Taber, administrator, was entitled to collect his pay."[9] Having himself been captured at San Patricio, Pittman was tolerably hazy about what happened to those members of the company who were at Agua Dulce, but there seems no reason to doubt that Johnson died there rather than at Goliad, since he does not turn up with other survivors on the rolls of Burke's company.

Nelson Jones
Listed on Pittman's roll, and a signatory of the Convention roll at Refugio, Jones was captured at Agua Dulce and rather confusingly seems to appear in the *New Orleans Commercial Bulletin* list of Matamoros prisoners as "James Wilson, aged 23, born in corner Spring and Sullivan streets, New York." First appearances to the contrary, there is no doubt that this is the same man, for "N. Jones" is listed as a prisoner in both *The National Banner and Nashville Whig*, of Nashville, Tennessee, in its issue for May 13, 1836, and the *Kentucky Gazette*, of Louisville, Kentucky, on May 23, 1836. "James Wilson" would seem to be a transcription error for "Jones, Nelson."

Lewis H. Kerr
Kerr is listed both on Pittman's roll and in the *New Orleans Commercial Bulletin* list of Matamoros prisoners as "Lewis H. Kerr, aged 33, born in Pennsylvania." He was apparently captured with Pittman at San Patricio.

John Kornicky
Appearing on Pittman's roll as J. Kornickey, this man was evidently Polish, and a note in the Nashville *Union* of November 24, 1835, mentions that he and John F. Beck had just left for Texas. He almost certainly returned from San Patricio with the guns on about February 15, rather than following Grant down to the Rio Grande, for he appears to have been one of four Polish gunners killed at Encinal del Perdido on March 19.

John H. Love
A Georgian, he came to Texas with Reuben Brown and initially joined Captain Benjamin Lawrence's United States Independent Cavalry Company, before transferring with Brown to Lewellen's company and following Grant down to the Rio Grande. At San Patricio in the early hours of February 27, he was with Frank Johnson and Daniel Toler when Urrea attacked. Love succeeded in escaping with them, first to Goliad and then to San Felipe.

Samuel W. McKneely
This soldier is listed on Pittman's roll as Samuel W. McNeely; on Chenoweth's as S. W. McNeilly, and in the *New Orleans Commercial Bulletin*

list as "S. W. McKinly, aged 17, born in East Feliciana, Jacksontown, La." He originally enlisted with Chenoweth, transferred to Lewellen's company, and was captured at San Patricio. He and Reuben Brown escaped together from Matamoros in December 1836, and when Brown wrote of his adventures in 1858, McKneely was a member of the Louisiana legislature. In 1874 he was living in Point Coupee Parish, Louisiana.

Andrew J. Miller

Identification of this soldier is uncertain. General Land Office file Fannin Donation no. 387 has certificate no. 547, which states that Miller "participated in the battle under Grant and Johnson." GLO file Fannin Bounty no. 430 similarly has bounty warrant no. 2057, which says he was "killed with Grant and Johnson."[10] Pittman's list certainly includes a soldier named Miller, who is noted to have escaped, only to be killed with Ward's command. However no first name is recorded for him on the roll, and it seems more likely that the man referred to may have been James Miller.

James M. Miller

In his 1858 account Reuben Brown remembered that one of his companions was "James M. Miller, nephew of Gov. Stephen Miller, of South Carolina." This is probably the soldier who appears on Pittman's roll, since Frank Johnson stated that he and John Love escaped with him from San Patricio, but "Miller, who joined Fannin, was butchered with his command"—which accords with Pittman's note that Miller "escaped and [was] killed with Major Ward." It is quite possible, however, that Brown may have been mistaken as to this man's name and that he is actually the same Andrew J. (James?) Miller already recorded.

Thomas S. Mitchell

At the time of his enlistment Mitchell was a resident of Power and Hewitson's colony in Texas and Reuben Marmaduke Potter refers to him as an Irishman, but the *New Orleans Commercial Bulletin* list describes him as "Thomas S. Mitchell, aged 24 years, born in Coswell, Milton County, North Carolina."[11] Whatever the truth of the matter, he was captured with Pittman's party at San Patricio but was either released or, like Brown and McKneely, succeeded in making his escape from Matamoros at some unknown date.

David Moses

Listed on Pittman's roll with the annotation "killed," Moses was one of those who escaped from the debacle at Agua Dulce. The next day Lewis T. Ayers recorded in his journal: "I walked out this morning, and saw a man approaching the house with great caution. I went toward him and called him to me. He proved to be a volunteer by name of Moses who made his escape from an engagement which took place yesterday about 20 miles beyond San Patricio between the other portion of the small force which composed the party of Col. Johnson, Grant, &c., Col. Grant commanded and was killed, as also Major Morris and most of the men. I took Moses to my house and gave him his breakfast, after which I went with him to Goliad. One horse carried our baggage. . . . We arrived at Goliad about 8 o'clock."[12] Presumably Moses later died with Fannin's command.

Robert Randolph

Randolph is listed on Pittman's roll with the annotation "killed"—probably at Agua Dulce. Harbert Davenport, however, was of the opinion, on what seem tenuous grounds, that he was the same man who witnessed an 1837 claim filed in respect of a Goliad victim named George Cash.

James Reed

Listed on Pittman's roll with the annotation "killed," Reed also appears on the *Telegraph and Texas Register* roll for Burke's company, enlisting with it on March 5, having escaped from Agua Dulce, only to die at Goliad.

William Scurlock

Listed on Pittman's roll, he was born in Chatham County, North Carolina, on October 22, 1807, and lived for a time in Tennessee and Mississippi before settling in San Augustine, Texas, in 1834. He set out his service in an affidavit enclosed with his pension application made on October 15, 1870: "He was a soldier in the army of Texas from the 17th of October 1835 to the 4th of October 1836, first as a private in the company of Captain Henry Augustin, then a member of Captain Llewellyn's Company. He was present at the taking of San Antonio in December 1835, afterward joined the company of Captain Burke, attached to the command of Col. Fannin, under whom he remained until the massacre of his command. After making his escape he returned home and secured a company and joined the command of Col. Thos. J. Rusk, under whom he served until the 4th October 1836." Missing from this recital is the fact that he joined Burke's company only after escaping from the fight at Agua Dulce; fought at Encinal del Perdido on March 19; and afterward avoided being murdered with the rest of Fannin's command through being employed as a hospital steward. Returning to San Augustine after the revolution, he died there on January 31, 1885. His brother, Mial Scurlock, also enlisted with Henry Augustine's company to fight at Bexar and later died at the Alamo.

Randolph De Spain
This soldier is listed on Pittman's roll as R. D. Spain with the annotation "killed" and on the *Telegraph and Texas Register* roll as one of Burke's company killed at Goliad, indicating that he escaped from Agua Dulce and enlisted with the other survivors in Burke's company.

John Tyler
Tyler appears on Pittman's roll with the annotation "killed." Harbert Davenport was of the opinion that he was the J. Tylor listed in the Land Office Muster Rolls under Captain Wyatt's company, but it seems more likely that the latter may have been a different James Tyler, who was at one time misidentified as an Alamo defender.

J. W. Wentworth
All that is known of this soldier is that he appears on Pittman's roll with the annotation "killed."

J. Williams
Again all that is known of this soldier is that he appears on Pittman's roll with the annotation "killed."

PEARSON'S COMPANY

Captain Thomas K. Pearson
Originally from Philadelphia, Pearson was described by Reuben Brown as being connected with the theatre when he raised his company in New Orleans. Lewis Washington also declared that he and King "were, I

believe, of the histrionic profession, as well as some of those attached to their respective commands."[13] Arriving at Paso Cavallo in November 1835, he and his men escorted the famous eighteen-pounder cannon salvaged from the wreck of the *San Felipe* to Bexar, but left it in the Alamo when they marched away with Grant. Pearson put his oratorical skills to good use in the confrontation at Refugio and afterward went down to the Rio Grande. At San Patricio he was called upon to surrender but at first refused and started shooting; then, seeing that the house they occupied would be burned, "the men Called Surrender; and in going out to give themselves up . . . [were] Shot or lanced, among them Capt. Thos. K. Pearson, Dr. J. Hart, Benjamin Dale, Liet. Cooney of New York" (see Chapter 7 for fuller details).

Lieutenant Henry Cooney

On the December 17 list of officers proposed by Frank Johnson to be commissioned in the Federal Volunteer Army, Cooney appears as second lieutenant of Pearson's company.[14] In the fight at San Patricio, McMullen stated that one of the men killed with Pearson was "Lieut. Cooney of New York."

Sergeant William Langenheim

Born in Braunschweig, Germany, in 1816, Langenheim emigrated to the United States in 1830, came to Texas from New York in 1833 or 1834, and served in Nidland Franks's artillery company during the storming of Bexar. Afterward he joined Pearson's company and was in charge of the horse party at Julian de la Garza's rancho when they were surprised on February 27. He appears in the *New Orleans Commercial Bulletin* list of Matamoros prisoners as "Wm. Laugnheem, aged 29, born in Germany." After his release he enlisted for a time in the quartermaster department of the U.S. Army during the Seminole War, then became a newspaper editor in Philadelphia, and died there in 1874.

John F. Beck

Little is known of this soldier other than that he was one of those who escaped the fight at San Patricio only to be killed at Goliad. Since he does not appear on Pittman's roll it is presumed that he belonged to Pearson's company, although it should be noted that he came to Texas from Nashville with John Kornicky (see Kornicky profile).[15]

Gustav Bunsen

Herman Ehrenberg remembered him as "Dr Bunsen from Frankfort am Main, who had recently arrived with a company from Louisville, Kentucky." Bunsen subsequently transferred to Pearson's company and was a member of Langenheim's party guarding horses at Julian de la Garza's rancho on the night of February 27. As Phineas Mahan remembered, "the second volley grazed Baron Von Bunsen on top of the head. The last I saw of him alive was his endeavoring to remove the cover from his rifle, the next, dead, and his body horribly mutilated."[16]

Joseph Carpenter

In his 1858 account Reuben Brown recalled that one of those who went to the Rio Grande was "Carpenter of Tennessee"; the fact that he does not appear on Pittman's roll indicates that he probably belonged to Pearson's rather than Lewellen's company. At any rate he stuck with Grant to the end and, as Brown related in 1858, was killed at Agua Dulce: "Among others whom I recognised was one poor fellow named [Joseph] Carpenter, from Tennessee, who was fatally wounded, but not quite dead. When it was discovered that he was alive, one of the dragoons was ordered to finish him. He dismounted, and, while poor Carpenter was asking to have his life spared, he struck him on the head with his escopeta, and thus ended his existence."

John Collet

Collett was taken prisoner at San Patricio.[17] He does not appear on any of the lists of Matamoros prisoners and for some unknown reason was released or escaped, perhaps with Thomas Mitchell, on or about October 31, 1836.

George Copeland

This solder appears in the *New Orleans Commercial Bulletin* list of Matamoros prisoners as "George Copeland, aged 16, born in Philadelphia," having been captured with Langenheim's party at Julian de la Garza's rancho

Benjamin Dale

One of the Irish colonists from Refugio, Dale originally enlisted with Dimitt at Goliad but then transferred to Pearson's company and, according to McMullen, was one of those killed in the street with Pearson at San Patricio on February 27.

Dr. J. Hoyt

This man presents even more problems than Dr. Heartt of Lewellen's company, with whom he is sometimes confused. At first glance identification appears quite straightforward, since Morris referred to him as "Doct. Joit," and Reuben Brown remembered him in 1858 as "Dr. Hoyt of South Carolina." However, McMullen recorded the death with Pearson at San Patricio of "Dr. J. Hart." Despite the different initials, Harbert Davenport eventually came to the conclusion that he was the Dr. William M. W. Hart listed as assistant surgeon in Johnson's December 17 list of officers to be commissioned in the Federal Volunteer Army. He was noted at the time to be a member of the Mobile Greys, and bounty and donation grants were later issued to his heirs on the strength of his having been killed at San Patricio. The difficulty with this particular identification is that W. H. W. Hart is still recorded as being at Bexar on about February 14, in a "Return, made by Col. J. C. Neil, of the men remaining in the garrison of Bexar when he left."[18] If so, he and Dr. Hoyt cannot be one and the same, since the latter carried a dispatch to Fannin from San Patricio on February 6. Presumably Hoyt subsequently returned to San Patricio with Cooke's reinforcement, but if not, the "Dr. J. Hart" killed there may have been Charles Heartt.

Edward H. Hufty

Hufty was one of Langenheim's party surprised at Julian de la Garza's rancho on February 27. Mahan remembered that: "The first volley wounded Spence and Hufty . . . Hufty, brother of the bank note engraver of Philadelphia, managed to escape and joined Col. Fannin's Command at Goliad, where he was retaken and shot."

Phineas Jenks Mahan

One of the original members of Pearson's company, Mahan wrote a useful account of the February 27 fight at the rancho, where he himself was captured (Memorial no. 247, file box no. 68, Department of State, Texas State Library and Archives, Austin). He subsequently appeared in the *New Orleans Commercial Bulletin* list as "P. S. Mahan, aged 22, born in Philadelphia." According to Harbert Davenport, on the other hand, he was born in Bucks County, Pennsylvania, on January 22, 1814, and died at Houston, Texas, on May 3, 1875.

Horace Ovid Marshall

The classically named Marshall is included here solely on the strength of an article in the *Grand Gulf Advertiser* for May 5, 1836, which notes that a son of Mrs. Mary C. Marshall of that place was with Grant. It should however be noted that he originally enrolled in Captain John Chenoweth's company on January 14, 1836, at Bexar, and signed the Convention Memorial about February 5, 1836, while still a member of that company.

John C. McLanglin

Nothing is known of McLanglin except that a donation warrant was issued on the strength of his having "Fallen with Grant and Johnson."[19]

John C. McLeod

Originally this soldier was a British member of the New Orleans Greys. Little is known about him apart from a cryptic reference by Mahan to the fact that the whole of Grant's command "was killed, as far as I am informed excepting Col. Johnson, McLeod, Bryan, John Collett and Scurlock."[20]

Johan Spiess

Although remembered by Mahan as being called Spence or Spease, this soldier was Swiss and, perhaps for that reason, was not taken to Matamoros with the other prisoners from the fight at the rancho. Wounded with Hufty in the first volley, according to Mahan, "Spease" was afterward "released and went to the City of Mexico with Captain Alavez, a Mexican officer."

William Williams

The only reference to Williams appears to be in Mahan's narrative of the fight at the rancho: "The first intimation we had of their presence was a volley poured into our sleeping quarters in the corral. . . . Williams had succeeded in climbing over the corral, but was assaulted by a large number of cavalry and literally chopped up. He was an Englishman, and had fought at Waterloo. He had frequently said on our march that he would never become a prisoner."

Stephen Winship

A supplemental certificate issued by the adjutant general's office states that "Stephen Winship, belonging to Breece's Company, was killed with Fannin." However, he disappears from the records after the storming of Bexar; he is neither on the listing for Blazeby's company, which remained there, nor on the rolls for the San Antonio Greys or the Mobile Greys. This raises the strong possibility that he may have transferred to Pearson's company and died at San Patricio or Agua Dulce.

Notes

ABBREVIATIONS

AHA — American Historical Association

Co23 and 24 — Colonial Office (Bahamas)

Fo50 — Foreign Office (Mexico)

Fo566/110 — Foreign Office (Mexico) Consular 1837

Fo75 — Foreign Office (Texas)

Fo84/479 with Kennedy 1844 — Foreign Office (Texas) Correspondence

PTR   John H. Jenkins, ed., — *The Papers of the Texas Revolution, 1835–1836*

SHQ — *Southwestern Historical Quarterly*

Sons of De Witt Colony website — Document archives, *Sons of De Witt Colony Texas* website, http://www.tamu.edu/ccbn/ccbn/dewitt/dewitt.htm

Colonial Office and Foreign Office references (CO, FO) are in the National Archives (formerly the Public Record Office) at Kew, London, United Kingdom. The number following the initials identifies the subject; the number following the slash is a box (for unbound papers) or volume, within which material is arranged by date; some items also have folio or dispatch numbers (f, no.). Foreign Office records in Fo135/1 (Mission to Mexico 1823) and Board of Trade records in BT6/53 (Vera Cruz Consul 1824), also at Kew, were consulted but are not cited.

INTRODUCTION

1. Fo50/103 f86.

2. DeShields, *Tall Men with Long Rifles: Set Down and Written Out by James T. DeShields as Told to Him by Creed Taylor, Captain during the Texas Revolution* (hereafter cited as Taylor account), *Sons of De Witt Colony Texas* website, http://www.tamu.edu/ccbn/dewitt.dewitt.htm.

CHAPTER I. GONE TO TEXAS

1. Lawson, *Relation of British Foreign Policy to the Monroe Doctrine*, 84–86. Next in order of importance was Argentina, but it could not compete with the lure of Mexican silver.

2. *Hansard* (official transcript of parliamentary proceedings), Aug. 6, 1836.

3. Johnston, *Mission to Mexico: A Tale of British Diplomacy in the 1820s*, 39–40. Wavell, born in Edinburgh in 1785, had successively served in the East India Company's Bengal Army, the Spanish Army during the Peninsular War, and then for a time with the Chilean Army, before ending up in Mexico in rather dubious circumstances. Although he became a general in the Mexican service he actually spent his time in various speculative mining and other enterprises. He had an equally circuitous voyage to London, originally sailing from Vera Cruz on August 11, 1822, bound for Bordeaux. Unfortunately his ship was almost immediately captured and looted by pirates, so he then made his way to Savannah, where another ship carried him on to Liverpool, from where he arrived in London on November 16 and had an interview with Canning "a few days after my arrival."

4. Temperley, *The Foreign Policy of Canning 1822–1827*, 106–107, 138.

5. Ibid., 553.

6. London *Times*, Feb. 8, 1830. The author was almost certainly Henry Ward, who served as *chargé d'affairs* in Mexico between 1825 and 1827. As he had already written extensively on the subject then and afterward, these views were far from new.

7. F050/4

8. A. G. Wavell to S. F. Austin, Feb. 17, 1823, in Austin, *The Austin Papers* (*Annual Report of the American Historical Association 1919*), vol. 2, pt. 1, 576–80 (hereafter cited as Austin, with volume, part, and page numbers). A full account of the Poyais business can be found in Sinclair, *Sir Gregor MacGregor and the Land That Never Was*. Like Wavell, MacGregor was a veteran of the South American wars of liberation.

9. Wavell to Austin, May 22, 1823, Austin 2:1, 646–47.

10. Temperley, *The Foreign Policy of Canning 1822–1827*, 270–71n.

11. Ibid., 269.

12. Sparrow, *Secret Service: British Agents in France 1792–1815*, provides a good account of Huskisson's early career as a spymaster. Oddly enough he is probably best known as the first man to be run down and killed by a railway locomotive, on September 15, 1830.

13. Quote from DeShields, Taylor account, *Sons of De Witt Colony* website. Charles Grant (1778–1866) was a noted abolitionist and liberal member of Parliament from 1811 until he went to the House of Lords in 1835. In August, 1819, he became a privy councilor as chief secretary for Ireland; he was appointed vice president of the Board of Trade on January 31, 1823, and president of the board on September 3, 1827. He resigned in the following year but returned to govern-

ment in 1830 as head of the East India Company Board of Control. Subsequently he became secretary of state for the Colonial Department in April, 1835, and was elevated to the peerage on May 8, 1835, as Lord Glenelg.

14. Killearnan Parish Register. Strictly speaking James was a second cousin, but the family was so very closely knit that the distinction is unimportant.

15. Mackay, *Urquhart and Glenmoriston*, provides a thorough if sometimes erratic history of the Grants of Shewglie. See also Embree, *Charles Grant and British Rule in India*, 23–24; Barber, *The Black Hole of Calcutta*, 154–56; Edwardes, *The Battle of Plassey*, 68, 138. The wife was Margretta Beck, "a Dutch lady he married at the Cape (of Good Hope)." Alexander's only other bequest was to cancel a debt of £200 owed to him by one of his brothers, Patrick Grant of Lochletter.

16. Prior to 1791 William had been living with his uncle, Major Gregor Grant, at Lakefield House in Glen Urquhart, where he married Christian Bannatyne, an illegitimate niece of his aunt, Anne Bannatyne, on August 7, 1790.

17. Grant's wife, Margaret, was the daughter of another protégé of the elder Charles Grant; former regular army officer Captain John Urquhart, who was at the time assistant military secretary at the East India Company headquarters in Leadenhall Street. She and James Grant were married in St. Clement Danes church in the Strand, London, on July 22, 1812. Both parties falsely claimed on the license to be aged over twenty-one years.

18. James Grant's Will, Harris County, Texas, Probate Records, B:277–79.

19. Grant stipulated that Margaret Urquhart was to receive £100 sterling annually, "on condition that none of my children by her are to reside with her permanently nor my daughter Jamesina even temporarily."

20. In a letter written from New Orleans in March, 1824 (see next note), Grant refers to some friends as having returned from a six months "cruze" to the West Indies. This means he was in the United States sometime before October 1823, but since he was certainly still at home in the early part of that year, he must have come across in the summer—just when Canning was having instructions drawn up for Hervey.

21. J. Grant to S. F. Austin, March 23, 1824, Austin 2:1, 756.

22. Grant to Austin, July 24, 1825, Austin 2:1, 1155.

23. The quotation is taken from Ward's *Mexico in 1827*, 586, but evidently repeats arguments first aired in his earlier *American Designs upon Texas*.

24. F050/14. No trace of any response, far less any formal instructions, can be found in the surviving Foreign Office archives, but there is clear evidence of weeding and of drafts having been cut from the "Out" books (containing correspondence and instructions emanating from the department), which might otherwise have thrown interesting light on matters.

25. F050/20 folio 156.

26. Ibid., f175.

27. Ibid., f184.

28. Ibid., f248. H. Ward to G. Canning, March 25, 1826. "It was partly at my

instigation that the Countess [de Regla] interfered in favour of General Teran and it was principally owing to her exertions that General Victoria's dislike of him was overcome."

29. Ward tried to obtain a grant of £400 ($2,400) from the Secret Service fund to cover the cost of printing and the inevitable entertaining but received a frosty response from the permanent under secretary—that the book and map were allowable but that no part of the "Secret Service can be appropriated to the expenses of Balls or Fetes." Fo50/19 f34.

30. Grant refers to his association with Milam as early as January 31, 1825, which may point to the two of them having been introduced by Wavell; Austin 2:1, 1030.

31. Little seems to be known of George Nixon at this period, but he was later a land commissioner for the Galveston Bay and Texas Land Company and at the time of the Texas Revolution a prominent member of the "Nacogdoches land men" and major of the local militia.

32. Grant to Austin, May 13, 1826, Austin 2:2.

33. Ibid.

34. *Sons of De Witt Colony* Website. Captain John Austin was not related to Stephen Austin but was one of the filibusters who came to Mexico with Dr. Long in 1819.

35. Fo50/22 f67.

36. Fo50/4.

37. Fo50/19 f105. The reference to "other agents" appears in this instance to relate to properly accredited consuls rather than to clandestine operators.

38. H. Ward to C. Vaughan, April 5, 1826, C122/5, Codrington Library, All Souls, Oxford.

39. Edwards is quoted in Yoakum, *History of Texas,* 1:239. Davis, *Three Roads to the Alamo,* provides a detailed account of the Bowie claims and their background.

40. Quote in John Sibley to S. F. Austin, Feb. 18, 1827, Austin 1:1, 1604; Fo50/25 f188.

41. J. Kerr to S. F. Austin, Jan. 24, 1827, Austin 2:2, 1591–92.

42. S. F. Austin to B. J. Thompson, Dec. 24, 1826, Austin 2:2, 1539–41.

43. A badly tattered obituary for Grant's daughter Jamesina, which appeared in an unknown Australian newspaper about 1900, relates inter alia that Grant went "to Mexico at the . . . [Mex]ican war, a reward . . . by the Mexican . . . [h]e was arrested, and . . . [wi]th Edwards, was im[prisoned] . . . [ma]nagged to escape, but . . . murdered." The gaps, unfortunately, are substantial ones, and there appears to be a conflation of the Fredonian and Texan revolts, but there is no mistaking the significance of his connection with "Edwards." The purchase of the land at Matagorda surfaces in the diary of his brother's agent, James Ogilvie: "Found a Deed of Sale from one Jacob Betts to James Grant (late of Matamoros) 9____1826"; see Harriet Smither, "Diary of Adolphus Sterne" (*sic*), *Southwestern Historical Quarterly* 30:309 (the diary is hereafter cited as Ogilvie and the quarterly as SHQ).

44. Ostensibly this was the culmination of a long-running row that had com-menced some months before with the permanent under secretary over Ward's alleged extravagance, but although the correspondence in Fo50 appears quite heated, it has a somewhat contrived and unconvincing air and is clearly aimed at covering up the real reasons for Ward's recall.

45. Fo50/40 f296–300.

46. For the record, according to his will the children's names were Gregor, Marcos, Antonio, William, Guadeloupe, Cristina, "and the last born whose name I know not as she was not baptized when I left Monterey."

CHAPTER 2. REVOLUTION

1. Harris, *A Mexican Family Empire: The Latifundio of the Sanchez Navarros 1765–1867,* 163–66.

2. For the claim see Robert Bruce Blake Collection, Center for American His-tory, University of Texas, Austin (hereafter cited as Blake), 56:84–128.

3. Gammel, *Laws and Decrees of the State of Coahuila and Texas,* 357.

4. Ogilvie, SHQ 30:151.

5. Linn, *Reminiscences of Fifty Years in Texas,* 301.

6. Gammel, *Laws and Decrees,* 272–73.

7. Clarence Wharton, "Life of Santa Anna," cited on *Sons of De Witt Colony* website.

8. For the loan see J. Irwin to (?) Chapman, Feb. 1 (?), 1834, and W. S. Parrott to S. F. Austin, Sep. 18, 1834, both in Austin 3:1045, 1090.

9. G. De Witt to People of Gonzales, Apr. 15, 1835, Green De Witt Papers, box OS, box 8, folder no. 7, Texas State Library and Archives, Austin.

10. Barker, "Land Speculation as a Cause of the Texas Revolution," SHQ 10 (July 1906): 76–95; Davis, *Three Roads to the Alamo,* 355, 680.

11. Alessio Robles, *Coahuila y Tejas desde la consumacion de la independencia hasta el Tratado de Paz de Guadalupe Hidalgo,* 1:510.

12. Secondary sources err in describing him as *the* secretary of the legislature, an office actually held by José Maria Irala (or Yrala). As a deputy secretary, how-ever, Grant was responsible for cosigning congressional decrees prior to their formal approval by the state governor.

13. Gammel, *Laws and Decrees,* 357–62, 382.

14. Barker, "Land Speculation"; Gammel, *Laws and Decrees,* 412–13. Miller, *New Orleans and the Texas Revolution,* provides a good study of the importance of Texas land in underwriting loans to the provisional government during the revolution.

15. Ogilvie, SHQ 30:306–307.

16. Ibid., 149.

17. John Marie Durst was the brother of Joseph Durst, who served as alcalde of Nacogdoches during the Fredonian Rebellion.

18. See Chapter 9 for a fuller accounting of the land certificates and what hap-pened to them.

19. Davis, *Three Roads to the Alamo,* 424, quoting Spencer Jack.

20. De Witt to People of Gonzales.

21. Decrees in late April included the grant of exclusive navigation rights on the Colorado River to Ben Milam and the establishment of a Commercial and Agricultural Bank by Samuel Williams. Grant was a cosignatory to both decrees and intended to become a shareholder in the bank. Gammel, *Laws and Decrees,* 402, 406–407; Ogilvie, SHQ 30:149.

22. Gammel, *Laws and Decrees,* 404. The "capitalists" presumably included Grant, since there are various references in Ogilvie's diary to his claim against the state of Coahuila y Texas.

23. DeShields, Taylor account, *Sons of De Witt Colony* website.

24. F050/99.

25. Ogilvie, SHQ 30:307.

26. Ibid., 219–20.

27. Davis, *Three Roads to the Alamo,* 424.

28. Alessio Robles, *Coahuila y Tejas,* 1:24, called him a "jefe de las armas."

29. Ibid., 2:24

30. *El Mosquito Mexicano* (Mexico City semi-official newspaper), April 5, 1836.

31. Ogilvie, SHQ 30:219–20; Blake, 56:84–128; James Grant's Will, Harris County, Texas, Probate Records, B:277–79.

32. James Grant's Will.

33. Davis, *Three Roads to the Alamo,* 262–74, provides the best account of the outbreak of the disturbances.

34. R. B. Blake, "Dr. James Grant," *Handbook of Texas Online,* hopelessly confuses Dr. James Grant with an entirely different individual of the same name then resident in Nacogdoches, who joined with Bowie and afterward fought at the siege of Bexar. This James Grant, who styled himself "Santiago" rather than "Diego" in Spanish documents, was aged only twenty-eight at the time; census records of Nacogdoches from Bexar archives, Blake, 19:189, Apr. 30, 1835. Unlike Dr. Grant, he survived the revolution.

35. Davis, *Three Roads to the Alamo,* 428–31.

36. Austin proclamation, Sept. 18, 1835, in John H. Jenkins (ed.), *The Papers of the Texas Revolution, 1835–1836,* 1:456 (hereafter cited as PTR).

37. Barr, *Texans in Revolt: The Battle for San Antonio, 1835,* 12–13, 72. The infantry belonged to the Morelos Battalion, while the cavalry (with some later reinforcements) eventually included the following companies, all named after the districts in which they had been recruited: Ague Verde, 1 Alamo de Parras, 2 Alamo de Parras, Bavia, Bexar, Lampazos, 1 Nuevo Leon, 2 Nuevo Leon, Pueblo, Rio Grande, 1 Tamaulipas, 2 Tamaulipas. It should be noted however that Cos's official report refers to two companies from the Rio Grande. Presumably he was actually referring to the two from Tamaulipas.

38. Ward, *Mexico in 1827,* 317; F050/28.

39. J. Fisher to S. F. Austin, Oct. 20, 1835, typescript letter, George Fisher

Papers, Center for American History, University of Texas at Austin, 9–10. Miller, *New Orleans and the Texas Revolution,* provides an essential background.

40. P. Dimitt to S. F. Austin, Oct. 15, 1835, PTR 2:124–25.

41. S. F. Austin to President and Consultation, Nov. 5, 1835, PTR 2:321.

42. S. F. Austin to Consultation, Nov. 7, 1835, *Sons of De Witt Colony* website.

43. Franklin Hall, "Who Will Go with Old Ben Milam into San Antonio?" *San Antonio Express,* Feb. 2, 1930.

44. Linn, *Reminiscences of Fifty Years in Texas,* 123.

45. Miller, *New Orleans and the Texas Revolution,* 85–107.

46. London *Times,* May 26, 1836.

47. F050/93 f276.

48. Fisher to Austin, Oct. 20, 1835, typescript letter cited.

49. F050/93 f276.

50. Ibid. See also Miller, *New Orleans and the Texas Revolution.*

51. A full list of all thirty-one was printed in the *Times* together with Cramp's last letters. A quarter of the men were British subjects: four from England, three from Ireland, and one Canadian. Nine were from France or Germany, and the remainder were Americans, of whom eleven were from New York, New Jersey, Pennsylvania, and other northern states and one each from Maryland, Virginia, and Kentucky.

52. "I have received of Mr. John McMullen the sum of $300 for the payment or (succor) of the company of troops that have escorted me, which sum will be paid out of the revenues of the state." A. Viesca, Nov. 8, 1835, Audited Military Claims, Texas State Library and Archives, Austin.

53. J. Grant to S. F. Austin, Nov. 13, 1835, PTR 2:395–96. This would largely be echoed in a subsequent secret briefing given to the council by Don Pedro Miracle on December 5:

That he left Mier on the Rio Grande the 19th ult. and was dispatched by Canales (a lawyer of talents and influence) and by Molano, formerly lieutenant-governor of the state of Tamaulipas, Tobar, formerly a senator of the federal party in congress, and several other men of influence who live in Matamoros and in other parts of Tamaulipas—The objects of his mission are to see the governors Viesca and Zavala and ascertain from them what was the character and intention of the revolution in Texas, for so many reports had reached there on this subject that they were in doubt—He states that Canales has two hundred men at a place called Palo Blanco this side of the Rio Grande within two days march of San Patricio on the Nueces—that Molano and Tobar who live in Matamoros have everything arranged with the principal inhabitants of that place to take up arms the moment all is ready—That the governor of the former state of Tamaulipas, Vital Fernandez, has an understanding with General Mexía to join the cause—that General Lemus and his brother and many others of the principal men of

New Leon are also in the combination, and many of the officers who are now on the march against Texas—that the company of troops at Lipantitlan or San Patricio is also gained over and ready to join Gonzales or Canales when called on—He also says that the state of Jalisco (better known here by the name of Guadalaxara) has refused to submit to the decree of the 3d of October last, and that General Montenegro of the liberal party had defeated General Paredas in Jalisco. Also that the people of Morilla had represented against it, and were ready to resist—That Canales, Molano, Tobar, Lemur, and all the other liberals are only waiting to hear from Governors Viesca or Zavala, or both, as to the objects of the revolution in Texas—Should it be to sustain the federal system, they will all unite and rise in mass—take Matamoros—attack the troops that are coming on against Texas—revolutionize the whole state of Tamaulipas—appropriate the proceeds of the custom houses of Matamoros and Tampico to the expenses of the war, etc.—They all admit that Texas ought to declare independence in case the central government is firmly established, but that she ought first to make an effort, in union with the liberals, to save the federal system.—Such in substance is the information given by Captain Miracle. He was an officer of the army at Zacatecas—is a Columbian by birth—Governor Viesca has confidence in him.

54. Dimitt to Austin, Nov. 14, 1835, PTR 2:409.

55. Gammel, *Proceedings of the General Council,* 601. Interestingly, he did so as *Diego* Grant.

56. Coleman, *Houston Displayed; Or Who Won the Battle of San Jacinto,* 4–5.

CHAPTER 3. BEXAR

1. One of Grant's bounty certificates states that "James Grant served faithfully 4 mos. Nov. 1 1835–Mch 1836," Fannin Bounty no. 10016.

2. William T. Austin's account, "Siege and Battle of Bexar" (1844), *Sons of De Witt Colony* website. William Austin was the brother of the Captain John Austin who complained in 1826 of clandestine British activity in Mexico and Texas.

3. Ibid.

4. G. M. Patrick to M. A. Bryan, Aug. 8, 1878, in Lindley, *Alamo Traces,* 191. Davis, *Three Roads to the Alamo,* 481–83, is skeptical as to whether Bowie can have considered that he had any realistic chance of gaining command.

5. The accounts by Thomas Rusk, Herman Ehrenberg, and Creed Taylor (in DeShields) are all on the *Sons of De Witt Colony* website. Taylor's reliability as a source has been called into question, but fundamentally the problem is summed up by the title. The book is essentially a narrative history of the revolution based upon a series of interviews with Taylor in his old age. How much actually originated with Taylor and how much was interpolated by DeShields and his researchers is a moot point. Some material has certainly been plagiarized from other works, and there is a particular problem with erroneous dates. Neverthe-

less it appears fundamentally sound, particularly in recording contemporary attitudes and rumors.

6. R. C. Morris to S. Houston, Nov. 29, 1835, PTR 3:31–32. The other James Grant was also in the camp at this time, and confusingly, he too wrote to Sam Houston, demanding action: "I have been a long time expecting to hear from you or to have the pleasure of seeing you in camp, but it seems you will not come until all the men that are hear have left, for the want of some one to command. This army cannot find stand much longer under the present circumstances and if we are obledged to retreat from this place I am afrade it will have a very bade affect and give the Mexicans much confidence. We have plenty of men to take it if they had any faith in their commanders but all confidence is lost. I want you to write to me as soon as possible and remember the appointment that you promised to me which is now in your power to give me. I am willing to serve for in any capassity that you think would be beneficial to the country" (Grant to Houston, Dec. 1, 1835, PTR 3:64). Although the two men are not distinguished by Jenkins, a comparison of handwriting, spelling, and orthography leaves no doubt that this letter was written by James Grant of Nacogdoches rather than Dr. James Grant.

7. Gulick and Elliott, *Papers of Mirabeau Buonaparte Lamar* (hereafter cited as Lamar), no. 2169, Cooke. Lamar intended to write a history of the Texas Revolution and amassed a large collection of papers and personal narratives; these are identified first by document number and then by the name of the contributor. Lamar's notation at the bottom says: "Endorsed Manuscript of Col. Wm. G. Cook furnished me at Washington Febry 1844." Cooke also told substantially the same story in a letter to his brother dated August, 1839, and reproduced in the *San Antonio Light,* Apr. 21, 1940.

8. Johnson, *A History of Texas and Texans,* 1:352–53.

9. Ogilvie, SHQ 30:319–20.

10. Thomas "Mag" Striff account, PTR 3:390.

11. Gammel, *Proceedings of the General Council,* 766.

12. Full name of those in Johnson's report are Major Robert C. Morris, Colonels James Grant and William Austin, Adjutant Nathaniel Brister, and Captains John York, William Patton, Thomas Lewellen, John Crane, George English, and William Landrum; Lieutenant-Colonel Nidland Franks; and Captains William Cooke, James Swisher, Haden Edwards, Thomas Alley, Peter Duncan, J. W. Peacock, Thomas Breeze, and Plácido Benavides. Burleson's reserve comprised companies commanded by Captains James Chesire, Robert Coleman, M. B. Lewis, James C. Neill, John S. Roberts, Michael Roth, Juan N. Seguin, Peyton Splane, William Sutherland, and Henry Teal.

13. Austin, "Account of the Campaign of 1835," *Texana* 4 (Winter 1966): 287–322 (also accessible on *Sons of De Witt Colony* Website).

14. The Morelos Battalion mustered 246 men on October 3, but as many as forty may have been killed or wounded at Concepcion and in the Grass Fight. Lindley, *Alamo Traces,* 352–62.

15. *Sons of De Witt Colony* website.

16. Striff account, PTR 3:390. The best modern account of the storming of Bexar is Alwyn Barr's *Texans in Revolt: The Battle for San Antonio, 1835*, 44–59, but Stephen L. Hardin's *Texian Illiad: A Military History of the Texas Revolution*, 78–91, is also useful.

17. *Sons of De Witt Colony* website.

18. Military Rolls Collection, "Texas Revolution Rolls," box 401-714, Texas State Library and Archives, Austin.

19. Johnson's official report regretted his wounded but provided no details of the circumstances. Alessio Robles, *Coahuila y Tejas*, 2:84–85, simply states that Grant fought "con bravura y fue herido" (with bravery and was wounded). See also Striff account, PTR 3:390.

20. Sánchez Navarro, *La Guerra de Tejas*, 98–101, *Sons of De Witt Colony* website. There is some confusion over the identity of the defectors. They certainly included the Agua Verde company, and Sánchez Navarro specifically identifies one of the officers concerned as Captain Barragan of the Rio Grande company. Cos also refers in his report to the defection of two companies from the Rio Grande, but as there was only one company bearing that title, and it, together with Captain Barragan, later fought under Santa Anna at the Alamo, this is clearly a mistake for the two Tamaulipas companies.

21. Gammel, *Proceedings of the General Council*, 766.

22. Ibid., 674.

23. Dimitt to (?), Dec. 2, 1835, PTR 3:77–79.

24. Austin to General Council, Dec. 22, 1835, PTR 3:315–17.

25. S. Houston to D. C. Barrett, Dec. 15, 1835, PTR 3:201–202.

26. Houston to Bowie, Dec. 17, 1835, in Davis, *Three Roads to the Alamo*, 489.

27. J. C. Neill to Governor and Council, Jan. 6, 1836, in Hansen, *Alamo Reader*, 647–50.

28. F. W. Johnson to Secretary of State (RG-307), Communications Received, Texas State Library and Archives, Austin.

List of the Officers of the Volunteer Army of Texas to be Commissioned by the Provisional Governmt. Commander in Chief—Col. Francis W. Johnson, Second in Command—Col. James Grant, First Adjutant—Captn. N. R. Brister, Second Do.—Captn. J. S. Vaughan, Surgeon in Chief—Dr. Albert M. Levy of N. Orlean's Greys, Assistant Surgeon Wm M. W. Hart, Mobile do., Quarter Master—Captn. V. Bennett, Paymaster—Captn. Francis Adams, Store Keeper—Mr. John W. Smith, First N. O. Greys—Captn. Wm. G. Cooke, 1st Lieut. C. B. Bannister, 2d. Do. John Hall, Second N.O. Greys—Captn. Thos. H. Bree[ce], 1st. Lieut. J. J. Baugh, 2d. Do. Wm Blaseby, Third Compy. of Infy.—Captn. T. Lewellyn, 1st Lieut. J. Chineworth, 2nd Blunt Fourth Cy. of Do., Captn. D. N. Burk, Mobile Greys, Artillery—Lieut. Col. J. C. Neill, Captn. Almeron Dickinson, Captn. T. K. Pearson, Artillery-First Lieut. W. R. Carey, First Do. Joseph J. Johnson, Second Do. S. Y. Reams, Do. Do. Henry Coney, Native Troops—Captn. John Cameron, Major Morris has already got his Commission. Head Quarters Bejar Decr. 17th 1835 F. W. Johnson Com. in Chief Fed. Vol. Army of Texas.

29. DeShields, Taylor account, *Sons of De Witt Colony* Website.

30. F. W. Johnson to Hanks and Clements, Dec. 24, 1835, PTR 3:307.

31. *Sons of De Witt Colony* Website.

32. J. Robinson to Austin, Archer, and Wharton, Jan. 23, 1836, in Garrison, *Diplomatic Correspondence of the Republic of Texas,* 2:64–65.

33. S. Houston to J. Neill, Dec. 21, 1835, PTR 3:278–79.

34. Johnson to Council, Dec. 17, 1835, in Hansen, *Alamo Reader,* 642n46. Comparison with the list of officers in note 28 indicates that the blue uniforms were intended for the two artillery companies commanded by Neill and Pearson, the gray uniforms for the 1st and 2nd New Orleans Greys and the Mobile Greys, leaving the green "rifle" uniforms for Lewellen's company. Two hundred fur caps were also ordered, sufficient for all the infantry but not for the artillery. Sadly, neither these uniforms nor any of the other supplies ever materialized.

35. J. Neill to S. Houston, Jan. 14, 1836, in Hansen, *Alamo Reader,* 652–53.

36. Lamar, no. 2169, Cooke.

37. *Telegraph and Texas Register,* Jan. 23, 1836.

38. Gammel, *Proceedings of the General Council,* 753, 755, 788–89.

CHAPTER 4. CONTENDING CHIEFTAINS

1. S. Houston to H. Smith, Jan. 30, 1836, PTR 4:191; Johnson, *A History of Texas and Texans,* 1:377; Yoakum, *History of Texas,* 2:44.

2. Johnson, *A History of Texas and Texans,* 1:377; Barker, "Land Speculation."

3. S. F. Austin to D. G. Burnett, Oct. 5, 1835, Austin Papers.

4. Palmerston to T. Spring Rice (Chancellor of the Exchequer), Oct. 9, 1837, Broadlands Papers, University Library, University of Southampton, United Kingdom.

5. J. Fisher to S. F. Austin, Oct. 20, 1835, typescript letter, George Fisher Papers, Center for American History, University of Texas at Austin, 9–10. California apparently "had nothing to say" as it was allegedly dominated by the Jesuits.

6. S. Houston to J. Forbes, Jan. 7, 1836, PTR 3:436–37.

7. S. Houston to J. Collinsworth, Mar. 7, 1836, PTR 5:17–18.

8. B. Lundy, *The War in Texas,* on *Sons of De Witt Colony* Website.

9. A popular belief has grown up, largely spawned by historical reenactors, that the New Orleans Greys were wearing U.S. Army surplus fatigue uniforms, but contemporary letters and memoirs clearly point to their wearing ordinary working clothes and sealskin hunting caps rather than U.S. Army forage caps. *Fustian* is an older term for what is now known as jean, a cheap and durable material with a cotton warp and woolen weft or fill, popular with farmers and other workmen in the South and extensively used by the Confederate armies during the Civil War. Although normally marketed as gray, it usually oxidized in sunlight to a brownish dust color popularly known as butternut.

10. William Christy was in fact prosecuted (unsuccessfully) for his role in fitting out Mexía's Tampico expedition. Miller, *New Orleans and the Texas Revolution*,146–49, deals specifically with the case but is also useful generally on the matter of volunteers and supplies channeled to the rebels through New Orleans.

11. D. Maxey (ed.), *Fannin and His Men: Notes from an Unfinished Study of Fannin and His Men by Harbert Davenport 1936*, http://www.tsha.utexas.edu/supsites/fannin/nin/hd_home.html.

12. Quoted in Lundy, *The War in Texas*.

13. *London Patriot,* July 6, 1836.

14. Quoted in Lundy, *The War in Texas*.

15. Palmerston to T. Spring Rice (Chancellor of the Exchequer), Oct. 9, 1837, Broadlands Papers.

16. *Hansard,* Aug. 5, 1836.

17. "Charles Grant," *Oxford Dictionary of National Biography*. It is a measure of Palmerston's indifference to the matter, or rather his preoccupation with European and Near Eastern affairs, that Sir Charles Webster's two-volume *The Foreign Policy of Palmerston 1830–41* contains not one single reference to Texas or any other aspect of Anglo-American relations.

18. C. Elliot to H. U. Addington (Under Secretary), Nov. 15, 1842, FO75/4.

19. Oddly enough, although a confirmed Turcophile, Urquhart did publish a pamphlet in 1844 entitled *The Annexation of Texas: A Case of War between England and the United States*, which was highly critical of America's conduct toward Mexico.

20. F. W. Johnson to Council, Jan. 3, 1836, PTR 3:412–13.

21. Johnson, *A History of Texas and Texans*, 1:382–83.

22. Gammel, *Proceedings of the General Council*, 729–30.

23. Ibid., 740.

24. J. Neill and G. Jameson to Houston, Jan. 1, 1836 (letter by Neill, postscript by Jameson), Adjutant General (RG-401), Army Papers, Texas State Library and Archives, Austin; Hansen, *Alamo Reader,* 647.

25. H. Smith to W. Ward, Jan. 6, 1836, PTR 3:428.

26. Gammel, *Proceedings of the General Council*, 744.

27. Ibid., 746–47.

28. Ibid., 758.

29. J. C. Neill to Governor and Council, Jan. 6, 1836, PTR 3:424–25.

30. Gammel, *Proceedings of the General Council*, 759–61. Frank Johnson admirably summed up the situation when he remarked that "Governor Smith thought an expedition to Matamoros not only proper but necessary, when ordered by himself, but all wrong when ordered by the council."

31. PTR 3:467–68. The reference to the 1824 flag is intriguing as it appears to be the only verifiable reference to it actually being flown by Texian troops—or more accurately in this case by federalist troops.

32. Palmerston to C. Grant, Aug. 17, 1830, Broadlands Papers.

33. Gammel, *Proceedings of the General Council*, 764–68; W. R. Smith, "The

Quarrel between Governor Smith and the Council of the Provisional Government of the Republic," SHQ 5:269–346.

34. It is frequently asserted that Grant was independently authorized by the council to raise and lead an expeditionary force to Matamoros. In fact it is clear from Houston's letter to Smith of January 30, 1836, that the sole justification for this charge was the council's reluctant decision to honor a claim presented by John Gilbert for a wagon and team impressed by Grant when he marched from Bexar (PTR 4:191). It is perhaps worth emphasizing this point, for it is common in secondary sources to find the council condemned for having separately authorized James Grant, Frank Johnson, and James Fannin to command the Matamoros expedition. While there is certainly room for ambiguity over Fannin's position vis-à-vis Houston, at no time was Grant authorized to command anything, and Johnston's authority was explicitly restricted to the Bexar volunteers—under Fannin's overall command.

35. Gammel, *Proceedings of the General Council*, 778–79.

CHAPTER 5. HIGH NOON AT GOLIAD

1. Houston to Smith, Jan. 30, 1836, PTR 4:191; Johnson, *A History of Texas and Texans*, 1:375.

2. Dimitt to Robinson, Dec. 28, 1835, PTR 3:344–46.

3. Dimitt to (?), Dec. 2, 1835, PTR 3: 77–78; Johnson, *A History of Texas and Texans*, 1:364–65.

4. Lindley, *Alamo Traces*, 324–25.

5. Gammel, *Proceedings of the General Council*, 719–20.

6. The latter was not a mortar but a five-inch howitzer. The two were similar, but howitzers were mounted on field carriages, while mortars were set in solid wooden blocks. The December 13 list of artillery and small arms surrendered at Bexar included "2 four-pound cannon, mounted, 1 small brass do., 1 four-pound field-piece, 1 do. three-pounder, complete, 1 rammer, 1 cannon, four pounder, with carriage and rammer, 1 iron culverine of nine-inch calibre, mounted, 1 howitzer of five-inch calibre, 1 cannon, six pounder, 1 field-piece, four-pounder, 1 cannon, three-pounder, mounted, 1 ditto six-pounder, mounted, 257 carabines and muskets" (*Sons of De Witt Colony* Website).

7. Johnson, *A History of Texas and Texans*, 1:383.

8. DeShields, Taylor account, *Sons of De Witt Colony* website; Houston to Smith, Jan. 30, 1836; Yoakum, *History of Texas*, 2:460–70.

9. Dimitt to Smith, Jan. 10, 1836, PTR 3:465.

10. Lamar, no. 2169, Cooke.

11. Lamar, no. 1645, Brown.

12. "James H. Bowman, Fort of Goliad Jany 8th 1836," Permanent Council Papers, box 2-9/19, Texas State Library and Archives, Austin.

13. Lamar, no. 1658, McMullen.

14. *Texas Almanac*, 1858, on *Sons of De Witt Colony* Website.

15. Bowie to Houston, Jan. 10, 1836, in Yoakum, *History of Texas,* 2:57–58. Blount's promotion was premature; Houston was to write three months later: "There is a Blount in Washington, who deserves a Captaincy in the cavalry. . . . He only received a Lieutenancy when he should have been advanced"; S. Houston to J. Collingsworth, Mar. 7, 1836, PTR 5:17–18.

16. Ibid., 2:56.

17. Lamar, no. 2169, Cooke.

18. Houston to Smith, Dec. 30, 1835, PTR 3:374.

19. Houston to Smith, Jan. 30, 1836, in Yoakum, *History of Texas,* 2:460–70.

20. Yoakum, *History of Texas,* 2:58–59.

21. Lamar, no. 1645, Brown.

22. Neill to Houston, Jan. 14, 1836, in Hansen, *Alamo Reader,* 652–53.

23. Houston to Smith, Jan. 17, 1836, in Hansen, *Alamo Reader,* 656–57.

24. Gammel, *Proceedings of the General Council,* 729–30.

25. Lamar, no. 1645, Brown.

26. Yoakum, *History of Texas,* 2:44.

27. Gammel, *Proceedings of the General Council,* 678.

28. Houston to Morris, Jan. 20, 1836, in Yoakum, *History of Texas,* 2:459.

29. Houston to Smith, Jan. 30, 1836, in Yoakum, *History of Texas,* 2:460–70.

30. In his 1858 *Texas Almanac* account Brown claimed that after he was captured at Agua Dulce, General Urrea offered to release him if he would carry terms to Fannin at Goliad; "this proposition was doubtless the fact of their having found letters about me from Col. Fannin, with whom I had been on intimate terms, we both having come from the same section of Georgia."

31. See James Crisp, *Sleuthing the Alamo,* 27–60, for a detailed discussion of Houston's speed as reported by Ehrenberg.

32. Ehrenberg, *Sons of De Witt Colony* website.

33. Lamar, no. 1645, Brown.

34. In addition there must have been an unknown, but probably small, number of men down in Tamaulipas with Grant when this count was made.

CHAPTER 6. RIO GRANDE

1. Robinson to Austin, Archer, and Wharton, Jan. 23, 1836, in Garrison, *Diplomatic Correspondence,* 2:64–65; J. E. Winston, "New York and the Independence of Texas," SHQ 18:368–85.

2. C023/94 (Colonial Office, Bahamas), folio 381–82.

3. F050/97, f76. Under international law any warship not sailing under a recognized national flag was considered a pirate, to be hunted down by any warship of any nation. The Royal Navy had a duty to escort British vessels into or out of Matamoros, fighting its way past the Texian vessels if necessary; but if it was accepted that the Texians were legitimate belligerents, then the navy would not interfere.

4. C023/94, f407.

5. Gonzales to Price, Nov. 13, 1835, PTR 2:394–95; Winston, "New York and the Independence of Texas."

6. Co23/96, f102. A rummage by customs officers at Nassau turned up "4 cases containing 56 swords = 224; 1 case containing 44 pike heads; 1 case containing 29 lance heads; 46 pistols; 11 dirks; 27 muskets and rifles and 33 swords loose in the gun room and in the cabin 2 swords and 6 pistols."

7. Co24/20 passim.

8. Linn, *Reminiscences of Fifty Years in Texas,* 119–20; Hardin, *Texian Illiad,* 41–48.

9. Dimitt to Robinson, Dec. 28, 1835, PTR 3:344–46.

10. Ibid.

11. Since Johnson is emphatic that Grant brought only two guns away from Bexar, the third must have been taken from Goliad. Neill mentioned in a letter to Houston of January 14 that three guns had been sent there in return for three wagon loads of supplies. Hansen, *Alamo Reader,* 652–53.

12. Johnson to Fannin, Feb. 6, 1836, in "Archival Communications Fannin and Goliad Aug 1835–Mar 1836" (hereafter cited as Fannin communications), *Sons of De Witt Colony* website.

13. Lamar, no. 1658, McMullen. This narrative appears to have been submitted to Lamar by James McGloin, but according to the editor of his papers, C. A. Gulick, the handwriting appears to be that of another San Patricio colonist named John McMullen.

14. Lamar, no. 1645, Brown.

15. Johnson to Fannin, Feb. 2, 1836, not now extant but quoted in Fannin to Robinson, Feb. 4, 1836, Fannin communications.

16. Fannin to Robinson, Feb. 4, 1836, Fannin communications.

17. Johnson to Fannin, Feb. 2, 1836, not now extant but quoted in Fannin to Robinson, Feb. 4, 1836, Fannin communications.

18. H. Davenport, "The Men of Goliad," SHQ 48 (July 1939).

19. Johnson to Fannin, Feb. 2, 1836, not now extant but quoted in Fannin to Robinson, Feb. 4, 1836, Fannin communications.

20. Morris to Fannin, Feb. 6, 1836, Fannin communications. Numbers are taken from Urrea's journal and Vicente Filisola's *Memoirs for the History of the War in Texas,* 2:149–52, available at *Sons of DeWitt Colony* website.

21. DeShields, Taylor account, *Sons of De Witt Colony* website.

22. Before leaving Camargo, Benavides dispatched a messenger named Blas Herrera to Bexar with a letter warning: "At this moment I have received a very certain notice, that the commander in chief, Antonio López de Santa Anna, marches for the city of San Antonio to take possession thereof, with 13,000 men." Herrera arrived in Bexar at 1:00 A.M. on February 11, and in the discussion that followed, Travis reckoned "it will take 13,000 men from the Presidio de Rio Grande to this place thirteen or fourteen days to get here; this is the 4th day." Assuming that Travis was speaking as if it were still February 10, this means Benavides had sent off his warning from Camargo on February 6 before set-

ting off to meet Grant at San Patricio. Antonio Menchaca, *Memoirs,* in Hansen, *Alamo Reader,* 504–505.

23. Morris to Fannin, Feb. 6, 1836.

24. Lamar, no. 2169, Cooke.

25. Lamar, no. 1645, Brown.

26. Fannin to Robinson, Feb. 7, 1836, Fannin communications.

27. Ibid.

28. Robinson to Fannin, Feb. 13, 1836, Fannin communications.

29. Johnson to Fannin, Feb. 9, 1836, Fannin communications.

CHAPTER 7. "GO IN AND DIE WITH THE BOYS"

1. Lamar, no. 1658, McMullen. Once the revolution began, the Texians adopted the name Convention for the assembly serving as their provisional government; the innocuous earlier name Consultation implied a purely consultative body and reflected the absence of a legal basis for an assembly in Texas.

2. Creed Taylor is rather more out than usual in stating that it was on February 16, since both Cooke and McMullen explicitly stated that Grant left on the day after the reinforcement arrived. Since Fannin received Morris's appeal for assistance only shortly before 10:00 P.M. on February 7, Cooke must have set off from Refugio just before first light on February 8 and claimed to have reached San Patricio after marching all day. This agrees with Johnson's February 9 letter, urging Fannin to come forward instead of retreating. Presumably Johnson left with Grant shortly after writing it.

3. Evidence of the transfers can be found in a nominal roll of Lewellen's Company maintained by its first sergeant, Hutchins Pittman; see Land Office Muster Rolls in D. Maxey (ed.), *Index to the Military Rolls of the Republic of Texas,* http://www.mindspring.com/dmaxey/rep-cont.htm. Benavides was reported by Johnson to have forty-seven men on February 2; Fannin to Robinson, Feb. 4, 1836, Fannin communications.

4. Lamar, no. 2169, Cooke.

5. Lamar, no. 1645, Brown.

6. Lamar, no. 1658, McMullen.

7. Johnson, *A History of Texas and Texans,* vol. 1, transcript from *Sons of De Witt Colony* website; Lamar, no. 1645, Brown. One of the many mysteries surrounding this affair is the question of the money. Fannin complained to Robinson in a letter dated February 25 that Johnson had not accounted for two thousand dollars issued to Johnson at San Felipe before he changed his mind about accepting the post of agent, which post was later offered to Fannin himself. Some of this money may have been used to buy horses, but for years afterward there were persistent stories that "the Doctor brought a quantity of money, chiefly in gold to San Patricio, and if a certain person would speak out . . . we might come to the knowledge of what became of it"; Ogilvie, SHQ 30:223.

8. The date is uncertain but has tentatively been established by working back-

ward through Brown's original narrative and by a statement in his 1858 version that they had been absent from San Patricio ten or twelve days when they were ambushed at Agua Dulce on March 2. Taken literally the latter claim is impossible, but it would in fact make sense if he actually meant it was by then ten or twelve days since they had parted from Frank Johnson at Santa Rosa.

9. Lamar, no. 1645, Brown.

10. Lamar, no. 1658, McMullen.

11. Urrea's diary entry for February 29 states that "according to our lists I had on this day 199 infantry and 183 cavalry," to which should be added six soldiers of the Yucatán Battalion who died of exposure on February 25 and the five cavalrymen killed or wounded at San Patricio on February 27. Urrea's diary and official report are both in C. E. Castañeda (ed.), *The Mexican Side of the Texas Revolution* (Dallas: P. L. Turner, 1928), accessible on *Sons of the De Witt Colony* website.

12. Ibid.

13. Johnson, *A History of Texas and Texans*, 1:419–22. Hardin, *Texian Illiad*, 158, rather inexplicably accepts Urrea's story about Johnson's men defending Fort Lipantitlán.

14. Lamar, no. 1658, McMullen.

15. Phineas J. Mahan Memorial, no. 247, file box no. 68, Department of State, Texas State Library and Archives, Austin.

16. Johnson, *A History of Texas and Texans*, 1:419–22.

17. Fannin to Robinson, Feb. 22, 1836, Fannin communications.

18. Fannin to Robinson, Feb. 26, 1836, Fannin communications. Fannin's letters, supposedly dated February 25 and 26, state that he set off from Goliad late on the former date and abandoned the attempt on February 26 rather than February 27; but others, including his ADC, John Sowers Brooks, quite clearly state that the main body set off on February 26 and returned after holding a council of war "in the bushes" on February 27. Brooks also implies—perhaps mistakenly—that word of Johnson's disaster reached them while this council was actually in progress.

19. Santa Anna to Urrea, Mar. 3, 1836, in Hansen, *Alamo Reader*, 335–36.

20. The location, some five miles west of the present monument, is thoroughly discussed and described by Bill Walraven, "A Re-Evaluation of the Agua Dulce Battlefield Site," *Bulletin Nueces County Historical Commission* 2, no. 1 (Nov. 1989). I am grateful to Thomas Ricks Lindley for providing a copy of this important article.

21. J. Sowers Brooks to Father, Mar. 10, 1836, "Letters from La Bahia Jan–March 1836," *Sons of De Witt Colony* Website.

22. In Castañeda, *The Mexican Side of the Texas Revolution*, accessible on *Sons of the De Witt Colony* website. Urrea afterward stated there were forty-two killed, including Grant and Morris. Three of the Americans were taken prisoner and five escaped, which means that twenty-four of the dead were Mexicans, to which should be added a further three taken prisoner and perhaps a few more who may have escaped.

23. Newell, *History of the Revolution in Texas*, 76–77. While this is not credited as a firsthand account, Newell was not in the habit of writing creatively but stitched his book together from a largely unattributed assortment of letters and reports and so may well have picked up the story from one of the survivors' accounts.

24. J. Sowers Brooks to Father, Mar. 10, 1836.

25. Interestingly, in the 1858 version of his story Brown stated that Plácido Benavides was sent off to warn Fannin *before* he and Grant tried to rejoin their men. Although Benavides survived both the battle and the revolution, he did not survive the wave of anti-Mexican feeling that followed San Jacinto. He was forced into exile in Louisiana and died at Opelousas in 1837—which may be why he was effectively written out of the later version of the story.

26. In 1858 Brown recalled the fight only slightly differently, saying that "we dismounted, determined to make them pay dearly for our lives. As I reached the ground a Mexican lanced me in the arm, but Grant immediately shot him dead, when I seized his lance to defend myself. Just as he shot the Mexican I saw Grant fall, pierced with several lances, and a moment after I found myself fast in a lasso that had been thrown over me, and by which I was dragged to the ground. I could do no more, and only regretted that I had not shared the fate of all the rest of my party" (*Texas Almanac*, 1858, *Sons of De Witt Colony* website).

27. Potter's account formed part of his article "The Prisoners of Matamoros," which appeared in the *Magazine of American History* in May 1878. One reason for writing of Grant's death was to counter a quite different story that had earlier appeared in Yoakum's *History of Texas,* alleging that Grant had been taken alive and promised his freedom if he would first treat Urrea's "numerous" wounded. After a few weeks, however, he was taken out and bound to the tail and hind feet of a wild horse, which was then turned loose "leaving behind him, in a short distance, the mangled remains of poor Grant" (Yoakum, *History of Texas*, 2: 84–85). Although Yoakum's tale is full of circumstantial detail and referenced to an anonymous "Statement of the Death of Dr. James Grant: MS," Potter explains that "an Italian doctor, named Constanza, was expelled from Monterey for conduct unbecoming a physician and a gentleman, and a little later in the season he went to New Orleans with no kind feeling towards the people who had cast him out. By way of reprisal he furnished a sensation newspaper, which named him as authority, with a new version of Grant's death, which was afterwards taken up as authentic by Yoakum." Similarly, the otherwise hostile Creed Taylor related:

Our good historian Yoakum made many statements which later writers could find no one to verify. I met and associated with several of those who were at San Patricio before and after its capture by Urrea and have heard their versions of the occupation of the place by the Mexicans, and the events connected there and I never heard the story of Dr. Grant's death as related by Yoakum until after I had enlisted in General Taylor's army at Corpus Christi. I think it was while on the march to the Rio Grande, opposite Matamoros, where Fort Brown was built later, that I heard the story told around the campfire, by one of the soldiers from the "states." I took occasion then, as did every Texan present, to challenge the story and to denounce it as utterly false.

It is possible that Brown's statement, in both his later accounts, that he saw Grant's body repeatedly thrust through with swords was intended to confirm that Grant was indeed dead when Brown left him on the battlefield, and Father Molloy also informed Potter that "he saw Grant's sword, knife and jacket, and other articles known as his, brought in by the dragoons when they returned from Agua Dulce, and that he was undoubtedly killed on the same day and in the same field with the mass of his band."

CHAPTER 8. FROM SEA TO SHINING SEA

1. Houston to Collinsworth, Mar. 7, 1836, PTR 5:17–18.
2. William W. Thompson affidavit, Dec. 1, 1840, folder 5, box 2-9/6, Texas State Library and Archives, Austin; Davis, *Three Roads to the Alamo*, 547–48.
3. Houston to Fannin, Mar. 11, 1836, Fannin communications. Davis, *Three Roads to the Alamo*, 554–63, has a good account of the fall of the Alamo and was the first to discover Ramírez y Sesma's report describing how the defenders tried to break out. R. B. Winders's *Sacrificed at the Alamo: Tragedy and Triumph in the Texas Revolution* is a good single-volume study. Although dated, Walter Lord's *A Time to Stand*, and Stephen Hardin's *Texian Illiad* (see 36–49) are both still valuable. Hardin's account has been updated in his *The Alamo 1836: Santa Anna's Texas Campaign*.
4. Santa Anna, "Manifesto," 1837, among "Massacre at Goliad: Mexican Centralista Descriptions" (hereafter cited as Centralista descriptions), *Sons of De Witt Colony* website; and see Hardin, *Texian Illiad*, 166–74. Hobart Huson's *Refugio: A Comprehensive History of Refugio County from Aboriginal Times to 1953* contains the most detailed modern account of the battle and is available on the *Sons of De Witt Colony* website.
5. Vincente Filisola, *Memoirs for the History of the War in Texas*, Centralista descriptions.
6. On May 27 Pakenham reported to Palmerston "the steps I had taken with my colleague the French minister to induce the Mexican government to act with becoming humanity toward the prisoners taken in the course of the campaign in Texas . . . [and] the cruelty of the principal officers employed in the expedition, who it appears have caused to be put to death all the prisoners who had fallen into their hands. I am assured, and fear there is no reason to doubt the fact, that in one day (Sunday the 27th of March) upwards of four hundred were shot by order of General Urrea, I suppose in consequence of orders from his superior, General Santa Anna. . . . Great and lasting disgrace must fall upon the nation under whose flag such atrocities have been committed" (Fo50/99 f143).

To which the Foreign Office responded on August 15: "Your dispatch . . . unhappily confirms the reports that had already reached this country respecting the inhuman treatment which the prisoners taken in the course of the campaign in Texas have met with at the hands of the Mexican generals. HM's government were at first disposed to disbelieve the accounts which reached them of the barbarous atrocity mentioned in your dispatch; and it is with feelings of the greatest regret that they have since been convinced of the reality . . . which stains with much disgrace the character of the Mexican nation" (Fo50/97 f52).

7. Cass to Gaines, Jan. 23, 1836, PTR 5:125–27.

8. Gaines to Cass, Mar. 28, 1836, PTR 5:233.

9. S. Carson to D. Burnett, Apr. 14, 1836, in Garrison, *Diplomatic Correspondence,* 1:83. The detachment spoken of by Joe was actually a reinforcement sent to Urrea to enable him to take on Fannin's command.

10. See Hardin, *Texian Illiad,* 192–93, and his *The Alamo 1836: Santa Anna's Campaign,* 72–73, for convincing discussion of this point. Moore, *Eighteen Minutes: The Battle of San Jacinto and the Texas Independence Campaign,* provides an alternative view.

11. Pakenham to Palmerston, Jul. 1, 1836, Fo50/99 f210; Fehrenbach, *Lone Star: A History of Texas and the Texans,* 248–51.

12. Catlett to J. Pinckney Henderson, Apr. 29, 1837, in J. L. Worley, "The Diplomatic Relations of England and the Republic of Texas," SHQ 9:2–3

13. Fo566/110.

14. Palmerston to Spring Rice, Oct. 9, 1837, Broadlands Papers.

15. Worley, "Diplomatic Relations," 11–16; Adams, *British Interests and Activities in Texas,* 67–68; Drescher, *The Mighty Experiment: Free Labour versus Slavery in British Emancipation,* 169–73. Tolme, the British consul at Havanna, reported on the "Highest authority" that upward of fifteen hundred slaves had been shipped from Cuba to Texas over the past few years; Thomas, *The Slave Trade,* 641.

16. See Donald Graves, *Guns Across the River: The Battle of the Windmill,* for a splendid account of the affair. The Hunters took their name from a popular song about Jackson's 1815 victory at New Orleans—"The Hunters of Kentucky."

17. Kennedy to Aberdeen, Oct. 20, 1841, Fo75/2.

18. Kennedy to Aberdeen (private), Nov. 9, 1841, Fo75/2.

19. Although he did not identify the "leading member of the Anti-Slavery Society," Kennedy may have been referring to Lord Glenelg; after all, the comment about activities "more zealous than judicious" would certainly have applied to his late cousin, James Grant.

20. Kennedy to Aberdeen, Jan. 28, 1842, Fo75/3. Enclosed with Kennedy's letter was one written to him by Sam Houston, of the same date:

> Before your departure from this place, I must be permitted to make a request of you. Should you find it within your control, you will much oblige me by informing the British Government of the particulars touching the delay, and subsequent ratification of the Treaty on the subject of the "Slave Trade" by this Government. For the consummation of this business,

I cannot but feel that the Executive is under many obligations to you for the lights afforded him upon this subject by yourself. Owing to the representations of our agent at London, had you not been here, I am inclined to believe, or rather I am satisfied, that it would not have been ratified at the present session of Congress. In making this request of you, I claim the right of an apology, on the ground that our agent at London, Gen. Hamilton, has been recalled under a resolution of Congress. And with a perfect knowledge of our situation you will not suppose that an agent, such as would be desirable for us, will be sent to England, owing to the condition of our *finances*. Should I not have the pleasure of meeting you again, previous to your departure for England, I will anticipate the happiness of again meeting you in Texas; as I sincerely hope Her Majesty's Government may think proper to send you to Texas in some relation which may be agreeable to you, as your return will be to the people, and particularly to your very sincere friend, Sam Houston.

21. Hamilton to Aberdeen, Mar. 25, 1842, FO75/3. Exeter Hall was the headquarters of the British Anti-Slavery Society.

22. Kennedy to Aberdeen, Apr. 20, 1842, FO50/158.

23. Aberdeen to Elliot, Jul. 1, 1842, FO75/4.

24. Aberdeen to Kennedy, Sep. 29, 1842, FO75/3.

25. Kennedy to Aberdeen, Sep. 23, 1844, FO84/479. In a subsequent letter in October, he reported: "By a letter from a trustworthy Correspondent (Hugh Grant?), dated, New Orleans, October 24th, I am informed that, ' . . . large quantities of Military Stores, wagons, etc. were being forwarded, by the Government of the United States, to the Texan frontier on the Red River.' The writer surmises these preparations are 'to be intended to counteract Mexican movements.'"

26. Bankhead to Aberdeen, Nov. 29, 1844, FO50/177.

27. Kennedy to Aberdeen, Dec. 5, 1844, FO84/479.

CHAPTER 9. POSTSCRIPT

1. Kennedy to Aberdeen, Dec. 20, 1845, FO75/14 no. 36.

2. Mowat, *The Diplomatic Relations of Great Britain and the United States*, 132–37. In one of his invaluable intelligence reports, William Kennedy forwarded the text of a remarkable speech delivered by Senator Thomas Benton in St. Louis, Missouri, on October 14, 1844 (FO75/14 no. 36):

And I went further in my views upon Oregon than the exclusion of the British, and the preservation of our territorial rights. I looked across the Pacific Ocean, and I saw Eastern Asia full in sight. I traced an American Road to India* through our own dominions, and across that Sea!—I showed that a new route, almost exclusively American, was to be opened to Asiatic Commerce, and although the event has not yet fulfilled my expectations, nor the public mind advanced to my position, yet I still stand upon it and adhere to my vision of five and twenty years ago. I repeat again what I then said: I say the man is alive, full-grown, and listening to what I say (without believing it, perhaps) who will yet see the Asiatic Commerce traversing the North Pacific Ocean, entering the Oregon river, climbing the Western Slope of the Rocky Mountains, issuing from its gorges, and spreading its fertilizing streams over our widely extended Union!—The Steam-boat and the Steam-car have not yet exhausted their wonders. They have not yet found even their amplest and most appropriate theatres—the tranquil surface of the North Pacific Ocean, and the vast inclined plane which spreads East and West from the base of the Rocky Mountains. The magic boat and the flying car are not yet seen upon this ocean, nor upon this plane—but they will be seen there;—and St Louis, in Missouri, is yet to find herself as near to Canton as she now is to London—with a better and safer route, by land and sea, to China and Japan than she now has to France and Great Britain.

*American Road to India:—These words are in small capitals in the published Speech, which, I should suppose, had received the revision of Mr Benton himself, as it was printed, in a pamphlet form, at St. Louis Missouri, from which place I obtained the copy now in my possession.

3. C. Elliot to H. U. Addington (Under Secretary), Nov. 15, 1842, Fo75/4.
4. A. Lipscombe to R. Pakenham, Jun. 6, 1840, in Garrison, *Diplomatic Correspondence*, 2:899.
5. Ogilvie, SHQ 30:135, 312.
6. Harris County, Texas, Probate Records, B:280–81.
7. Adolphus Sterne noted in his diary on March 21, 1841, that John Sutherland had told him that Ogilvie was from "Muryshire Banff Scotland." Banff and Morayshire were two separate but adjacent counties immediately to the east of Inverness-shire. Much of what follows is reconstructed from Ogilvie's diary, which came into Sterne's possession after Ogilvie's death in 1840 and was erroneously identified as Sterne's when the first installment was published by the Southwestern Historical Society in 1927. The confusion arose in part because Sterne, recognizing the diary's usefulness, resolved to emulate Ogilvie by keeping one of his own.
8. Ogilvie, SHQ 30:149.
9. Harris County, Texas, Probate Records, B:277–79.
10. Ogilvie, SHQ 30:231.
11. Ibid., 30:154–55.
12. Ogilvie to Pakenham, Aug. 20, 1839, in Garrison, *Diplomatic Correspondence*, 2:600. A *sitio* equated to 4,428 acres of land.
13. Lipscombe to Pakenham, Jun. 6, 1840, in Garrison, *Diplomatic Correspondence*, 2:899.
14. Headright grants of 1,476 acres were awarded to those declaring their intention to settle in Texas; bounty grants, as we have seen, were awarded for

service, in this case during the taking of Bexar in December 1835. In total, according to the documents lodged by Toler, James Grant was entitled to one head-right claim, one bounty claim, and one donation claim in his own right, totaling 4,036 acres. In addition, Toler apparently proved Grant's entitlement to four of the five soldiers' claims, totaling a further 1,280 acres.

15. Harris County, Texas, Probate Records, B:483–84.

APPENDIX: GRANT'S MEN

1. H. Davenport, "Men of Goliad," SHQ 43:1–41; D. Maxey (ed.), *Fannin and His Men: Notes from an Unfinished Study of Fannin and His Men by Harbert Davenport 1936*, http://www.tsha.utexas.edu/supsites/fannin/hd_home.html.

2. Miller, *New Orleans and the Texas Revolution*, 76–77.

3. Harris County, Texas, Probate Records, B:280. See also Chapter 9.

4. Land Office Muster Rolls, 38, in Maxey, *Index to the Military Rolls of the Republic of Texas*. "I do hereby certify that the foregoing is a true copy of the original muster roll of Capt. Thomas Llewellyn's Company now in my possession, the original being in pencil, and I do hereby further certify that the remarks opposite to the names are correct to the best of my knowledge and belief: Given and signed at San Antonio, Texas, this the 17th day of April, AD 1850: H. M. Pittman, First Sergeant, Capt. Llewellyn's Company, Texas."

5. I am grateful to Ron Strybos of Texas for information as to Brown's later career with the Confederate Army and as to his burial place.

6. A partially reconstructed roll of Fannin's men appeared in the *Telegraph and Texas Register*, Nov. 9, 1836.

7. The claim of being an Alamo defender is in Groneman, *Alamo Defenders*, 34. The convention roll was a petition soldiers at Refugio signed, demanding representation at the convention scheduled for March 1 at San Felipe.

8. Unreferenced note by Davenport, in Maxey, *Fannin and His Men*.

9. Comptroller's Military Service Records no. 259, Texas State Library and Archives, Austin.

10. T. L. Miller, "Fannin's Men: Some Additions to Earlier Rosters," SHQ 61:522–32.

11. Potter, "Prisoners of Matamoros."

12. Lamar, no. 336, Ayers.

13. Narrative originally in *Georgia Citizen* (n.d.), reprinted in *Texas State Gazette*, June 1853, accessible at *Sons of De Witt Colony* Website.

14. See note 28 to Chapter 3 of the present volume for the list.

15. Miller, "Fannin's Men."

16. Phineas J. Mahan Memorial, no. 247, file box no. 68, Department of State, Texas State Library and Archives, Austin.

17. Ibid.

18. Maxey, *Index to the Military Rolls of the Republic of Texas*.

19. Davenport, in Maxey, *Fannin and His Men*.

20. Phineas J. Mahan Memorial.

Bibliography

BOOKS, ARTICLES, AND PAMPHLETS

Adams, Anton. *The War in Mexico.* Chicago: Emperor's Press, 1998.

Adams, E. D. *British Interests and Activities in Texas.* Baltimore, 1910.

Adams, E. D. "Correspondence from the British Archives Concerning Texas, 1837–1846." *Southwestern Historical Quarterly* 16–21 (1913–17).

Alessio Robles, Vito. *Coahuila y Texas desde la consumacion de la independencia hasta el Tratado de Paz de Guadalupe Hidalgo.* 2 vols. Mexico: 1945.

Austin, Stephen F. "General Austin's Order Book for the Campaign of 1835." *Southwestern Historical Quarterly* 11(July 1907): 1–56.

———. *The Austin Papers.* Comp. and ed. Eugene C. Barker. 3 vols. Washington, D.C., and Austin: American Historical Association and University of Texas, 1919–26.

Austin, William T. "Account of the Campaign of 1835 by William T. Austin, Aid to General Stephen F. Austin & Gen. Ed Burleson." *Texana* 4 (Winter 1966): 287–322.

Barber, N. *The Black Hole of Calcutta.* London: William Collins, 1965.

Barker, Eugene C. "Land Speculation as a Cause of the Texas Revolution." *Southwestern Historical Quarterly* 10 (July 1906): 76–95.

———. "The Texas Revolutionary Army." *Southwestern Historical Quarterly* 9 (April 1906): 227–61.

Barr, Alwyn, *Texas in Revolt: The Battle for San Antonio, 1835.* Austin: University of Texas Press, 1990.

Boyle, Andrew A. "Reminiscences of the Texas Revolution." *Southwestern Historical Quarterly* 13 (April 1910):285–91.

Brands, H. W. *Lone Star Nation: The Epic Story of the Battle for Texas Independence.* New York: Random House, 2005.

Brown, Gary.*Volunteers in the Texas Revolution: The New Orleans Greys.* Lanham, Md.: Republic of Texas Press, 1999.

Castañeda, C. E. (ed.), *The Mexican Side of the Texas Revolution.* Dallas: P. L. Turner, 1928.

Chartrand, Rene. *Santa Anna's Mexican Army 1821–48.* Oxford: Osprey, 2004.

Coleman, Robert. *Houston Displayed; Or Who Won the Battle of San Jacinto.* Velasco (Brazosport, Tex.), 1837.

Crisp, James E. *Sleuthing the Alamo: Davy Crockett's Last Stand and Other Mysteries of the Texas Revolution*. New York: Oxford University Press, 2005.

Davenport, Harbert. "The Men of Goliad." *Southwestern Historical Quarterly* 43 (January 1939): 1–41.

Davis, William C. *Lone Star Rising: The Revolutionary Birth of the Texas Republic*. New York: Free Press, 2004.

———. *Three Roads to the Alamo: The Lives and Fortunes of David Crockett, James Bowie, and William Barret Travis*. New York: Harper Collins, 1998.

DeShields, James T. (comp.). *Tall Men with Long Rifles: Set Down and Written Out by James T. DeShields as Told Him by Creed Taylor, Captain during the Texas Revolution*. San Antonio: Naylor Company, 1935.

Drescher, Seymour. *The Mighty Experiment: Free Labour versus Slavery in British Emancipation*. Oxford: Oxford University Press, 2002.

Edwardes, M. *The Battle of Plassey*. New York: Macmillan, 1963.

Ehrenberg, Herman. *Ehrenberg: Goliad Survivor, Old West Explorer*. Ed. Natalie Ornish. Dallas: Texas Heritage Press, 1997.

———. *With Milam and Fannin: Adventures of a German Boy in Texas' Revolution*. Austin: Pemberton Press, 1968.

Embree, Ainslie Thomas. *Charles Grant and British Rule in India*. London: Allen and Unwin, 1962.

Fehrenbach, T. R. *Lone Star: A History of Texas and the Texans*. New York: Macmillan, 1968.

Fraser, William. *Chiefs of Grant*. 3 vols. Edinburgh, 1883.

Gammel, Hans Peter Neilsen (comp.). *The Laws of Texas, 1822–1897*. 10 vols. Vol. 1: *Laws and Decrees of the State of Coahuila and Texas*. Vol. 2: *Proceedings of the General Council*. Austin: Gammel Book Company, 1898.

Garrison, G. P. *Diplomatic Correspondence of the Republic of Texas*. 2 vols. Chicago and New York: American Historical Association, 1908.

Graves, Donald E. *Guns across the River: The Battle of the Windmill, 1838*. Toronto: Robin Brass Studios, 2001.

Groneman, Bill. *Alamo Defenders: A Genealogy, the People and Their Words*. Austin: Eakin Press, 1990.

Gulick, Charles Adams Jr., and Katherine Elliott (eds.). *The Papers of Mirabeau Buonaparte Lamar*. Austin: A. C. Baldwin and Sons, 1921; reprint, New York: AMS Press, 1973.

Hansen, Todd (ed.). *The Alamo Reader: A Study in History*. Mechanicsburgh, Pa.: Stackpole Books, 2003.

Hardin, Stephen L. *Texian Illiad: A Military History of the Texas Revolution, 1835–1836*. Austin: University of Texas Press, 1994.

———. *The Alamo 1836: Santa Anna's Texas Campaign*. Oxford: Osprey, 2001.

Harris, Charles H. *A Mexican Family Empire: The Latifundio of the Sánchez Navarros 1765–1867*. Austin: University of Texas Press, 1975.

Haynes, Sam W. *Soldiers of Misfortune: The Somervell and Mier Expeditions*. Austin: University of Texas Press, 1990.

Haythornthwaite, Philip. *The Alamo and the War of Texas Independence.* London: Osprey, 1986.

Huffines, Alan C. *The Blood of Noble Men: The Alamo Siege and Battle, An Illustrated Chronology.* Austin: Eakin Press, 1999.

Huson, Hobart, *Refugio: A Comprehensive History of Refugio County from Aboriginal Times to 1953.* 2 vols. Woodsboro, Tex.: Rook Foundation, 1953–55.

Jenkins, John H. (ed.). *The Papers of the Texas Revolution, 1835–1836.* 10 vols. Austin: Presidial Press, 1973.

Johnson, Frank W. *A History of Texas and Texans.* 5 vols. Ed. Eugene C. Barker. Chicago and New York: American Historical Association, 1914.

Johnston, Henry Mackenzie. *Mission to Mexico: A Tale of British Diplomacy in the 1820s.* London, 1992.

Keay, John. *The Honourable Company: A History of the English East India Company.* London: Harper Collins, 1991.

Kennedy, William. *Texas: The Rise, Progress, and Prospects of the Republic of Texas.* London: R. Hastings, 1841.

Lamar, Mirabeau Buonaparte. *The Papers of Mirabeau Buonaparte Lamar.* 6 vols. Ed. Charles A. Gulick, Katherine Elliot, Winnie Allen, and Harriet Smither. Austin: Pemberton Press, 1968.

Lawson, L. A. *Relation of British Foreign Policy to the Monroe Doctrine.* London, 1922.

Lindley, Thomas Ricks. *Alamo Traces: New Evidence and New Conclusions.* Lanham, Md.: Republic of Texas Press, 2003.

Linn, John J. *Reminiscences of Fifty Years in Texas.* New York, 1886.

Long, Jeff. *Duel of Eagles: The U.S. and Mexican Fight for the Alamo.* New York: William Morrow and Company, 1990.

Lord, Walter. *A Time to Stand.* New York: Pocket Books, 1963.

Lundy, Benjamin. *The Life, Travels and Opinions of Benjamin Lundy.* Philadelphia: Augustus M. Kelley, 1847.

———. *The War in Texas.* Philadelphia: Published by author, printed by Merrilew and Gunn, 1837.

Mackay, William. *Urquhart and Glenmoriston.* Inverness: Northern Counties Publishing, 1893.

Miller, Edward L. *New Orleans and the Texas Revolution.* College Station: Texas A&M University Press, 2004.

Miller, Thomas Lloyd. "Fannin's Men: Some Additions to Earlier Rosters." *Southwestern Historical Quarterly* 61 (April 1958): 522–32.

Moore, Stephen L. *Eighteen Minutes: The Battle of San Jacinto and the Texas Independence Campaign.* Lanham, Md.: Republic of Texas Press, 2004.

Morris, Henry. *The Life of Charles Grant.* London: John Murray, 1904.

Mowat, R.B. *The Diplomatic Relations of Great Britain and the United States.* London: Edward Arnold and Company, 1925.

Nevin, David. *The Texans.* New York: Time Life Books, 1975.

Newell, Chester. *History of the Revolution in Texas, Particularly of the War of 1835 &*

1836, Together with the Latest Geographical, Topographical and Statistical Accounts of the Country, from the Most Authentic Sources, Also, an Appendix. New York: Wiley and Putnam, 1838.

Nofi, Albert A. *The Alamo and the Texas War for Independence, September 30 1835–April 21 1836.* Conshohocken, Pa.: Combined Books, 1992.

Oxford Dictionary of National Biography. Oxford: Oxford University Press, 2004.

Phillips, C. H. *The East India Company: 1784–1834.* Manchester: Manchester University Press, 1940.

Potter, Reuben M. "The Prisoners of Matamoros." *Magazine of American History* (May 1878).

———. "The Fall of the Alamo." *Magazine of American History* (January 1878).

Reid, Stuart. *The Texan Army 1835–46.* Oxford: Osprey, 2003.

Roberts, Randy, and James S. Olsen. *A Line in the Sand: The Alamo in Blood and Memory.* New York: Free Press, 2001.

Sinclair, David. *Sir Gregor MacGregor and the Land That Never Was.* London: Headline, 2003.

Smith, W. Roy. "The Quarrel between Governor Smith and the Provisional Government of the Republic." *Southwestern Historical Quarterly* 5 (April 1902): 269–346.

Smither, Harriet (ed.). "Diary of Adolphus Sterne" (Ogilvie journal). *Southwestern Historical Quarterly* 30 (October 1926–April 1927): 139–55, 219–32, 305–24.

Sparrow, Elizabeth. *Secret Service: British Agents in France 1792–1815.* Woodbridge, Suffolk: Boydell and Brewer, 1999.

Temperley, Harold. *The Foreign Policy of Canning 1822–1827.* London: 1925.

Thomas, Hugh. *The Slave Trade: The History of the Atlantic Slave Trade 1440–1870.* New York: Picador, 1997.

Urquhart, David. *The Annexation of Texas: A Case of War between England and the United States* (pamphlet). London: 1844.

Walraven, Bill. "A Re-Evaluation of the Agua Dulce Battlefield Site." *Bulletin of Nueces County Historical Commission* 2, no. 1 (November 1989): 45–49.

Ward, Henry. *Mexico in 1827.* 2 vols. London: H. Colburn, 1828.

Webster, Sir Charles, *The Foreign Policy of Palmerston 1830–41.* London: G. Bell and Sons, 1951.

Winders, Richard Bruce. *Sacrificed at the Alamo: Tragedy and Triumph in the Texas Revolution.* Abilene, Tex.: State House Press, 2004.

Winston, J. E. "New York and the Independence of Texas," *Southwestern Historical Quarterly* 18:368–85.

Worley, J. L. "The Diplomatic Relations of England and the Republic of Texas." *Southwestern Historical Quarterly* 9 (July 1905): 1–40.

Yoakum, Henderson. *History of Texas from Its First Settlement in 1655 to Its Annexation to the United States in 1846.* 2 vols. New York: Redfield, 1855.

WEBSITES AND ONLINE PUBLICATIONS

Maxey, D. (ed.). *Fannin and His Men: Notes from an Unfinished Study of Fannin and His Men by Harbert Davenport 1936.* http://www.tsha.utexas.edu/supsites/fannin/hd_home.htm

——. *Index to the Military Rolls of the Republic of Texas.* http://www.mindspring.com/~dmaxey/rep_cont.htm.

Handbook of Texas Online. http://www.tsha.utexas.edu/handbook/online/search.html

Southwestern Historical Quarterly. http://www.tsha.utexas.edu/publications/journals/shq/online

Sons of De Witt Colony Texas. http://www.tamu.edu/ccbn/dewitt/dewitt.htm

Index

Viesca, Augustin, 34, 36, 40, 41, 46

Ward, Henry, 16–19, 76, 152, 179, 200n 6, 202n 29; Fredonian revolt 20–25; recalled, 25, 203n 44
Ward, Major William, 97, 110, 149
Wavell, Gen. Arthur Goodall, 8, 11–12, 179, 200n 3; Fredonian revolt, 18–19, 21, 23–24, 25

Wentworth, J.T., 192
Westover, Capt. Ira, 100, 114–15, 139
Williams, J., 192
Williams, Samuel M., 34, 36, 111, 174, 175
Williams, William, 196–97
Winship, Stephen, 197
Wyatt, Capt. Peyton, 94–95

Zacatecas, 34
Zorro, *See* Canales, Antonio

ISBN-13: 978-1-58544-565-3
ISBN-10: 1-58544-565-7

52995

9 781585 445653